The Author

Richard P. Olson has served as pastor or staff member of churches in Massachusetts, South Dakota, Wisconsin, Colorado, and Kansas. He has been a pastoral counselor and a teacher in college. Most recently, in early retirement years, he was the Distinguished Professor of Pastoral Theology at Central Seminary, from which he retired in 2016.

He received his bachelor's degree from Sioux Falls College, his M.Div. and STM from Andover Newton Theological School, and his Ph.D. from Boston University (in social ethics). He was also a fellow in the American Association of Pastoral Counselors.

He and Mary Ann, his wife of sixty-eight years, have three daughters, six grandchildren, and five great-grandchildren. In 2018, they moved Oakwood Village at Prairie Ridge, a retirement community in Madison, Wisconsin.

This is the twenty-second book for which he is author or co-author, the most recent being *Laughter in a Time of Turmoil*; *Side by Side: Being Christian in a Multi-faith World*; *A Guide to Ministry Self-Care: Negotiating Todays' Challenges with Resilience and Grace*; *Celebrating the Graying Church: Mutual Ministry Today, Legacies Tomorrow*; and *The Grandparent Vocation: Wisdom, Legacies, and Spiritual Growth*.

When encountering a book by Richard Olson, readers can count on several things: relevance, impeccable scholarship, practicality, and inclusivity. In this latest work, Dr. Olson does not disappoint. The matter addressed is of immediate relevance, especially to pastors but also to others of us with commitment to and concern about the Church and an increasingly polarized society. The author has done his homework thoroughly, with citations and quotations from the breadth of other scholars who address these matters. Olson's approach is readily applicable to ministry, inclusive of well-crafted questions useful for reflection and discussion. He is intentionally inclusive in language and spirit. In this, his twenty-second book, Dr. Olson draws on his own extensive experience and wisdom yet also includes the voices and stories of thirty younger ministers whom he interviewed. The result is instructive, interesting, and effective. I highly recommend *Rowing Together through the Rapids*.

Rev Tarris (Terry) Rosell, Ph.D., D.Min
Professor of Pastoral Theology—Ethics & Ministry Praxis, Central Seminary
Clinical Professor Emeritus, History & Philosophy of Medicine,
University of Kansas School of Medicine

Engaging all the key issues facing churches and congregational leaders, this recent book from a wise and seasoned pastor/scholar helps us understand the ecclesial landscape. Significant research and thoughtful interviews inform what I would commend as an essential pastoral manual for those entering the uncertain waters of the life of the church. It provides much needed hope without false assurances.

Molly T. Marshall, Ph.D.
President of United Theological Seminary of the Twin Cities

Employing the image of the church as a leaking ship moving through the rapids of change, the author explores a library of scholarship in text and footnotes, structures a logbook of naming the changes, dialoging with teachers and pastors rowing the leaky boat now, and creates a journal of creative questions to personalize for the reader a hopeful journey. This is an excellent viewpoint for church leaders and students who care about the community and mission of the Christian Church.

Ronald E. Mach, Pastor and Assistant to Bishop, ELCA, Retired

In *Rowing Together through the Rapids*, Dr. Olson speaks as one who loves the church and longs for it to live into its full potential within a changing context. Drawing on decades of experience as a pastor and seminary professor and in conversation with younger pastors he interviewed, he draws readers into considering some of the most significant issues facing the church today. Its steep decline is analyzed within larger societal trends, offering perspective to discouraged pastors. Contemporary challenges are considered with thoughtful graciousness and explored as new opportunities for ministry. I gladly recommend this hopeful and encouraging book.

Rev. Ruth Rosell, Ph.D.
Director of the Buttry Center for Peace and Nonviolence
Associate Professor of Pastoral Theology Emerita
Central Seminary, Overland Park, Kansas

Richard P. Olson's *Rowing Together through the Rapids* provides pastors and church leaders with both a survey of the current state of the American church and practical tools for the future. Olson weaves decades of experience with the latest data, observations of experts, and dialogue with Gen-X and Millennial church leaders to define the current reality and to learn from practitioners who are charting a way forward. This book is a helpful companion for anyone navigating the rapids of ministry.

Evan Duncan, Senior Pastor,
Baptist Church of West Chester, Pennsylvania

This is not the time of bold predictions about the future of the church in America. This is the time of authentic, vulnerable, challenging, truthful, fresh expressions of the Spirit of God at work in the church. Dr. Richard Olson peels back the layers of chaos and change to reveal the stories and experiences of pastors all under the age of 50 who are fulfilling the vows of their ordination in compelling and hopeful ways. No one ever said pastoral ministry would be easy, but this book shows again and again—there is no other vocation like it! Take, read, and inwardly digest.

G. Travis Norvell, Pastor,
Judson Memorial Baptist Church, Minneapolis, Minnesota

What makes *Rowing Together through the Rapids* unique is that Dr. Olson has specifically sought out the experiences, views, and values of Gen X and Millennial pastors. Dr. Olson turns to those who are in the thick of congregational ministry right now, to ministry among "nones and dones" outside the church, and how this is shaping Gen Z and the future. *Rowing Together* encourages conversation and collaboration on the challenges and opportunities younger generations of ministerial leaders and spiritual seekers are facing. As a Regional Executive Minister, this book offers a useful tool for lay leaders, pastors, and judicatories to support pastors and new ministries, as Christianity shifts into a new era.

Rev. Mindi Welton-Mitchell
Regional Executive Minister, American Baptist Churches of Wisconsin

Not often can one discover a resource that has the breadth of years that Olson offers in this one. Olson, a retired professor, pastor, and a sage, invited himself into today's conversations about where the church is and where it might be going in the future. Weaving in many interviews from people in ministry serving on "Main Street" in our communities, he presents topics by sharing stories and inviting the reader to engage with evocative questions after each chapter. Like Paul who has borne witness of Christ encouraging young Timothy to remain steadfast, Olson encourages us to be hopeful because Christ's church is still alive in the world!

Donald Ng,
who was Senior Pastor of First Chinese Baptist Church, San Francisco
and served as President of American Baptist Churches, USA in 2014-2015.

Rowing Together through the Rapids

HOPEFUL CONVERSATIONS FOR
TODAY'S AND TOMORROW'S CHURCH

RICHARD P. OLSON

© 2025
Published in the United States by Nurturing Faith, Macon, GA.
Nurturing Faith is a book imprint of Good Faith Media (goodfaithmedia.org).
Library of Congress Cataloging-in-Publication Data is available.

ISBN: 978-1-63528-252-8

All rights reserved. Printed in the United States of America.

Scripture quotations (unless otherwise noted) are taken from the Holy Bible, New Revised Standard Version, Updated Edition (NRSVue). Copyright © 2021 by the National Council of Churches of Christ in the United States of America. Used by permission. All rights reserved worldwide.

Scripture quotations marked (An Inclusive Version) are taken from The New Testament and Psalms: An Inclusive Version. Copyright © 1995 by Oxford University Press, New York. Used by permission. All rights reserved.

Dedication

In Memory of
Lee Regier
Ron Erickson

And in Honor of
Barbara Regier
Marjorie Erickson
Ministry Friends for a Lifetime!

And with Profound Appreciation for
My Life Partner, Mary Ann Olson
And Our Daughters, Julie Willems Van Dijk, Lisa Michalec, Laurie Johnson

They were good "PKs"* back then and have been wonderful companions, caregivers, and supporters ever since

*Preacher's/Pastor's Kids

Acknowledgements

This book is a combination of—and a dialogue between—my history as a pastor and professor and the wisdom and experience of many other people. I express my thanks and indebtedness.

Many authors have provided wisdom. However, there are three I particularly note. First, the late Loren Mead, founder of the Alban Institute, astutely discerned, described, and prescribed ministry for what he called "the once and future church." This book re-explores his insights and wisdom some thirty years later. Second, Eileen R. Campbell-Reed, former Central Seminary colleague, has studied widely and contributed on many issues, among them pastoral imagination and flourishing, ministry during the pandemic, and women in ministry. In this book, I rely on her insights frequently. Third, Bob Smietana has been a great help. His 2022 book, *Reorganized Religion: The Reshaping of the American Church and Why It Matters*, identified so clearly many church-wide issues that I was addressing in local ministry that I found myself citing his book, quoting him, and turning to resources he mentioned again and again.

A key component of what I offer in this book is a conversation with Gen X and Millennial pastors about their experiences and insights in their current ministries. First, my thanks to those who helped me find and enlist those pastors. I am grateful to Nathan Huguely, Jerrod Hugenot, Mindi Welton-Mitchell, Lauren Ng, and Rachael Lawrence for identifying Gen X or Millennial pastors, some of whom agreed to visit with me.

I had at least one good talk, an hour or more long, with each person listed below. With some, I had several conversations. I did not stay strictly within the age parameters for a few of these pastors, especially those with unique specialties or expertise. (The questions that shaped our conversations may be found in the Appendix.)

Before I list these pastors, let me explain why they are listed as they are. When I use information and quotes from the interviews in the writing of this book, I identify these pastors by first name only. Before including their words in my book, I sent a draft of what I had written to each contributor and asked for permission to include it. In most cases, these pastors graciously granted permission. Occasionally, some asked that I use a pseudonym to protect their identity or their church's privacy. (For the chapter that explores discouragement, the temptation to resign from ministry, termination, and self-care, I use pseudonyms for everyone, unless they specifically asked me not to do so.)

In preparing this acknowledgement page, I again asked each of these pastors how they would like to be listed. I wondered if some would want family or colleagues to know about their contribution to this work. Below is how each of them answered. Some added titles or other information, and some did not. I have listed each person as they responded to my inquiry. My deepest gratitude to each of the following for their contributions about ministry in today's world:

Anita Peebles
Amber Naylor
Cindy Boyer
Cody Knapik
David Harris, Jr.
Rev. Dr. Debbie Buchholz
Edris
Evan Duncan
Rev. James Hill, Jr., pastor of churches in Missouri and Connecticut for twenty-five years
Jason C
Rev. Dr. Jason Mack
Jennifer Harris Dault
Jessica
Joanna
Jonathan Elsensohn
Jonathan D. Lawrence
Kathy
Melissa Newberry
Mia Chang
Rev. Michael Strickland
Rev. Michele Turek
Molly
Peter Assad
Peter C
Rev. Randy Van Osten
Rev. Dr. Rob Kirbach
Rev. Dr. Seth David Clark
Rev. Tim Schaeffer
Rev. Dr. Chaks Zadda

I am also grateful to those who accepted this project and saw it through publication. I appreciate being accepted and published by Good Faith Media, Nurturing Faith, and Faithlab LLC. I am especially grateful for the guidance of Carol Brown and Faithlab's editors and graphic designers. It is wonderful to bring this long-term project to completion! To all these who helped make it possible, my profound gratitude.

Contents

Introduction 1

Understanding Our Changing Past and Present

Chapter 1: I Don't Think We're in Christendom Anymore 7

Chapter 2: Sailing against the Wind in a Leaky Boat 21

Keeping the Faith—Ongoing Church Practices

Chapter 3: Spiritually Hungry in a World of Possibility 37

Chapter 4: Crying in the Chapel 51

Chapter 5: Singing God's Praises in a New Key 64

Chapter 6: An Alternative to Illiterate Proof Texting 79

Chapter 7: Flourishing in the Wilderness; Renewing in the Exile 93

Exploring Issues and Missions— Possible New Ministry Opportunities

Chapter 8: Seeking Racial Shalom in a Changing Nation 110

Chapter 9: Mother God Comes Close 131

Chapter 10: A Visible Church for an Invisible People 146

Chapter 11: A Humble Journey: Marriage, Family, Gender and Sexuality Today 163

Chapter 12: Faithfulness in a Frail Creation: What Can a Congregation Do? 181

Chapter 13: Figure Skating on Thin Ice: Navigating the Political Divide 194

Finally, Sisters and Brothers, Grace and Peace 207

Appendix: The Questions That Shaped My Interviews 212

Bibliography 214

Introduction

Dear Pastor, Dear Church Leader, Dear Friend,

I follow your work with love, longing, and hope. For many years, I served in a pastoral role and (on most days) I enjoyed that role. For me, ministry was at its best when I was growing personally, spiritually, and professionally, and when a congregation was growing with me. Friendship and support with other ministers and church leaders were important parts of that.

In this book, I offer you a conversation about church and ministry, then and now. I hope that the "bifocals" of long experience and present encounter will provide us with some "aha" moments. Through these bifocals, we will look at the life of the church in the past and the opportunities and challenges present in the church today. We are indeed in a time of great change and challenge. And we are in a time when there is great uncertainty about what comes next.

As we journey together, I will share about my experience in parish ministry from 1960 through almost the end of the century, a period followed by nearly twenty years of seminary teaching. Through those many years, I have lived through vast changes. Some of those changes were invisible to me at the time but are much clearer now as I look back.

Sometimes, I was discouraged. Even though my colleagues and I worked hard and gave all that we had, it sometimes seemed that the church was weaker when we finished than when we began. I was not alone in that feeling. For example, Loren Mead, founder of the Alban Institute, anticipated some of the signs and changes before many of us even noticed. In his book, *The Once and Future Church*, Mead reflected on what was happening in the church in the 1980s and 1990s.[1] Since that time, many of the changes he noted have accelerated.

Then there was the pandemic!

On the pages that follow, I will attempt a two-way conversation about church and ministry today. As one partner, I will bring my experience. I will reflect on what we did well, what mistakes we made, and where we failed. I will also explore perspectives on the influences of the times in which I lived.

The other partner in this conversation is the cadre of dozens of Gen X (those born 1965-1980) and Millennial (those born 1981-1996) pastors who visited with me about their ministries today.

Here is a little background about my own story: throughout my ministry, I tried very hard to be a well-trained pastor and teacher of pastors. This included graduate education beyond my seminary degree as well as extended Clinical Pastoral Education. Near the end of my local pastorate career, I was invited to a seminary to teach what is variously called Pastoral Theology, Applied Theology, or Practical Theology. (When my seminary president and professor of theology, Molly Marshall, and I were on a panel together, I might tease and say to her, "I teach practical theology, and, Molly, you teach…?" She would go along with my gag and answer, "Impractical theology." Eventually she would move to a more accurate description of her field of study. "Constructive theology," she would say.) Some of my teaching was in the "Ministry Praxis" classes where students would complete supervised ministry service and reflect on that in an academic setting.

We mostly called our department "pastoral theology," but we might have also said that we were working in the field of ecclesiology. We were studying and living out what it meant to be church.

For the next twenty years, I learned more about the fascinations and mysteries of church and ministry by studying and teaching, as well as by learning from my students. This body of knowledge was (and is) always growing and changing. To stimulate my growth, I was also a member of two professional societies: the American Association of Pastoral Counselors and the Society for Pastoral Theology. I will bring what I have experienced, learned, and discovered in all these experiences and encounters to my side of our conversation.

The other partners in our conversation are the present-day pastors I interviewed. To facilitate dialogue, I designed a set of interview questions about the experience and ministry of a pastor. (See the Appendix for a list of my dialogue questions.) Then I searched for persons to interview. I focused on Gen X and Millennial pastors. In a few cases, I spoke with pastors who did not fall in those specific categories, but who had specialized training or experience that I thought might be helpful.

Two denominational staff members, two regional leaders, and a seminary official sent invitations to lists of people they selected. I also put this invitation on my own Facebook page. When someone volunteered to be part of a conversation, I sent my questions and asked them to suggest a time to talk. I then called the person, and we would visit for an hour or more about ministry. My list of questions would typically guide our conversation.

I did all these interviews by phone, except for one. (There was one local pastor who came by my office.) As we talked, I would type out as complete a summary of what they were saying as I could. When I called a person, I knew only their name, phone number, and time zone. In conversation, I would learn more about their location and type of ministry, and I would gather information about how the pandemic had affected their work. Then our conversation would normally move to other related topics of interest.

Originally, I had hoped for at least a couple dozen of these conversations. Eventually, I had thirty. Twelve of the conversations were with women and eighteen were with men. There were at least six denominations represented. I did not interview any megachurch pastors; the size of worshipping congregants ranged from a dozen or so to about two hundred.

I talked with pastors in all four time zones. I spoke with at least three Asian American pastoral leaders. I learned that one interviewee was African American from something he said midway in our conversation. The spectrum of persons interviewed could have been wider, but I went with the volunteers who emerged through the process of gathering a pool of people to talk with. All the pastors were under the age of fifty, and all were actively engaged in ministry. The pool was what might be called a "convenience sample."

I enjoyed these talks. I was grateful for the openness and candor with which these pastors spoke. When I sent a thank you note, I often learned that my conversation partner enjoyed it as well. There was frequent comment on how good it was to be listened to about their work. At least a few told me that they saw the significance of their little churches and ministries in a new light after talking with me! Two had recently finished Doctor of Ministry dissertations. I was able to read both dissertations to my benefit. When asked, I helped one person get in touch with an acquisition editor and provided a little help in writing a proposal. I also learned that two pastors had written books based on their ministry interests and concerns. You will hear from these conversations in the following chapters.

Recently, I have been in touch with each of those pastors again to ask their permission to quote them and to check my accuracy in hearing what they said. These new pastor friends comprise the second partner in this conversation.

I have said there are two parties, but there are really three parties in this conversation. The third party is a variety of resource people—scholars, local and regional leaders, researchers, and practitioners. I will also rely on their work in these pages. The insights of these wonderful partners will enrich our conversation immeasurably!

Here are the topics we will explore in this book:

First, we will devote two chapters to wide overviews.

- "I Don't Think We're in Christendom Anymore." We will look back over the last fifty to seventy-five years focusing on what ministry and church life was and why it changed.
- "Sailing against the Wind in a Leaky Boat." We will take a broad look at ministry in our present situation and consider the immediate prospects for the church.

Next, we will look at certain aspects of church and ministry that seem to have new urgency today.

- "Spiritually Hungry in a World of Possibility." How to respond to spiritual searching by the those who are "spiritual but not religious" as well as those already in our faith communities.
- "Singing God's Praises in a New Key." How to guide worship that speaks to each generation and its needs.
- "Crying in the Chapel." How to provide community and pastoral care for the lonely and the hurting.
- "An Alternative to Illiterate Proof Texting." How to foster biblical literacy.
- "Enduring the Exile; Flourishing in the Desert." How to address fatigue and burnout in pastor and people and engage renewal strategies.

Then we will explore additional issues and missional opportunities in this new and different age of church. These include:

- "Seeking Racial Shalom in a Changing Nation." Engaging the changing racial and ethnic makeup of our country.
- "Mother God Comes Close." Welcoming the new day of women in ministry and adopting inclusive theological language.
- "A Visible Church for an Invisible People." Exploring fresh outreach with persons with disabilities.

- "A Humble Journey: Marriage, Family, Gender, and Sexuality Today." Caring for the changing lives of individuals and families, including gay and transgender persons.
- "Faithfulness in a Frail Creation: What Can a Congregation Do?" Becoming more deeply involved in creation care.
- "Figure Skating on Thin Ice: Navigating the Political Divide." Offering prophetic witness and conversation in a politically polarized nation and church.

Weighty topics all! Our hope is that there will be food for thought and discussion—as well as stimulation for new ministry initiatives.

You might wonder about this book's title, *Rowing Together through the Rapids*.[2] That image came from an experience I had some years ago. I once went on a white-water rafting trip with my friend and brother-in-law, Don. A few of us were taken in an inflatable raft on a three-day journey down a mountain river.

Every time our oarsman pulled the boat to shore for a time to stretch and walk around, I saw him intensely visiting with other oarsmen who were there. I asked him what they were discussing. He told me that they were telling each other what they knew about what was ahead.

Though each of them did this trip several times over the summer, each time was a little different. For example, the early season trips might have snow run off and the river might be high and wild. If the summer was dry, places in the river might have become so shallow that it would be difficult to get through. In conversation, they were offering each other insight about what was ahead. They were providing guidance about the best way forward on this particular day.

We, of various ages and experiences, are rowing through these rapids of ministry together. We have the opportunity to learn from each other, encourage one another, and provide assurance. I will be grateful if this "little life jacket of a book" might help us make the trip without capsizing! Welcome aboard! It's going to be quite a ride!

FOR REFLECTION AND CONVERSATION

1. What is your greatest joy in your present ministry or church life? What is your greatest disappointment or frustration?

2. Who is your "go to" person when you are puzzled, disappointed, or frustrated? How does this help?

3. What were your strongest areas of preparation for your present ministry or church life? What issues or needs do you face for which you feel unprepared?

4. Of the topics mentioned above, which ones do you look forward to exploring and conversing about? What other topics interest you?

NOTES

[1] For a summary overview and his key works, see Loren B. Mead, *The Once and Future Church Collection* (Bethesda: The Alban Institute, 2001).

[2] I didn't know until much later that there was a similarly titled book on a related subject: Tod Bolsinger, *Canoeing the Mountains: Christian Leadership in Uncharted Territory* (Downers Grove: IVP Books, 2015).

CHAPTER 1

I Don't Think We're in Christendom Anymore

WHERE ARE WE, AND HOW DID WE GET HERE?

I thank my God for every remembrance of you,
always in every one of my prayers for all of you,
praying with joy for your partnership
in the gospel from the first day until now.

Philippians 1:3-5

There are always mysteries when leading a church community. Why is this effort working and not that one? How did we end up in this particular situation? Where do we go from here? What guidance is available?

In this chapter, we will explore those questions from a long-term perspective, focusing on memories, recollections, and insights from the past. What gifts did we bring to the life of the church? What mistakes did we make? What did we happen to get right? We will also consider the impact of the pandemic. Together, these older experiences and reflections provide perspective, offer food for thought, and raise questions as we explore ministry and church life today and into the future.

THE WAY IT WAS—PERSONAL RECOLLECTIONS

A LOVE STORY

I was too young to realize it at the time, but I was part of a church that came back to life. In 1942, when I was eight years old, my minister father came to serve a bedraggled congregation in a small county seat town on the plains of northwestern South Dakota. The church consisted of eight discouraged members meeting in a weather-beaten and dilapidated old building. They had been battered by drought and depression, and they were barely holding on.

My father worked patiently with them, restarting the Sunday School and summer Vacation Bible School. He joined and worked with community organizations. In addition, he made many calls on farmers and ranchers in that sparsely settled area. These were people he understood well, having been born on a homestead himself. One rancher remembered that my dad visited on the day he was butchering. My dad stayed and helped; "good help too," the rancher told me. Further, my father was present for people in the crises, pains, spiritual hungers, and tragedies of their lives. There was at least some growth and a few signs of life in the church when he died, far too young, just a couple of years into this ministry.

His successor, the Rev. Jeanie Sherman and her large foster family, came and built well on my father's foundation. Gradually, the little church prospered. We built a modest but more adequate building and grew to more than one hundred members, both European-Americans and Native-Americans. I will tell more about this part of the story in chapter 8.

As young people, many of us were deeply influenced by what we experienced in this little church. I was one who responded to the community, message, and call I experienced there. I became a local church pastor and, later, a seminary professor.

My Ministry Journey

My ministry as a local church pastor started after seminary graduation in 1960 in another small town in South Dakota. Over time, my places of ministry ranged from Boston to the Colorado Rockies. There was great variety in those congregations from one that had all farmers to another that was an inner city "Old First Church." Still another was in a university community, and another was a young congregation in a stable, but once fast-growing, suburb. One of these churches had a Latinx congregation as part of its life, and another hosted and sponsored Laotian refugees. There are many memories—rich worship, winsome children and youth groups, exciting witness-through-the-arts events, fruitful mission trips, wedding and marriage ministries, vocational discovery ministries, and prophetic encounters focused on community and social issues such as school desegregation.

In these congregations, though, something else was going on. In contrast to the steady growth of my home church, I discovered that it was more and more difficult to attract people to faith in God and church involvement. Sometimes, it was even difficult to find people who had respect or appreciation for the church. Often, our church communities struggled to maintain a steady membership. As I looked back at the end of forty years of parish ministry, two of the smaller churches I had served had closed. My once vital home church had sold its building (it became a hunting lodge) and merged with a tiny community church. The larger congregations where I had been a pastor continued to survive, but with diminished people and resources.

A WIDESPREAD PHENOMENON

Over time, I learned that the congregations I had served were not unique in this regard. This decrease and decay were common to virtually all religious groups and, indeed, to many organizations. What's more, this downward turn seemed to be nationwide. (The same thing had been happening in Europe well before this time. However, faith, witness, and growth were still flourishing in many parts of the global south.)

I had begun serving my first church full time, after seminary pastorates, in 1960. Though I didn't know it at the time, that year marked the all-time high in church membership in the United States. American church membership had grown from about forty-five percent in 1890 to around eighty percent in 1960. All denominations and religious groups—Catholics, Protestants, and Jews—had experienced this surge.

But things were about to change, and the decline continues to the present day.

The Many Twentieth-Century Changes

There are many explanations for this decline. First, it's important to note that there were vast societal and cultural changes happening in America during the twentieth century. Many new things were happening. There was the increased availability of inexpensive family cars, a broad highway system, and many interesting places to go. Further, a technological revolution brought television into the American home. At first, there were just three network choices, but the options quickly expanded. Computers and programmable cell phones opened new worlds of knowledge, choice, and experience.

These changes, including the rise of professional sports and entertainment, invaded time and space once devoted to church and religion. In my childhood and youth, Sunday morning and evening was available time for worship, youth groups, Bible studies, and all manner of religious activities. But soon there were many other ways to use that time. As a pastor, I remember a Sunday morning when a couple of lay leaders kidded me, saying that if I didn't finish my sermon promptly within the allotted time, they were going to start one of the crowd chants for the local professional football team. The telecast of that game would start promptly at noon, and they didn't want a long sermon to get in the way of the game. But at least they were there; thousands had passed on worship that morning to tailgate, relax, and eat and drink in anticipation of the game.

With all these innovations and options, there was also a change of attitude. For many, Sunday worship and Sunday School had been a given, an assumption, an expectation. Now it became one choice among many! Often, the choices were hard. Families had to decide between worship and Christian education for their children on Sunday mornings or popular organized team sports that met at the same time.

Theologian Phyllis Tickle notes there were thought revolutions of many kinds going on during this century. Albert Einstein, with his theory of relativity, and other scientists were expanding the world of scientific investigation. New ideas sometimes led to uncertainty, and that uncertainty began to erode the religious certainty that had seemed secure in the past.

There were also developments in the field of biblical scholarship. People were exposed to new ideas about the cultural setting of the Bible, the transmission of the biblical text, ancient languages and issues in translation, and the mutual influence of ancient religions on each other. Scholars were talking openly about what could be known with certainty about the historical Jesus. These conversations and studies raised questions that sometimes began to erode a traditional confidence and trust in scripture.

Other changes were happening in the religious world. Many of these changes were the products of earlier historical movements. The Pentecostal Azusa Street revival in Los Angeles earlier in the century had opened the door for a vast and worldwide charismatic movement. The development (and popularity) of Alcoholics Anonymous and other twelve-step programs invited trust in a generic "higher power" and opened the door for a different sort of religious/spiritual experience. Others were drawn to the meditative practices of Zen Buddhism and other eastern religions. If that were not enough, there was also experimentation with hallucinogenic drugs as a door to religious ecstatic experience.[1]

Churches found themselves facing questions that had once been assumed settled. Among many others, these issues included the ordination and leadership of women. Further, churches found themselves responding to the skyrocketing rates of divorce and remarriage, realties often found even in the lives of religious leaders. Also, there was the opportunity to reexamine traditional attitudes on homosexuality and gender. It was, indeed, a new day.

These trends and changes have continued into the twenty-first century, and they have accelerated. While we attempt to understand how these changes have affected churches and ministers, we are invited to consider why some churches and denominations flounder—and why other churches and denominations flourish?

"Big Picture" Concepts of These Changes

Let's examine these changes and innovations from a different angle. While we sometimes see these changes as simply random, unrelated happenings, it is more likely that all this change reflects a sweeping historical movement. Here are three "big picture" ways to understand what has been happening.

A Perfect Storm with a Shock and Two Aftershocks

Harvard sociologist Robert Putnam and his associates described the 1960s and the years following as "A Perfect Storm," a storm that yielded a shock and two aftershocks. According to Putnam, these disruptions have profoundly affected all sorts of organizations and institutions.[2]

What was the perfect storm of the 1960s? Many things were happening at the same time. We have mentioned a few of these, but there were many others. There was a huge baby boomer population redefining itself through drug experimentation, changing sexual mores, and different and new understandings of morality. There were the tragic assassinations of both John Kennedy and Robert Kennedy as well as Martin Luther King, Jr., and Malcolm X. There was the unpopular and polarizing war in Vietnam. There were civil rights challenges and uprisings, both during King's life and in the wake of his death.

During this decade, Pope John XXIII had called the Vatican II Council which led to changes which some Catholics found exciting and fresh, and other Catholics found disheartening and concerning. Sales of religious books plummeted by one-third in this decade. Of the books that did sell, some of those books explored the theme of "The Death of God."[3] All of this had a huge impact on churches and other religious institutions. Weekly church attendance decreased from forty-nine percent in 1958 to forty-two percent in 1969, by far the sharpest decline ever recorded.[4]

Even more telling was the response to a statement regularly included in opinion polls. Respondents were asked to agree or disagree with this statement: "The influence of religion in America is growing." From 1957 to 1970, there was a marked decrease in agreement with that statement.

1957: sixty percent agreed;
1964: forty-five percent agreed;
1965: thirty-three percent agreed;
1967: twenty-three percent agreed;
1968: eighteen percent agreed;
1970: fourteen percent agreed.[5]

This was a change, the scholars noted, seemingly "from God's country to godless country!"[6] The political, military, and religious turmoil had an impact on all American institutions, and it is what Robert Putnam called "the perfect storm." This perfect storm resulted in a shock to every religious, social, and civic organization in America.

According to Putnam, this shock was followed by two aftershocks. The first aftershock was the rise of religious conservatism. With widespread moral, religious, and spiritual confusion, there was a marked decline in historic protestant churches, and there was corresponding growth in conservative churches. Perhaps, in those confusing times, people were looking for guidance, foundations, and firm stands on religion and morality. They perhaps believed that the more conservative-evangelical churches would provide this. A good bit of this growth was in churches that described themselves as "nondenominational."

The second aftershock was the subsequent disaffection with religion in general. A good part of this disaffection was likely the result of unhappiness with the prominent support by some conservative religious leadership of certain political causes and candidates. The reaction was strongest among those under the age of thirty.

These two aftershocks help us understand where we are today. They also highlight some of the current challenges for churches and their leaders. (We will talk more about that in our next chapter.)

There is yet another impact from the 1960s that is important for our understanding. Robert Putnam and Shaylyn Romney Garrett share a significant insight about this period:

> ...mainstream America entered the Sixties in an increasingly 'we' mode—with communes, shared values, and accelerating efforts toward racial and economic equality—and we left the Sixties in an increasingly 'I' mode—focused on 'rights,' culture wars, and what would be almost instantly dubbed the 'Me Decade' of the 1970s... Americans entered the 1960s moving toward community, but midway through the decade abruptly changed direction and left the 1960s behind, moving toward individualism.[7]

A Longer View—Revivals and Awakenings

William McLoughlin, a Brown University historian, took a longer view. He examined the history of American religion, and he did this by exploring revivals and, particularly, awakenings in the American experience.

It is important to be aware of the distinction between these terms. A revival, McLoughlin noted, "is the Protestant ritual...in which charismatic evangelists convey 'the Word' of God to large masses of people who, under this influence experience what Protestants call conversion, salvation, regeneration, or spiritual rebirth."

By contrast, "Awakenings—the most vital and yet most mysterious of all folk arts—are periods of cultural revitalization that begin in a general crisis of beliefs and values and extend over the period of a generation or so, during which a profound reorientation of beliefs and values takes place." While revivals affect the lives of individuals, "awakenings alter the world view of a whole people or culture."[8] He went on to describe these vast awakenings he discerned in American history.

McLoughlin believed that awakenings begin with a "crisis of legitimacy and deviations from old rules. Old norms cease to make sense." People "begin to doubt their sense and their sanity and to search about for new gods, new ways to perceive and comprehend the power that guides the universe.[9]

He further observed that there had been at least three such awakenings in America. The First Awakening took place over 1730-60. It marked the end of European styles of church organization and introduced an experiential, democratic, pan-Protestant community of faith called evangelicalism.

The Second Awakening happened over 1800–1839. In this period, Calvinist theological dominance ended. New understandings of free will, voluntary systems for church membership, and benevolence work came into being.

The Third Awakening occurred from 1890-1920 and had two distinctive expressions. One was the embracing of the "social gospel" movement with an emphasis on social justice and progressive politics. The other was the earlier mentioned Pentecostal movement with emphasis on miraculous transformation.

In the 1970s, McLoughlin speculated that we might be in the beginnings or in the middle of the "Fourth Great Awakening." He speculated that this awakening had begun in the 1960s. (This is the same decade that Putnam described as "the Perfect Storm"!) McLoughlin's book on awakenings came out in 1978, and he died in 1992.

Once again, he suggested that America was in a time of reorientation, a time of pondering who we are as a people and what we want to be, and, therefore, a time of challenge and change. In his opinion, the 1990s would see a consensus emerge. McLoughlin anticipated that enough people would have changed—been converted—to restructure institutions and politics on a vast scale.

He wrote,

> Such a reorientation will most likely include a new sense of the mystical unity of all mankind and of the vital power of harmony between man and nature. The godhead will be defined in less dualistic terms...of an absolutist sin-hating, death dealing 'Almighty Father in Heaven' and more in terms of a life-supporting, nurturing empathic, easy going parental (Motherly as well as Fatherly) image. There will be growing harmony with mother earth. Self-sacrifice rather than self-aggrandizement will become a dominant value. Cooperative effort will multiply.[10]

Wherever we are, religiously and politically, we can see that this awakening has stalled, is floundering, or is struggling to take shape. At any rate, the outcome is not yet apparent.

But what if McLoughlin was right about suggesting that our views and behaviors are impacted by these awakenings? If that's true, his perspective may offer us insights and wisdom about our life together and our ministries today. We do our ministry in a time of questioning and upheaval. And who knows? Perhaps, in this time of struggling and questioning, we may see the dawn of something new, including our witness and life as church leaders! The Fourth Great Awakening may still be in process.

A Still Longer View—the Five-Hundred-Year Rummage Sale

There is one other view that has an even longer frame of reference. The Right Reverend Mark Dyer, an Anglican bishop, has suggested that perhaps the way to understand what is happening to twenty-first century Christians is that somehow every five hundred years or so, the church feels compelled to hold a giant rummage sale! This is when the church "cleans out its attic."

Using that image, consider what the previous "rummage sales" might have been. About five hundred years ago (the 1500s), there was the Protestant Reformation. Doctrines, practices, and the structure and divisions of the church were all changed. These changes resulted in revitalized practices, outreach, renewal, and an expanding influence for both Protestants and Catholics.

Five hundred years before that (the 1000s), there was the "Great Schism" where the Church divided into the Eastern Orthodox and Western Roman Catholic branches. Issues that felt important and divisive led branches of the church to pursue their own life and mission and ways to more effective witness and influence within their respective expressions.

Five hundred years before that (the 500s), there was the fall of the Roman empire and the coming of the "Dark Ages." But there was also Pope Gregory "the Great." He is called "Great" because he led the church into some sense of coherence in those troubled times. Most of all, he is remembered for guiding Christianity into the monasticism that would "protect, preserve, and characterize it during the next five centuries."[11] The Dark Ages were not as dark as they would have been had not monasticism preserved learning from the past and offered education to those in its settings.

Five hundred years before that (the time of Jesus and the New Testament Church), there was the formation of the Christian church as a way for followers of Jesus to be faithful, paralleled by the emergence of the synagogue for Jewish believers. Five hundred years before that (500 BCE) was the exile and the return of Jews to Palestine, an important time of change for the faith leaders and people of our heritage. Five hundred years before that (1000

BCE) was the establishment of the kingships in Israel. Clearly, there were momentous changes in each of those five-hundred-year rummage sales!

If we are, indeed, in that kind of "rummage sale" moment today, what can we learn from the past? What should we do in this moment? A careful look at history might lead us to the understanding that, as in the past, the structures of institutional Christianity may need to change. It is even possible that some of those structures may collapse. For that matter, some of these structures may need to be shattered and set aside.

Out of that shattering and the change of a five-hundred-year rummage sale, Phyllis Tickle observes, there are always (or, at least, *usually*) three consistent results or corollary events. First, a new and more vital form of Christianity will emerge. Second, the organized expression of Christianity (churches, institutions, denominations) will be reconstituted into something else, something less rigid. Third, when the "incrustations of an overly established Christianity" are broken open, the faith will spread dramatically into new geographic and demographic areas.[12]

All of this will be strange and upsetting. Phyllis Tickle helps us make sense of this moment: "Intellectually, politically, economically, culturally, sociologically, religiously, psychologically—every part of us…has been reconfiguring, and these changes are now becoming a genuine maelstrom around us"[13]—because we may be living in the next five-hundred-year rummage sale.

Postscript: And Then the Pandemic

Up to this point, we have been discussing gradual changes over the last sixty to seventy-five years. Younger pastors will have started their ministries in this diminished but familiar "churchscape." (We will speak more about that in the next chapter.)

As if we needed even more change, in early 2020, the Covid Pandemic came. In February 2020, the World Health Organization named this emerging disease, and in March declared it a pandemic. States and cities immediately began establishing regulations to employ "social distancing." In many places, churches and schools were shut down. Church leaders were challenged to be ministers and lead churches in a time unlike any other.

This national and worldwide experience—this pandemic—had a clear beginning. However, the ending was both extended and unclear. As we learned more and more about the transmission of the virus, the value of masks, the development of testing, and the efficacy of vaccinations, the impacts of the pandemic slowly eased.

But in March 2020, the question for every church and every church leader, experienced or brand new, was "How do we do ministry now?" The most immediate awareness was focused on what we could NOT do: we could not make hospital calls; we could not comfort those in nursing homes; we could not console the bereaved; we could not conduct in-person funerals. Jonathan, one of the young pastors I interviewed, recalled, "I did my first Covid funeral at the end of March, and no one could come: no friends, no family, even the body was brought directly from the hospital."

Further, we could not gather in person for worship, choir practice, discussion or prayer groups, pastoral counseling, or board meetings. We wondered: how is it possible to be church, to worship God, to care for each other, and to serve our community in a time like this? The younger pastors I interviewed shared a variety of experiences in this regard.

Many people who had been coming to worship out of custom or habit no longer did so. When the pandemic eased, some of those people came back. Some stayed away for a while but gradually returned, while others never returned. Meredith reflected on that time: "We really didn't lose anybody to the pandemic, but then in my older smaller congregation, there was a natural decline due to members passing away or moving." At the other end of the age range, three pastors told me they lost their youth groups. By the end of the pandemic, one group of young people had graduated or gone on to other activities, and the younger children and youth did not pick up on youth activities and take the place of the group that had left.

Ministers and churches began looking for a way to worship and do other activities remotely, engaging a variety of platforms. Probably many could relate to James who recalls, "This called for a skill set I did not have." As churches gained a bit of help and experience, it became clear that several parts of the worship experience could not happen in this medium: we could not shake hands, embrace, pass the peace, or even pass the communion elements or an offering plate.

Once churches had moved into remote worship and other activities, there were benefits they might not have anticipated. James further recalls, "A man in our church had passed away during the pandemic. His widow lives too far away to attend worship, but she watches every Sunday. This has allowed us to reach out to her. These broadcasts have blurred the lines of what is our neighborhood. We have some people active in the life of our church who don't live in our neighborhood. We have had so many people who want to stay connected to the church they have known."

Tim and others noticed a related benefit: "Actually Zoom attracted some people in some categories. People in their twenties and thirties all had attended multiple services online. They had left the church for some reason or another and were skeptical. This was a way to audition churches. How does the theology of this church align with their values?"

I was surprised at Cindy's response: "Covid was a very good thing for us. Through a grant, we were able to get technology in the form of tablets for senior citizens, so they could get on Zoom. Because of Covid, we connect with people who no longer drive. We also use those tablets to translate spoken words into written words for our hard of hearing members. It's not foolproof, but it helps."

No doubt about it; all of us left the pandemic changed in one way or another![14]

AND SO

It is possible that these long historical overviews and recent crises may answer some questions for church leaders today. At the same time, our current situation may raise additional questions.

I am reminded of the scene in the movie "The Wizard of Oz" just after the tornado. Dorothy looks around and says to her dog, *"Toto, I don't think we're in Kansas anymore!"* That comment may help us understand our current situation! Toto, I don't think we are in Christendom anymore! We are certainly not in the Christendom of widespread Christian belief, membership, participation, and influence. We are not in the Christendom I remember from my childhood and youth. In many ways, we are in a strange new world. We need a way of caring, witnessing, and being as we move forward.

As challenging as today may be, we find ourselves living and serving and leading in a world full of exciting ministry opportunities. As we continue our conversation, we will grapple with these fascinating challenges and opportunities.

FOR CONVERSATION AND REFLECTION

1. What is your first memory of church? What has changed since then? What has mostly stayed the same?

2. At the beginning of this chapter, I said that I would tell about some of the previous generation of church leaders' contributions and mistakes. What contributions did you notice? What mistakes?

3. What did I miss in describing the changes in society, culture, and church over the last decades?

4. With which of the "big picture" images (the perfect storm, great awakenings, rummage sales) do you most closely connect? What does it reveal for you?

5. How did you relate to the younger pastors' descriptions of responding to the pandemic? What was your experience?

6. In the present, what is most fulfilling for you as a church leader? What is most concerning or stressful?

7. At the beginning of this chapter, I cited Philippians 1:3-5 to provide guidance and perspective for our present church life and ministry. What scripture passages do you choose for perspective on ministry and church today?

NOTES

[1] Phyllis Tickle has described this century of changes in *The Great Emergence* (Grand Rapids: Baker Books, 2008), 63-76.

[2] Robert Putnam and David Campbell, *American Grace: How Religion Divides and Unites Us* (New York: Simon & Schuster, 2010).

[3] For example, see Thomas J.J. Altizer and William Hamilton, *Radical Theology and the Death of God* (Indianapolis: Bobbs-Merrill Co., 1966).

[4] Robert Putnam and Shaylyn Romney Garrett, *The Upswing: How America Came Together a Century Ago and How We Can Do It Again* (New York: Simon & Schuster, 2020), 138.

[5] Ibid.

[6] Ibid.

[7] Ibid., 301.

[8] William G. McLoughlin, *Revivals, Awakenings, and Reform* (Chicago: University of Chicago Press, 1978), xiii.

[9] Diana Butler Bass, *Christianity After Religion: The End of Church and the Birth of a New Spiritual Awakening* (San Francisco: HarperOne, 2012), 62.

[10] McLoughlin, 214.
[11] Tickle, 22. The descriptions of these "rummage sales" is also from Tickle.
[12] Ibid., 17.
[13] Ibid., 25.
[14] For a thoughtfully researched report of the impact of the pandemic on pastors, see Eileen Campbell-Reed, "Pandemic Pastoring: What It Was Like; How it Changed Us; Where We Go from Here," https://cdn.eileencampbellreed.org/wp-content/uploads/PandemicPastoring-Report-FULL-9-1-2022.pdf., accessed 19 August 2023.

CHAPTER 2

Sailing against the Wind in a Leaky Boat

"Who then is this, that even the wind and the sea obey him?"

Mark 4:41b

Down through the centuries, the church has been portrayed as a small boat on the sea of the world with a mast in the form of a cross. Indeed, since 1948 this has been the logo of the World Council of Churches. Sometimes this image is accompanied with a prayer: "Dear Lord, be with us—our boat is so small, and the ocean is so large!" This little boat seems to be a fitting symbol for church and ministry in the world buffeted by the forces we mentioned in the last chapter. We have been through storms. Our faith communities have been battered by rough seas, and we are sailing into strong winds.

What is it like to be a pastor or church leader today with the changing status of Christianity and church involvement? Are there any predictions about our future? What perils and tasks await us? Are there ways to counter these trends? What promises can we claim for our present and for our future? We will explore these questions in this chapter.

The Present

For years there has been a steady increase of those who check "none" to identify their religious preference surveys. It has grown from about five percent of the population in the 1970s to around twenty-five percent or more today.[1] This increase of "nones" is spread among all age groups but is larger among the younger cohorts. For example, among the "Silent Generation" (those born 1928–1945), eighty-four percent identify as Christian, and half go to church weekly. Among Millennials (those born 1981–1996), forty-nine percent identify as Christian, and twenty-two percent go to church weekly. Forty percent of Millennials claim no religion. The next generation is Generation Z (those born 1996–2011). Looking at this generation, researchers identify religious and spiritual interest but a general distrust of organized religion—and little involvement in religious instruction or worship. Instead, the researchers suggest that they see evidence of "faith unbundled." By this they mean that young people increasingly construct their faith by combining elements such as beliefs, identity, practices, and community from a variety of religious and nonreligious sources.[2]

As I visited with Gen X and Millennial pastors, I found acceptance and understanding of our present situation. Instead of negative criticism of "the way things are," these younger pastors offered remarkable insights about the life and health of the church today.

Here are some of their responses:

Amber: "I connect to the nones. I understand the response of nones."

Evan observed, "For most ministers, this age feels like a dramatic change. I am better with nones and dones ["Dones" are those individuals who, in answering a religious survey, indicate that they are *done* with religion.] I am better with lots of questions and with those who are disgruntled or wounded. We know there are a lot more of those folks. To me this doesn't feel foreign; these are my people. That is where we are going."

Evan further reflects: "I was in seventh grade when 9/11 happened, and I experienced the instability, fear, and evaporation of institutional trust. People could fly a plane into these buildings! This deeply impacted my generation. We had questions about God and access to all kinds of answers. The world felt fragile, and we carried a new level of anxiety with us. We entered a different kind of reality. For the church to continue to do things as usual was to ignore what had happened."

Jonathan concurs and reflects, "I grew up in the none-done generation. Among the people I grew up with, I was the only one who had a religious component that was active. It didn't take root in any of them. I have been a minister-of-sort to my friend group; they brought their life concerns, deaths, breakups, and relationship losses to me. I guess I was in the role of chaplain for them."

"After entering the professional ministry, I was called into weddings, funerals, and baby dedications with these 'none' friends. If people wanted to have a wedding that had a coherence to it, wanted words to be said over their loved ones, or wanted their children consecrated, they turned to me. The hunger is there. For those who didn't grow up in faith, they don't know what to do with it. Their children have questions that they, their parents, are unequipped to answer."

Reflecting on his time of ministry, Peter A. observes, "It's remarkable how many values of Christianity they (nones and dones) subscribe to such as love for neighbor, concern for the refugee, or health care for all. The irony is that they want the values of Christ's kingdom but not the church that should represent those values."

These ministers are experiencing and addressing what religious journalist Bob Smietana notes: "In other words, America's grandparents go to church; their grandkids do not. America's grandparents are white and Christian; their grandkids are not. These two groups of older and younger Americans are living in what are essentially different universes when it comes to race and religion…"[3]

In the past, churches have maintained steady membership and grown numerically in several ways: attracting and discipling new converts, welcoming Christian people moving into their community, and educating and nurturing the faith of children of the families in the church.

However, "drop-ins" to a church in today's world are relatively infrequent, and the birth rate among all generations is shrinking to bare maintenance of our nation's population. In churches with an older adult predominance, the chances of having a significant number of people under age eighteen is very small. Growth from the nurturing of children of families in the church will likely be small, and probably non-existent for many religious groups.

For many congregations, the present experience may be a church of mostly older adults. This does not need to cause despair. As a member of the Silent Generation myself, I fervently hope that churches don't give up on ministering with and claiming the gifts of older adults. There can be vigorous churches of elders who still have much leadership, creativity, energy, and care to offer. Moreover, much of religion's "safety net" and disaster response is done by older adults. However, to do ministry with the elderly well, American churches will need to overcome their tendency toward ageism. But that is another story to tell, a story that I have tried to communicate elsewhere.[4]

The Future—Pew Research Center Demographic Projections

We have been talking about the present. What does the future hold?

In a widely publicized study, the Pew Research Center made note of the percentages of people who have changed how they describe their religious affiliation or lack thereof. Researchers then asked: If this religious affiliation change pattern continues at the present rate, or accelerates, or decelerates, what will the population makeup look like in 2070?

In the current American population, they estimated that sixty-four percent were Christians. They estimated the unaffiliated, the nones, at thirty percent. Both of those numbers are higher than the numbers we suggested earlier, but in this study the researchers included children of both groups. Adherents of non-Christian religions measured about six percent of the American population.[5]

What will the American population look like in 2070? Depending on whether the present rate of religious preference change decreases, maintains, or increases, research projections suggest that the number of Christians of all ages will decrease from sixty-four percent to between fifty-four and thirty-five percent. Nones will increase from around thirty percent to fifty-two percent. Finally, they suggest that non-Christian religious populations will probably grow to about twelve or thirteen percent of the population.[6]

Some media reports of this study focused only on the most extreme possibility—that in 2070, only thirty-five percent of the population would identify as Christian of any type. However, the compilers of the study were much more measured. They made clear these are not forecasts, but projections based on present and possible trends. Further, they readily acknowledged that there could be events "such as war, economic depression, climate crisis, changing immigration patterns, or religious innovations" that could change current religious switching trends. Whether these types of events happen or not, there could also be another Christian revival or reawakening.[7] However, without some such dramatic change, the future of religion in America will probably be within one of the scenarios the researchers have described.

Pastoral Experience in the Middle of This

The assessment of Bob Smietana is straightforward and sobering: "The average American church is shrinking and shrinking fast."[8] Twenty years ago, average attendance at worship services in the United States was 137 people. Today, it is sixty-five. Church membership reflects a similar decline.[9] Furthermore, thousands of churches close every year. Some estimates place this number at four to five thousand church closures annually.

Scott Thumma, director of the Hartford Institute for Religious Research, notes that half of the churches in the country are "in a precarious situation with doubtful prospects." He continues: "Certainly, there is evidence of pockets of vitality in new church plants, minority-led and immigrant congregations and in communities with a clear mission and sense of purpose." But for many, there is a need for radical self-examination. To survive and, more than that, to thrive, Thumma concludes that "congregations and religious leaders must embrace a willingness to change and an attitude of innovation and adaptation to maintain a vibrant and diversely sized congregational presence in the future."[10]

Leading a church today may require significant changes for many ministers. For example, some church leaders may be required to serve as part-time or bi-vocational ministers. In other cases, churches may need to reconsider the ownership and use of buildings and facilities. Finally, some church leaders may be called to assist a church in closing. Here are a few thoughts about these possibilities based on my own experience, the research of other practitioners, and the insights of the church leaders I interviewed.

Transitioning to Bi-vocational or Part-time Ministry

For many churches, the journey into the future will involve reconsidering how to manage resources of people, property, and finances. It may be that a church's pastoral leadership position will need to become part-time. Of course, this is nothing new; it is as old as the New Testament church. Several times in the New Testament, we read about the Apostle Paul working at his trade and supporting himself while carrying on his missionary activity. In Acts 18:3, we are told that Paul was a "tentmaker." Living in seaport community, it's possible that he might have also been a sail maker or a sail repairer. Paul reports that he earned his own living while serving and placed his example before his readers in 1 Corinthians 9:14–18 and 2 Thessalonians 3:7–10. In these passages, Paul challenges other believers to be as committed to doing their part in the church's life and witness as he has.

African American and immigrant churches have traditionally been open to part-time leadership in their churches—and it may be time for others to embrace that same approach. G. Jeffrey MacDonald is a pastor and free-lance journalist who *accidently* discovered and experienced this. He subsequently observed many churches with part-time pastors and wrote helpfully about this in his book *Part-Time Is Plenty: Thriving without Full-Time Clergy*.[11]

His accidental discovery happened in a church in Newbury, Massachusetts. Having exhausted their endowment and unable to pay a full-time pastor, this congregation had decided that it was necessary to close.

They invited MacDonald to come and lead a few final worship services. Within a few weeks, however, the church decided not to disband but to continue with a radically different ministry model. Their plan was to reduce the minister's hours from forty hours a week to ten hours a week. The church also eliminated the church administrator position. They decided that members would receive training to provide leadership in other areas of church life. Eight years later, according to MacDonald, the church "is thriving by several measures."

He makes it clear that this change was not because he was any "rescue hero or turnabout guru." The survival of the church was rather the result of the church learning and discovering as they went along together. From this experience, MacDonald went on to observe many other churches that had part-time ministers with good results. He began to study those churches and discerned wise practices and patterns.

This leads to MacDonald's basic thesis: "Congregations *can* experience *more* vitality, not less, after switching to part-time clergy. They can get there by following a few tested steps and principles, no matter where they're located or what denomination they belong to."[12]

How can this kind of transition lead to growth and vitality? It starts with the belief that members of the congregation have ministry gifts to offer. As the Apostle Paul explains in 1 Corinthians 12:7: "To each is given the manifestation of the Spirit for the common good."

Anticipating this kind of change, the church negotiates with a pastor regarding the number of hours of employment and the types of ministerial activities the pastor will provide. Then the congregation members identify what ministries and organizational and administrative tasks they will provide. Through ongoing conversation, training, and guidance, both the pastor and the members grow in their understanding of new roles and responsibilities.

The basic role of the part-time pastor is to help the congregation reclaim and practice "the priesthood of all believers." In short, it is the responsibility of the pastor to help the congregation become a community of ministers with their varying gifts and contributions.

This basic role of a part-time pastor may require at least three possible sub-roles. First, the pastor will be an equipper—helping to build up congregational capacity for effective ministry. Second, the pastor will be an ambassador—representing the congregation to the wider community in various settings. Third, the pastor will be a multi-staff team member—

contributing reliably whatever specific responsibilities are needed from the pastor.[13]

MacDonald further notes that being a part-time minister is actually good for the minister! He suggests that serving in a part-time capacity helps ground the minster, spiritually anchoring the minister in the work of worship, Bible study, and preaching. He also suggests that serving part-time provides financial grounding, allowing the minister to pursue other avenues of work that might provide compensation. In MacDonald's case, while serving as a part-time pastor, he felt free to pursue his work as a free-lance journalist. His compensation for his part-time ministry provided a small but steady income during seasons when he was not able to land journalism assignments. He suggests that many part-time ministers might experience something similar in their situations.[14]

As simple as this new approach sounds, both churches and denominations will be required to rethink their understanding of both church and ministry. What MacDonald proposes, though, is a hopeful method well worth re-thinking and re-strategizing. Others have been open to MacDonald's suggestions. One regional denominational leader is leading his region in an exploration of part-time ministry. During his recent sabbatical, the Rev. Jerrod Hugenot studied and wrote a guidebook for churches with part-time and shared ministries. Based on his experiences in New York State, he has conducted workshops on these topics. In his presentations, he often reflects on the insights found in MacDonald's book.[15]

One possibility for other part-time employment to supplement a part-time pastor's salary might be a chaplaincy position. While we might think first of military chaplains or hospital chaplains, opportunities for chaplaincy have multiplied in recent years. Dr. Trace Haythorn, former Executive Director for the Association for Pastoral Clinical Education, notes the varied settings that currently engage chaplains. Veterinary clinics are looking for chaplains. There is a chaplain at the huge Atlanta airport. There are chaplains serving in the court system and at ports in New York City. There are chaplains for bicycle messengers and chaplains serving at racetracks. Tyson Foods and other corporations employ chaplains to provide care and service for employees.[16]

A chaplain has the role of being a spiritual and caring presence to all people of whatever religion or none. Many of these chaplaincies, particularly the new and experimental ones, will likely be part-time positions with part-time pay. These types of positions may be opportunities for ministry and employment for those who find themselves serving as a part-time pastor of a congregation.

Among the younger ministers with whom I spoke, a number are doing part-time or bi-vocational ministry. Though none were part-time chaplains, a number had other employment. Meredith, for example, had been a receptionist for a chiropractor and is serving in a part-time position with for her denominational region. Cindy is now an occupational therapist. Jessica teaches English to refugees. Jeremy is a professor at a small Catholic college. For a year, Randy accepted a twenty-five-hour-a-week appointment while running a coffee house ministry in another city. The church required him to keep a log of the hours he worked and his activities on behalf of the church. Based on his documentation, at the end of the year, his church was able to offer him a modest full-time salary.

Some fulfill their part-time ministry while taking care of family responsibilities (without additional employment). Edris has two children, ages eleven and four. Mark serves one church part-time and another church "very part-time." Primary income is provided by his wife who works for Starbucks, and he takes care of many of the parental responsibilities. Joanna is about to move from three-fourths time to one-half time. She plans to spend her additional time writing, speaking, or consulting.

While I did not ask, I gathered that these pastors did not specifically select part-time ministry. Rather, they accepted it as something a small church would need and something that they were able and willing to provide. There was one exception. During his Ph.D. studies, Jeremy requested, and was granted, ordination to a teaching ministry. Teaching religion in college is his ordained calling and his main source of income. He also serves in a one-quarter time ministry with a church. There, he leads worship, teaches confirmation classes, makes hospital calls, and attends a monthly council meeting.

His responsibilities resemble what I heard from others. The churches seemed to need leadership in worship, preaching, the teaching of Bible classes, pastoral counseling, and occasional hospital and bereavement care. Part-time ministers are able and willing to fulfill these responsibilities. In the words of one of these pastors, "The church pretty much runs itself. They know each other very well."

Because Jeremy had specifically chosen part-time bi-vocational ministry, I asked him to share more about that. He responded:

> On the one hand, having a part time minister allows congregations to keep going when they otherwise couldn't. It also allows persons who cannot do full-time ministry to do pastoral ministry. However, it probably postpones some of the conversations that congregations may need to be having. The nice part is the additional income. I teach in a small college that could not give us substantial raises for a long time. The tough part is that busy times of the college year and the church year are the same. For example, the end of the fall semester and Advent-Christmas time. There are times when it feels overwhelming. In most instances, I do find it enriching. Sometimes the things I am talking about with the students overlap with what I am talking about with the church. I wanted to be ordained to teaching ministry because I felt this was my calling. This arrangement helps me to balance these two aspects.

Reconsidering Church Buildings and Facilities

Increasingly, churches will need to think not only about staff and pastoral leadership; they will also need to think about the buildings in which they meet. I talked about this at length with Jason M. who wrote his Doctor of Ministry dissertation on this topic.[17] His dissertation explores the process of a church going through this decision-making experience while participating with a cohort of other churches. This process was guided by the RootedGood organization[18] using the "Good Futures Accelerator" that the organization provides. Jason is also available to help churches work on these decisions about their property.[19]

Many churches now have a larger building than they need and must ask important questions: Is our building an asset or a liability? Is it possible to change our building from a liability to an asset, or even a blessing? How did we get here, and what are the possibilities for the future?

It is always good to remember our history. Jason points out that, following World War II, there was a huge baby boom and corresponding growth in churches. There was an obvious need for Christian education space. Jason explains that, in 1959, at the peak of this season of building, churches invested the equivalent of four billion dollars in today's currency in church buildings. Further, as we noted in the previous chapter, 1960 was the peak of religious membership and attendance. Churches were building at the height of the growth, just before decline began.

Following that peak of church membership and attendance, societal upheaval affected all sorts of organizations (including churches). Beginning in the early 1960s, attendance began declining. And that decline continues today. As many as 100,000 church buildings will be sold or repurposed throughout the United States by 2030. This may mean that in any given neighborhood, over the near future, a third or more of present church properties will no longer be churches.[20]

For any church with unused—and expensive—space, an urgent concern is turning that liability into an asset. Even more, a church needs to consider further how to change that asset into a blessing for the surrounding community.

Jason suggests that churches have a range of options:

- Keep doing what we are doing, [eventually] sell our building to the highest bidder, and give the money to a good cause.

- Make small changes, like renting out space to other churches or non-profits, generating a little money to help us keep going for a little longer.

- Completely rethink how we use the building without making major remodels.

- Completely remodel the building into something else with a guarantee that some of the space will be reserved for the church.

- Completely remodel the building for some other use while the church meets somewhere else.

- Completely remodel the building for something and consider it our legacy to our neighborhood.[21]

Many communities need housing, both marketplace and affordable housing. However, there may be other community needs where a church space would be helpful. The basic step for a congregation moving in this direction is to listen. It is crucial to understand the needs of the community—and it is essential to talk with neighbors, folks on the street, businesspeople, social service providers, and governmental leaders. The central question is important: Is there some way for our building, our land, or our other property to bless this community?

If a church decides to remodel the building to help provide community housing, for example, it is important to partner with a developer early on. There are many details, procedures, regulations, and negotiations along the way where expertise will be needed. Ideally, the church will lead in making decisions, but a knowledgeable and active partner is essential.

Good stewardship of buildings and property can take ministry into new paths!

Leading a Church through Closure

As we noted, thousands of churches close each year. It is important to realize that this does not necessarily identify failure for either people or pastor. Churches have stages of life, just as individuals do. A church's lifespan may not be unlimited. A church may have come into being to respond to a new opportunity, a particular population, or a specific mission. When that has been achieved, when the intended constituency has moved on, or when the original recipients of that mission no longer need it, it may be time for a church to close.

Gail Cafferata, an Episcopal priest, experienced the closing of a church she had loved and served for nine years. As she reflected on her experience, she interviewed other pastors who had gone through a church closure. She reported on her discoveries and guidance in a book, *The Last Pastor: Faithfully Steering a Closing Church*.[22]

An amateur sailing enthusiast, Cafferata uses a nautical theme to frame her work. Indeed, she finds sailing to be a useful interpretive metaphor for a church moving toward the mission of closure. She writes:

> The gifts of all the baptized are needed to keep the ship working and safe on its journey. When the congregation confronts strong winds or crosscurrents, the company of the faithful moves their ship ahead by loving God and one another…[Judicatory persons are the coast guard, to come and help with process "when a church calls out in distress."]…As in a sailboat, the wind of the Holy Spirit lifts the sails of the congregation and propels it forward. Wind fills our faces with hope and expectations for a good future. When the wind shifts, a

good skipper follows it…There is no easy way…God's "mark" isn't the survival of a congregation. It's being and becoming more and more the people God is creating us to be even if that means leaving the ship that carried us with peace, joy, and hope, for so long and so far.[23]

A transformational pastor is needed to lead this process of discernment and decision. This pastor will need to be "differentiated" from the conflict and the storms blowing all around. A knowledge and practice of church-family systems theory will be most helpful. The pastor will lead this slow, torturous process to closure. The pastors who do this well "guide with their rudder—the gospel of resurrection faith—inviting their congregation to look to Jesus Christ and imagine for themselves a new future after death."[24]

According to Cafferata, at the end of this process, there needs to be a "good enough death," that is, a closing ritual or celebration. This event would celebrate the church's past and present ministries, provide an opportunity to thank God and others, make it possible for the church to leave a legacy, and console those who have been part of the ministry.[25] That sentence is so important! If a church must close, the closing can be painful and disillusioning—or the closing can be hopeful and empowering. The ministries of the past need to be celebrated. And the saints who served—living and dead—need to be named, recognized, and thanked.

It is so helpful for the church to "leave a legacy." Closing churches have found various ways to do this. One church, whose real estate was sold, gave the money to support several causes it had served over the years. Among other things, it gave a seminary an endowment for a "Chair of Congregational Health." It was the hope of this church that this professor would prepare future ministers to respond to churches in crisis as they had been. At least two other churches, in my knowledge, gave their buildings to fledgling young congregations. In these cases, both receiving congregations were thriving immigrant groups. A legacy like that gives hope and eases the pain.

Leading a church through closure comes at a cost to the pastor leading the process. Gail Cafferata found within herself, and within other pastors, feelings of failure, fragility, and self-blame. This might spill over to the pastor's relationships with family members and close friends. It may lead to a need for therapy and a renewed engagement or enlargement of the pastor's spiritual practices.

For some pastors, this experience of closing a church may impact their ministerial career. Some may experience a lack of respect from others or delays in finding the next ministry opportunity. All in all, Cafferata gives us an important look at a painful, but common, process many churches will face over the coming years. Thankfully, she also models how to do this difficult process well.[26]

I raised questions about church closings with the younger pastors that I spoke with. Two of them are aware that this is imminent for them within the next few years. Both churches have sold their buildings and are embedded in another church's building. These congregations were able to continue financially as they drew down funds from their building's sale to keep going. Closure at some point in the fairly near future seems likely. Another pastor, serving as a bi-vocational minister with a somewhat healthier and pluckier little congregation, expressed the hope that she would never have to close a church.

Only one minister I interviewed had already experienced a church's closing. At my request, I visited with David at length about his experience. He graduated from seminary in 2018. After a year of discernment, he accepted a call and began ministry in June of 2019. He sensed that the church wanted a fresh new start. Though there were still some unresolved feelings about a former pastor, the congregation hoped that this newly ordained pastor would attract younger families with children and help the church move forward.

David said the church understood that it needed to allow time for this to happen. Then the pandemic hit. He recalls, "This threw a wrench into any momentum. Within nine months after my arrival, the pandemic shut down everything and put any possible program on pause." At this point, he could only relate to members virtually. The vulnerability of this older membership during the pandemic started to stir some thoughts, doubts, and questions about the future of the church.

Toward the end of the lock-down period of Covid, the church started planning for its two-hundredth anniversary. This was an occasion to reflect and re-imagine what church is like and could be like in the future. In 2021, they held that two-hundredth anniversary celebration. There were a variety of events, including an open house, a meal, a Sunday morning worship service when a previous long-term pastor preached, and a reception. The occasion was marked with festive music, some historical pieces, and a recognition from the denomination. There was celebration of past and present as well as thinking about the future of First Baptist.

As 2021 passed into 2022, in the aftermath of the celebration, there was a more somber assessment of the state of the church and its future. While there were many thoughts about possibilities, there was also uncertainty, discouragement, and concern about its long-term viability. These conversations took place through the summer and into the fall. There were discussions about possibilities of merging with some other congregation or selling the property and becoming a house church. These conversations were conducted by the executive committee of lay leaders from the congregation in consultation with their judicatory staff. Ultimately, this group recommended that the congregation should close the church.

David's role at this time was mostly being available to the grieving people who had been there the longest. I asked what this had entailed. He responded: "Listening skills, being able to hear what people were saying and feeling, offering pastoral care, knowing how to be there for them. They were facing giving up a church they had known all their lives." He added, "In retrospect I wish I had done more—being proactive in distributing information to the congregation, urging more transparency, better communication, more helping people be aware throughout the process." However, his mentors and those who knew the history of the church assured him that what he had done was fitting and helpful.

Eventually, the meeting was held for the congregation to vote on the recommendation to close. He recalls, "Some people were visibly distraught. Some abstained from voting. Of those voting, the vote did pass."

The last worship service at First Baptist Church was the first Sunday in November 2022. Understandably, it was more somber than the anniversary celebration had been. David recalls, "I think it was a funeral that left people feeling unsettled. People in the church were still processing some of the questions about what comes next. There was still a lot of anger and frustration. Both the pastor of the Korean church that met in our building and I preached. I focused my sermon on the legacy of First Baptist, both in its history and in the present. I wanted them to know that in this season of uncertainty, First Baptist Church has been faithful throughout its history."

"I had many conversations after the service about what people were feeling. We took a picture of the members at the worship center. Some were ready to move on to the next stage of their spiritual journey, wherever it would take them. However, there was uneasiness and uncertainty for a lot of congregation members."

"After that service," David said, "I was officially relieved of duties."

I asked David how being part of this had affected him. He responded, "This was my very first church. I didn't expect it to end this way! Early on, those feelings were very strong. What could I have done, more or better? How could I have used other skills to keep the church from closing? Pretty strong feelings. There was a lot of beating myself up for sure."

David was wise to listen to the counsel of a retired long-term pastor of the church, as well as his local clergy association friends, and members of the regional staff. Eventually he was able to conclude this was not his fault. He had done what he could.

AND SO

This chapter has explored several aspects of being church and doing ministry in the present day. There are many other considerations that we will explore in the following chapters. As we move forward, we will talk about some of the other essentials of church life: spiritual growth, community building, pastoral care, worship, environmental concerns, and much more. How can we be the best we can be? And how can we be empowered to touch the heart of a changing world?

FOR CONVERSATION AND REFLECTION

1. Does this chapter describe what you are experiencing in church and ministry? Where does your experience differ?

2. Are you, or have you been, a bi-vocational pastor or part-time pastor—or have you been part of a church with one? How did your experience compare with what this chapter described?

3. Are you aware of a church's closing? Have you experienced the closing of a church? How did that experience compare to the stories in this chapter?

4. What is most rewarding in your life of faith, church involvement, and/or ministry in the last five years? What is most disappointing, painful, or frustrating?

5. What subject(s) do you most hope will be explored in our next conversations?

NOTES

[1] Linda A. Mercadante, *Belief Without Borders: Inside the Minds of the Spiritual but not Religious* (New York: Oxford University Press, 2014), 1-2.

[2] Springtide Research Institute, *The State of Religion & Young People: Navigating Uncertainty* (Farmington, MN: Springtide Research Institute, 2021), 43-60.

[3] Bob Smietana, *Reorganized Religion: The Reshaping of the American Church and Why It Matters* (New York: Hachette Book Group, 2022), 14.

[4] Richard P. Olson, *Celebrating the Graying Church: Mutual Ministry Today, Legacies Tomorrow* (Lanham: Rowman & Littlefield, 2020).

[5] Pew Research Center, "Modeling the Future of Religion in America," https://www.pewresearch.org/religion/2022/09/13/modeling-the-future-of-religion-in-america/ accessed 8 December 2022.

[6] Ibid.

[7] Ibid.

[8] Smietana, 147.

[9] Ibid.

[10] Scott Thumma, "Exploring the Dynamics and Challenges of Congregational Size," *Theology Today* 78, no. 3 (October 2021). https://journals.sagepub.com/doi/pdf/10.1177/0040576211030245. Summarized in Smietana, 147. See also https://religionnews.com/2021/11/16/why-the-minichurch-is-the-latest-trend-in-american-religion/.

[11] G. Jeffrey MacDonald, *Part-Time Is Plenty: Thriving without Full-Time Clergy* (Louisville: Westminster John Knox Press, 2020).

[12] Ibid., 2-3. Italics his.

[13] Ibid., 70-88.

[14] Ibid., 133-35.

[15] Jerrod H. Hugenot, https://www.abc-nys.org/uploads/1/1/8/7/118772542/parttimeandsharingpastorsguide__.docx

[16] Trace Haythorn, "Plenary Address," Spiritual Caregivers Conference, sponsored by the American Baptist Home Mission Society, Kansas City, Missouri, 19 September 2022.

[17] Jason Mack, *Designing a Future Beyond the Building: Exploring the Strengths and Weaknesses of the Design Thinking Process for Churches Rethinking Their Building and Property*. A Dissertation Submitted to the Faculty of the Central Baptist Seminary Department of Doctor of Ministry in Candidacy for the Degree of Doctor of Ministry in Creative Leadership, 2022.

[18] Good Futures Accelerator| Make Good With RootedGood.

[19] Jason may be contacted at revjasonmack.com.

[20] Mark Elsdon, ed., *Gone for Good? Negotiating the Coming Wave of Church Property Transition* (Grand Rapids: Wm. B. Eerdmans Publishing Company, 2024), 1, 5.

[21] Jason Mack, "Church Redevelopment Presentation."

[22] Gail Cafferata, *The Last Pastor: Faithfully Steering a Closing Church* (Louisville: Westminster John Knox Press, 2020).

[23] Ibid., 3-4.

[24] Ibid., 63.

[25] Ibid., 100.

[26] Ibid., 105-159.

CHAPTER 3

Spiritually Hungry in a World of Possibility

...the fruit of the Spirit is love, joy, peace,
patience, kindness, generosity,
faithfulness, gentleness, and self-control.
Galatians 5:22-23

Rowing through the rapids of our ministries in the twenty-first century surfaced two important questions: What in the world has happened? And where are we now? Now, it is time to ask the central question: How do we do ministry in this changed and changing setting?

One realization provides us with a good starting place. Though participation in "organized religion" has indeed decreased, there is still interest and curiosity about spirituality. People are interested in spiritual beliefs, theological questions, spiritual practices, and spiritual growth. If we listen carefully to the people who are "spiritual but not religious," we can hear their curiosity and interest.

We begin this chapter with a summary of reflections and insights from some who have listened to the "spiritual but not religious." I will then report on my conversations with the young pastors that I talked to. Our question is important: How can we best address the spiritual hunger present in our world today?

REFLECTIONS FROM SCHOLARS ON THE CURRENT RELIGIOUS ATMOSPHERE

Linda Mercadante, The Spiritual but Not Religious

A few years ago, Linda Mercadante, a professor of historical theology and a formerly "spiritual but not religious" person herself, wanted to learn more. She noticed that there was much publicity about the growth of "nones." She also noticed, however, that there was not much investigation about who they were, what they believed, or what had brought them to this place.

Mercadante set out to discover answers to these questions by interviewing nearly a hundred Spiritual But Not Religious (SBNR) people of all adult ages in one-to-two-hour conversations that she recorded, transcribed, and analyzed.

She attempted to have these conversations with people from all adult cohorts. However, though she worked hard to recruit them, she had the smallest response with Millennials (those born after 1981). She sensed this was because many had never had a "religion of their youth," but rather "illustrated well the widespread declining involvement in and authority of organized religion in the United States."[1]

Mercadante found a variety of attitudes among the SBNR people she interviewed and described them in several broad categories:

- Dissenters who "largely stay away from institutional religion,"
- Casuals, persons for whom "spiritual practices are primarily functional,"
- Explorers, who "seem to have a spiritual 'wanderlust,'"
- Seekers who "are actually looking for a spiritual home," and
- Immigrants "who had moved to a new spiritual 'land' and were trying to adjust to this new identity and community."[2]

I recently heard Dr. Mercadante reflect on what she heard in all this listening. She says that she heard very few stories of religious distress. Often people said they missed the potlucks where everyone was so friendly. They remembered that they just liked coming together and not feeling unwelcome. She heard few complaints about religious community, nor were these people narcissistic commitment-phobes. Her interviewees were not unhinged, lazy, or terribly unhappy. They were not less engaged than the average church member, though their focus and commitment might have been more local. Further, they were not against belief.

What she often found were people wrestling with spirituality and with specific beliefs. She also heard a good bit about what they *don't* believe. What was often being rejected was the person's impression of evangelical Christianity, whether accurate or not. She heard discussions on exclusivism, absolute truth, and whether there is a personal intentional involved God. She also heard questions about sin, about heaven, and especially about hell. Many wondered whether community is necessary for spiritual growth.

Mercadante experienced an openness and willingness to talk in response to her respectful inquiry. At times, she experienced inaccurate perceptions of religion. At other times, she experienced more openness to further investigation, growth, and change. She came away with the conviction that these folks needed to be heard, that they needed a listener, and that it was important for Christian people to hear them.

In the light of this, what is a helpful way of relating to persons who identify as spiritual but not religious? One of Mercadante's suggestions is not to apologize for faith, but to be realistic. As she points out, a person has to be strong and brave to be a Christian. She went on to provide other suggestions: Ask about their experience and beliefs. Listen respectfully. Help identify and name their spiritual struggles. Don't preach. Aspire to respond in a Christlike way.

She further counsels us to be prepared: "Do your homework about what you believe, what you commit to and why. If you don't, you may be stumped." She guides us to witness to what we believe "in" rather than belief "that." Mercadante wryly reminds us that "the church has not specialized in humility." Trustful, respectful conversation about values and faith is an important gift to all participants. She further notes that we cannot and should not avoid these conversations. Some nones and dones are members of our own families![3]

Ryan P. Burge, Different Kinds of Nones

Ryan Burge is a pastor and social scientist who has carefully analyzed recent surveys about nones to gain insight and guidance for ministry. He points to some important information and clues he found that is helpful for our purposes. For example, he notes that Pew Research surveys have discovered that nones describe themselves in three different ways. On surveys, they can check "atheist," "agnostic," or "nothing in particular." This last category ("nothing in particular") is the largest category of nones. He notes that if there were five people who were nones, one would be an atheist, one would be agnostic, and three would be nothing in particular.

This is of interest for at least three reasons. First, "'Nothings in particular' are one of the largest religious groups in the United States." Second, "They are the fastest growing religious group in the United States."[4] Third, Burge discovered that this group is significantly open to change. This insight comes from his analysis of a panel survey conducted by the Cooperative Congressional Election Study. A panel survey asked the same questions of the same people over a period of time. It can thus identify whether people are open to changing their minds or beliefs.

The particular panel that Burge analyzed had asked questions about religious affiliation of the same people in 2010, 2012, and 2014. He discovered that four in ten "nothing in particular" people changed their affiliation over this four-year period. About thirteen percent became atheist or agnostic, nine percent moved toward a non-Christian faith, but more than sixteen percent now identified as Christians, four years after the first survey.[5] Though that number still represents a small shift, the likelihood of positive response to Christian outreach and witness is larger among the "nothings in particular" than with the other nones (atheists and agnostics). Therefore, it is wise ministry to pay close attention when learning that a person is a "nothing in particular none." That self-description may suggest that they are uncertain, undecided, and wondering. These are people who might respond to open-ended conversation, interest, care, and hospitality.

James Emery White, The Importance of Cause

It has been noted that the invitation to the Christian faith is threefold: it is an invitation to Christ's *person* (relationship, forgiveness, salvation); it is an invitation to Christ's *people* (community, acceptance, fellowship); and it is an invitation to Christ's *purpose* (offering care to the needy and hurting, working for a more just society, finding meaning in life).

Growing out of his effective ministry with nones, James Emery White examined these three aspects of Christian invitation, seeking to discern which of the aspects had the greatest appeal. He was also interested in discovering if the effectiveness of those appeals had changed over time. He explained that, in the 1950s and 1960s, effective evangelistic outreach was *direct proclamation* of the gospel. From Billy Graham's crusades to many local churches' efforts, "presentation led the way." During that time, people were typically invited to Christ's *person*.

From the 1990s and into the early 2000s, *community* became an important strategy. As White explains it, "People wanted to belong before they believed. Skepticism was rampant and trust had to be earned. Once enfolded into that community, Christ was often met in its midst."

Now, he notes, the world has changed again: "From the 2010s forward, *cause*...became the leading edge of our connection with a lost world, and specifically with the *nones* in terms of both arresting their attention and enlisting their participation in community and relationship." Local or world hunger, human trafficking, or the environmental crisis are the some of the causes which nones might embrace. (White also points out that it is important not to be on the wrong side of causes that these spiritual but not religious folks might hold dear.)[6]

The importance of cause in our witness is an important insight. At the same time, this may also be a time when acceptance, welcome, and community are vital aspects of witness and important points of contact.

Josh Packard, The Door to Generation Z

Josh Packard, Executive Director of Springtide Research, a nonprofit agency that focuses on Generation Z (those born between 1996 and 2011), points to the need for conversation, particularly conversation of a certain kind. As researchers interview young people and young adults, they hear lively spiritual curiosity and interest in investigation and experimentation, but little interest in institutional involvement. The key to trust, he notes, is not so much expertise as a religious leader, but rather an openness to a relationship of mutual respect and searching.

Packard continues, "The best way to think about this generation is that they're trying to construct faith lives out of the pieces left laying around by their deconstructed parents. [And so] the best way to reach that group is not to show them a house that's already built but to get in there and help them build something for themselves."[7]

YOUNGER PASTORS ON ENGAGING NONES AND DONES

When I raised this topic with the pastors I interviewed, I heard more about dones. Several spoke of reaching out to persons who had left their church. According to the interviews, some dones had had serious disagreements with a former pastor; others were so connected to a previous pastor that when that pastor left, they were left with a sense of loss. Others were suffering the after-effects of church conflicts that had not been productive.

Seth experienced a different type of done. He came to a church of mostly older people who had come from Laos. They had raised their children in this church years before. When Seth reached out to these young adults, they expressed gratitude for this grounding. However, they showed no interest in returning.

I encountered several strategies for relating to dones.

Rob reflected: "At two different times, I engaged a demographic I called 'Recovering Christians,' people who had been hurt or alienated by church but possibly still felt a love for God. They had no interest in relating to a church. I felt drawn to them and saw in them an opportunity to relate to people who had a capacity for belief."

"My means for drawing them back was to invite them to a strategically designed Bible study that would engage them, their experience, and their questions. I would bring a variety of perspectives on Bible study. Further, I would bring a background of literature as we considered faith that could be more real. At the very least, I engaged these people and invited them to consider the possibilities of a reconstructed, repurposed faith and involvement."

Jason C reflected on cooperative efforts to care for nones, dones, and others: "We started doing some experimental programs. One was a midweek inter-church 'breathing space.' We would create a space for busy people and mark the space out. In doing that, we would share a simple meal, then have prayer stations, or perhaps a quiet time in the chapel. We initially reached out to people in orbit around the church, somewhat connected to church. There was attendance of about eight to twelve the first year, fifteen to twenty-three the second year, and then Covid hit."

As he reflected on this and other efforts, Jason C observed, "A lot of churches are looking for the right program that will hook people in. The question is whether or not you can help people make real and authentic connections with each other. That is how we begin to realize the true presence of the incarnate Christ, the presence of the Spirit."

Tim shares this perspective: "Those who grew up in the church and those who are new all seem to articulate the same basic need—to be part of community. To be not only accepted, but embraced, totally accepted, including beliefs, theological and political, the way you express yourself, and more. These are the things people freely share when they are really part of a community."

Thinking about relating to nones, Michael reflected, "My experience with nones, connecting with them in ways that were meaningful and spiritual, was a long relationship-building process. There was so much distrust and skepticism. Church for a lot of folks was just not relevant. Things like funeral ministries, and weddings and such, opened doors and led to conversations I would not have foreseen."

"For example, two weeks ago, I was messaged by someone who had attended a couple of weddings and his grandmother's funeral. These were scattered contacts over nearly eight years. Now, all these years later, perhaps for the first time in his life, he is thinking, 'Maybe I need something more in my life, and maybe a religious person can lead me in.' When he got to that place, to my surprise and joy, I was the person he reached out to."

SPIRITUAL CARE FOR THOSE INSIDE THE CHURCH

It is also important to realize that those who remain within church life have a similar hunger. A person's participation in church may be consumed by responsibilities. There may be a need to step back, rest, and reflect. A gracious invitation and care for the member's spiritual growth, practices, questions, and searching may be gratefully received. To be the caregiver needed for times like these, the minister needs to be attentive to one's own spiritual life as well. We need to keep growing, learning, discovering, renewing, and becoming!

Scott Thumma, Professor of the Sociology of Religion at Hartford International University, suggests that "the true task facing pastors and lay leaders is that of reminding wayward members of the benefits of spiritual education, the joy of community, and the richness of fellowship with other believers."[8]

SPIRITUAL INTENTIONS AND PRACTICES

If we aspire to be an intentional center of spiritual exploration, there are a number of possibilities to consider. These are ways that have been developed in other times and places and may also hold possibility for the present. We will talk about Bible study and worship in later chapters. For now, let's consider some other doorways.

Being a Spiritual Friend, a Spiritual Director, or a Spiritual Peer

Perhaps ministers or people in the church could prepare and offer themselves as spiritual directors, spiritual friends, or spiritual peers. These people could offer guidance with individuals or in small groups. As the Spiritual Directors International website notes, "Spiritual direction or companionship inspires people to experience authenticity in their lives as they connect with and explore the ground of all being, that deepest of truths which is beyond life and death and goes by many names, including God, and no name at all."[9]

While specific training for this type of ministry is normally required, some people have simply grown into this role and others turn to them for counsel. What does a spiritual director do? As explained by Marjorie Thompson, a spiritual guide "listens to us…helps us notice things…helps us respond to God with greater freedom…points to…disciplines of spiritual growth…loves us…prays for us."[10] Spiritual direction and spiritual friendship can range from rather structured and hierarchical relationships to informal, supportive, and nondirective relationships. For the spiritual searcher who does not want even that much direction, two people can covenant to become spiritual friends or spiritual peers. They commit to each bringing one's own journey to a selected partner. They also covenant to be open and offer concerned listening, agreeing to support the other's questions, investigation, growth, and journey.

Spiritual Retreat Centers

A spiritual leader will want to know about places of spiritual renewal that may be nearby and open to visitors and searchers. There are probably many places such as monasteries and retreat centers where people can go for reflection, exploration, study, and discovery. Some of these centers have the explicit commitment to welcome each guest as they would welcome Christ. These retreat experiences can range in time from a day to weeks, or they may be open-ended. People who visit these centers may simply want solitude to reflect, think, and pray, or they may want to have a wise person from the center with whom to visit, ask questions, and seek direction from time to time. Perhaps the center or guide can offer spiritual discovery rituals, spiritual exercises, or times of community worship and prayer.

Study Resources for Spiritual Growth

Some people may want to reflect on life and on their own journey. Others might want a door into what wise spiritual people have discovered and experienced in the past. If so, there are helpful resources to assist. I will mention two sets of these resources that have been widely and helpfully used. First, the "Practicing Our Faith" organization describes its work as offering "a way of life for a searching people."[11] This organization has developed the idea of "Practices" which they define as "things Christian people do over time in response to and in the light of God's active presence for the life of the world."[12] The practices they have selected, explored, and described include the following:

honoring the body;
hospitality;
household economics;
saying yes and saying no;
keeping Sabbath;
testimony;
discernment;
shaping communities;
forgiveness;
healing;
dying well; and
singing our lives.

This group has prepared books and other resources for many of these practices as ways to experience God's presence in the world.[13]

Much earlier, Richard Foster wrote a widely-read and enduring book on developing discipleship, *Celebration of Discipline*. Foster spoke of inward disciplines (meditation, prayer, fasting, study); outward disciplines (simplicity, solitude, submission, service); and corporate disciplines (confession, worship, guidance, celebration.).[14] This book has met a widespread hunger and has been in continuous publication for many years.

Reading and practicing what these books say can be enriching by oneself, more so with another person, and perhaps even more so with a small group of fellow seekers.

Spiritual Traditions

Over recent years, I have been increasingly drawn to and influenced by the Celtic tradition of spirituality. It embodies much of what I had been feeling—for example, the idea that we are guided by two books: the Bible and creation. In Celtic spirituality, there is an invitation to be aware of—and in communion with—God all about us and within us. There is a practice of sacred hospitality for others. This is epitomized in the concept of the *anam cara*—soul friend, a person who is totally available for deep friendship that might include spiritual counsel and conversation. Celtic spirituality is a calming, open-minded, open-hearted strengthening practice in my life.[15]

Another spiritual tradition was mentioned by Rob in my interview: "As a local pastor, I found a lot of encouragement in Benedictine spirituality and monasticism in my ministry. Their sense of hospitality, welcoming each as Christ, the incorporating of contemplative prayer into my life and into worship. I found this to be quite enriching. It has a sense of authenticity."

A Not So Familiar (to me) Spiritual Tradition—Charismatic Experience

There is another spiritual tradition that has been transformational for many. I am nudged to this awareness by Loren Mead, beloved founder of the Alban Institute. Through the 1970s, 1980s, and 1990s, he worked tirelessly listening to, consulting with, and encouraging churches. In the 1990s, he wrote a series of books about what he sensed was already happening, His first book was titled *The Once and Future Church*. Mead spoke of his mission: "I believe I am working for the church that God is calling into the future."[16]

Near the end of his career, Mead's rector in his home parish asked him, "Would you put together your ideas about what the church must face in the next generation or two to rebuild its life for the future?"[17] Then, he was asked to put those insights in a sermon and preach that sermon to his parish congregation. He did that, and he later wrote about those challenges. One of the challenges surprised me: "To Discover a Passionate Spirituality."

Mead recalled that in his and his colleagues' interviews, they had discovered many persons, faithful church members, who could describe powerful and personal experiences of God, often life-changing events, but they had never been asked to share these experiences with their pastor or congregation.

He concluded that there is a discomfort in structured religion about "the unpredictable power of the Spirit who comes without regard to our plans."[18] This led him to believe that for a church to receive all that God has in store, it needs to find a way to welcome and encourage both forms of spirituality— the charismatic form and the more structured and formal traditional forms I have been describing. He suggested that "traditional and charismatic spirituality are polar opposites, and that the health of the body depends on our finding a creative way for them to coexist within the churches."[19]

Harvey Cox also called attention to this form of spirituality. Growing out of his long fascination with "religion of the heart," he offered a thoughtful look at the vast growth of Pentecostalism all over the world, even while participation in other religions was decreasing. At least one part of the appeal, he claimed, was their "primal speech," sometimes described by scholars as "ecstatic utterances," "glossolalia," "speaking in tongues," or "praying in the Spirit." Cox observed that "in an age of bombast, hype, and doublespeak...that seem to have emptied and pulverized language, Pentecostals learned to speak with another voice, 'the language of the heart.'"[20]

Cox recalled that in nearly every spiritual tradition in human history, when the mystics tried to describe their profound religious experiences, their ability to describe it evaded them. He reflects, "Confronted with this verbal paralysis, what can people do? They sing, they rhapsodize, they invent metaphors, they soar into canticles and doxologies. But ultimately, words fail them and they lapse into silence. Or they speak in tongues."[21]

This "primal religious speech," he notes, is akin to the mysticism of various religions. And it is discussed in Paul's writings to the New Testament churches, particularly in I Corinthians 14, where he offers counsel about its wise and courteous use in what seems to have been a common and frequent experience. Further, in Romans 8:26, he reflects "Likewise the Spirit helps us in our weakness, for we do not know how to pray as we ought, but that very Spirit intercedes with groanings too deep for words." This is part of the spiritual journey that should be attended with openness and care.

Wider Searchings—Multiple Religious Belonging and Practice

As enriching and helpful as many people have found these various practices and disciplines, the spiritual but not religious person—or even a person grounded in the Christian tradition—may be bringing more wide-ranging inquiries to their quest. For example, some might bring experiences, thoughts, and questions about other religions and experiences they have had. Perhaps they feel a connection to multiple religious traditions and have experienced multiple religious practices. As a group of inter-religious scholars define this, "Multiple religious participation is the conscious (and sometimes unconscious) use of religious ideas, practices, symbols, meditations, prayers, chants, and sensibilities derived from one tradition by a member of another community of faith for their own purposes." Or, more simply, this is a way "in which people of faith engage in communities and practices of more than one religious tradition."[22] For example, participation in yoga, mindfulness meditation, or presence in the rituals of varying religious traditions is widespread and common. The conversation a person may want to have will undoubtedly bring to the surface what they have experienced, what they believe about it, and what you believe about it.

Quite unexpectedly, I experienced this at least once. I was asked to chair the planning committee for a Baptist-Muslim dialogue event. I did not anticipate how I would be enriched by my relationship with the Muslim members of that committee or that I would feel myself drawn, from time to time, to Friday prayer at a nearby Mosque. Being with fellow believers during their prayers, kneeling with forehead on the floor, or standing shoulder to shoulder in solidarity and prayer touched something deep in me. I am no longer able to be involved in that community, but I remember those times with gratitude and longing.[23]

NOT ONLY WHAT, BUT HOW?

As I consider how to carry on these conversations, the scripture offered at the beginning of this chapter offers guidance: "The fruit of the Spirit is love, joy, peace, patience, kindness, generosity, faithfulness, gentleness, and self-control." (Galatians 5:22) How do I converse? I do so as a spiritual person where these qualities are part of my being. This may involve being ecumenical to the core which, in turn, means being actively aware of what resources other faith communities offer those on spiritual quests.

How are we to carry on these conversations? The way any kind and generous host would!

FOR REFLECTION AND CONVERSATION

1. How would you describe your conversations with spiritual but not religious persons? Are you willing to discuss mutual spiritual journeys and spiritual searches? How would you describe your church community in this regard?

2. How would you describe the "spiritual atmosphere" of the faith community where you participate? Do people have the opportunity to explore and strengthen their spiritual journey and spirituality? Is there openness? Trustworthiness? What are your leadings in this regard?

3. Which possibilities suggested in this chapter feel most comfortable to you? Which feel strangest or most challenging?

4. It is understandable for someone to feel defensive and want to argue or debate with a person who misunderstands and misrepresents your faith. In this chapter, following the lead of persons who have written out of their experience, I advocate listening in a hospitable, non-defensive, conversing way. What do you think? Should this be the way? What will you need to respond in this manner?

5. Has your journey had any movements from less (or no) religious participation to more active religious engagement? Have you ever moved from questioning and searching to more active faithing? If so, what do you discover from reflecting on that journey? What was most helpful to you? What was not helpful?

NOTES

[1] Linda Mercadante, *Belief Without Borders: Inside the Minds of the Spiritual but not Religious* (New York: Oxford University Press, 2014), 46.

[2] Ibid., 53-63.

[3] Linda A. Mercadante, "Missing the Mark with the Spiritual but Not Religious," workshop, 21 September 2022, "Space for Grace" conference of the American Baptist Home Mission Society, Kansas City, Missouri.

[4] Ryan P. Burge, *The Nones: Where They Came From, Who They Are, and Where They Are Going* (Minneapolis: Fortress Press, 2021), 100-101.

[5] Ibid., 118-119.

[6] James Emery White, *The Rise of the Nones: Understanding and Reaching the Religiously Unaffiliated* (Grand Rapids: Baker Books, 2014), 99-101. In these three paragraphs of quotes, summary, and paraphrase, I have used italics where White does.

[7] Quoted in Bob Smietana, *Reorganized Religion: The Reshaping of the American Church and Why It Matters* (New York: Worthy Publishing, 2022), 95.

[8] Quoted in Smietana, *Reorganized Religion*, p. 78.

[9] https://www.sdicompanions.org/ accessed 22 January 2023.

[10] Marjorie Thompson, *Soul Feast: An Invitation to the Spiritual Life* (Louisville: Westminster John Knox, 1995), 110-111.

[11] https://practicingourfaith.org/

[12] Dorothy C. Bass, ed., *Practicing Our Faith*, 2nd ed. (San Francisco: Jossey-Bass, 1977), 5. Italics hers. Many of the practices are also described in an entire book.

[13] https://practicingourfaith.org/practices/ accessed 23 January 2023.

[14] Richard Foster, *Celebration of Discipline* (New York: HarperCollins, 1978).

[15] Two excellent resources that provide introduction to and guidance in Celtic spirituality are John Philip Newell, *Sacred Earth, Sacred Soul: Celtic Wisdom for Awakening What Our Souls Know and Healing the World* (New York: HarperOne, 2021) and John O'Donohue, *Anam Cara: A Book of Celtic Wisdom* (New York: Harper Perennial, 1997).

[16] Loren Mead, *The Once and Future Church Collection* (An Alban Institute Publication, 2001), 15. (This volume includes all three books Mead wrote on this subject: *The Once and Future Church; Transforming Congregations for the Future*; and *Five Challenges for the Once and Future Church*, as well as conversations and updates about these books.)

17 Mead, *The Once and Future Church*, 368. This and the following two notes are from *Five Challenges for the Once and Future Church*, originally published in 1996.

18 Ibid., 311.

19 Ibid., 316.

20 Harvey Cox, *Fire from Heaven* (Reading, MA: Addison-Wesley), 82.

21 Ibid., 92.

22 Peniel Jesudason, Rufus Rajkumr, Joseph Prabhaker Dayann, eds., *Many Yet One? Multiple Religious Belonging* (Geneva, Switzerland: WCC Publications, 2016), 10, 1.

23 I have written of this in *Side by Side: Being Christian in a Multifaith World* (Valley Forge: Judson Press, 2018).

CHAPTER 4

Crying in the Chapel

A NEW KIND OF COMMUNITY AND CARE

If one member suffers, all suffer together with it;
if one member is honored, all rejoice together with it.
Now you are the body of Christ and individually members of it.
1 Corinthians 12:26-27

Springtide Research Institute has done extensive study of Generation Z (those born 1996-2011). In addition to their discoveries about these young adults' spirituality, researchers discovered another important insight. They speak of Generation Z as "America's loneliest generation"—lonely, isolated, and stressed. In their surveys, more than a third, sometimes a half, agreed with the following statements: "I have nobody to talk to," "I feel completely alone," "I feel no one understands me," "No one really knows me well," and "It is difficult for me to make friends." Further, they observed that the responses were similar whether the young person attended religious gatherings or not.[1]

Generation Z people are not the only ones! There is much isolation and loneliness throughout our society. As Diana Butler Bass notes: Google "longing for community," and you will get more than ten million hits![2] Over the last decades, our society has experienced many changes that isolate us. Extended families living close together are rare. Education, employment, and military service have spread people across the country and world. In our present society there seems to be less emphasis on community, mutual care, and altruism. Instead, there is more emphasis on competition, glamour, consumption, and achieving a pinnacle of success. We seem to be choosing individualism over community.

Granted, there are brief exceptions when there is compassionate response to a region devastated by a fire, flood, hurricane, or earthquake. However, too soon we return to our isolated ways. We divide easily into suspicious sub-groups, whether politically, religiously, economically, or ethnically. Even in seemingly compatible groups, we aren't doing all that well. Many people, young and old, who participate in religious communities still express feelings of loneliness and isolation.

United States Surgeon General Vivek Murthy claims that loneliness is a public health hazard as well. For example, he said that poor or insufficient connection to other people is as deadly as smoking fifteen cigarettes a day. This loneliness increases the risk of heart disease by twenty-nine percent, stroke by thirty-two percent, and dementia by fifty percent.[3]

Of course, no church will have the answer to all these problems. But there is an opportunity here. This is an invitation for a church to be aware, sensitive, and responsive to each person it encounters and to reach out to locate, identify, and relate to others. If a church accepts this call, there are two spreading branches to explore. One branch is to be alert to all the friendship, support, and acceptance opportunities they have to offer. The other branch is to be sensitive and redemptive to persons' needs and issues. Let's explore these two branches in turn.

This pervasive loneliness and its cost are not news to the young ministry colleagues with whom I visited. My questions for these three chapters—on spiritual enrichment in Chapter 3, community-pastoral care in this chapter, and worship in Chapter 5—were all answered against the backdrop of an awareness of loneliness.

Nearly everyone spoke of the intense isolation during the pandemic, of the setbacks to worship and group life, and of the hesitancy to venture back. David spoke of people "staying in their Monday to Saturday silos," hesitant to come out. At least three pastors spoke of the core of the leadership in their youth groups graduating or moving on during the pandemic and the seeming impossibility of reviving that youthful community again.

Evan moved from doing mostly youth and young adult ministry to a church with many older adults. He recalls, "Pastoral care for senior adults was challenging for me. I had no experience. Then I learned that their loneliness and needs were about the same as for twenty-year-olds. They often wondered about the same concerns. *I don't know if I can trust my body. I don't know what the future holds. I can no longer control things. There is instability. Where do I fit in?* That is what people are searching for across the board. Regardless of age, there is a need for support and for people to know you."

"When I asked students, 'Why did you stay?' I heard, 'Somebody called me by name and asked me to come back.' Noticing people, wanting to be with them, wanting them to come back. Twenty-year-olds want it;

eighty-five-year-olds want it. I think you have something that brings value to everyone else."

There are circumstances that exacerbate the loneliness. Anita, who serves in Seattle, notes, "The Northwest really lends itself to introversion, particularly through the grayer times of the year, fall and winter. There is a lot of loneliness, but it is very hard to build community. People open up very slowly here. This makes it very hard for people who don't know how to reach out to each other."

"Further, Seattle is a pass-through city with a lot of young professionals coming here briefly from other places. Our church is also located right near a university, colleges, and a gay and lesbian neighborhood. Young adults are regular for a few years, then they are gone."

There was also a sense that we have practices, such as "Sunday best," that get in the way of the deep community people desire. Jason observes, "There is a public attitude of dress and attitude that 'all is well' that gets in the way of deep sharing community." Rob concurs: "The historical perception is that we need to clean ourselves up to go to church. The hunger seems to be 'comfortably vulnerable' and 'safely vulnerable,' and these are oxymorons. This desire to be accepted is sometimes at odds with what an institution might expect."

COMMUNITY

Atmosphere, Welcome, Transparency, and Open Invitation

An important commitment for a church to make is that, as the Benedictines would say, we welcome each person who comes into our community as we would welcome Christ. When someone comes to worship or to an event or attends a group in our church, the person needs to be welcomed, introductions made with names repeated, and as much attention and information offered as fits the comfort level of the guest. Further, we should not wait at a church building for people to come. Friendship, care, and hospitality can be offered by Christian people wherever they find themselves.

I was once part of a church where leaders prepared a brochure asserting that we were "the end of your search for a friendly church." I wondered how often we lived up to that promise. Perhaps if we had lived that motto well, we would not have had to put it in print! That particular church was in a new suburb that had been growing for a number of years. Many young families were moving into the area and finding a way to connect with other people. Perhaps, at that time, the brochure touched a hunger and need that was fitting. The question is: How can we be that kind of church for people in today's world?

Joanna has encountered many people who really cry out for a friendly church. She speaks of "people who want to have faith but have been hurt in the past and told they are not really Christian." This may have had to do with sexual or gender identity, topics that we will discuss later, or it may have been for other reasons. She also encounters university students with questions, such as, "Look at Job; why is God so terrible?"

The pastors with whom I visited found a variety of people in need of this hospitality. Cindy reflects, "We have had people who have been incarcerated and folks with drug and alcohol issues. We work with one woman who is at risk of losing her daughter. We try to find ways of trying to be supportive without feeding into behavior that does not need to be supported." Joanna's community has accompanied several parents through various struggles with their children.

When asked about the pastoral care needs in her community, Meredith responded, "All the grief we have gone through. We experienced grief in selling our building and moving. And there is loss of life. We have many funerals. For my community, it is processing grief and loss."

Further, some pastors encountered many people who were ready to talk about mental health crises in their own lives or among people they cared about. Anita reflected, "Perhaps there is less stigma in talking about mental health in Christian spaces now. Depression and anxiety were big topics in youth groups this last year. We talk a lot about suicidal ideation, depression, mental health care, and welfare in general. Mental health is a topic for all ages. We led small groups for parents of adult children with mental illness. Often, we would hear, 'I don't have any other place where I can talk about this and wrestle with it.'"

Peter C, who now teaches in a public high school, was seeing a gradual improvement in the performance of students in his classes after the pandemic. However, when he spoke with the counselors and nurses in his school, they told him that they were seeing no improvement at all. Among the students in that high school, the inability to relate and the mental health episodes were of epidemic proportions and not improving. There is need aplenty.

Food and Survival

Cody responded to my question about needs for pastoral care by saying that it was about survival in his community. He reflected, "We had a very big spike in helping people survive and thrive with food, fuel, and other things. The most frequent issue I experienced is how people are trying to make it, in a mostly older population, with the cost of living. Our area has the second highest gas tax in the nation. There are lots of questions about how to spend the same amount of money when everything is increasing in cost."

He noticed that "toward the back end of the pandemic I had a small amount of marriage counseling, not only for people in my congregation but from the community as well" that might have come out of his church's care and presence in these survival crises.

Churches "communicate community" with food in different ways. One way is simply inviting people, or welcoming those who drop by, to join in a meal. Perhaps it is a potluck dinner at the church or an annual Thanksgiving dinner for those who would otherwise be alone. It might be providing a meal for a college student or a youth group. It might be as simple as inviting a visitor to go out for a Sunday noon meal after a worship service. In the next chapter we will report about churches that have combined a worship service and a meal.

Other churches, like Corey's, offer a Food Pantry where people can stop by and pick up some essentials. A study of congregations' economic practices showed that about half of congregations have a food pantry or some other way of distributing food.[4] A food pantry I observed recently is a lovely example of this ministry. This particular pantry, intentionally located in a "food desert," did not accept federal funding because of restrictions that would be placed on the number of times people could come for help. The church found financial support from other sources.

Sarah, a recent college graduate and volunteer who checked people in, welcomed them warmly, and learned the number of people in their household. (This would determine the quantity of food they could select.) She told me, "I would not want to help in a pantry that has to turn hungry people away; I couldn't do that." All who came were treated with kindness and respect, an expression of God's grace that brings people together. When a box of donuts broke open, a volunteer offered them to all close by. When a child spilled a drink and looked worried, another volunteer quietly mopped it up. There was warm community between the volunteers serving and the people receiving this service.[5]

Ryan Burge and the small Illinois church he serves (along with his university teaching and research) found another way to offer food community. His church began packing brown paper sacks filled with weekend food for schoolchildren who were struggling in their community. They started small, but they now provide about three hundred of these bags of food each weekend, serving three schools in their neighborhood.

Some members suggested they put a religious tract in each bag. Burge refused. He recalled, "For me, the purpose of those bags was not to try to bring people to Christ. It was to show those kids that someone they don't even know loves them and wants to help." So, instead, they included a note explaining who was providing the bags and why they were doing it. The note invited them to call if they ever needed help. At least once, they had such a call. A grandmother needed a warm coat for her grandson. It happened that the church was having a rummage sale. They invited the woman to come and take what she needed, and she did so, with the church's welcome and blessing.[6]

Other churches offer hospitality through community gardens. Some people enjoy planting and growing a garden. Others enjoy receiving food. The community garden might add rhubarb plants and berry bushes from which any can help themselves.

There are many community opportunities when we invite others to share our food.

Being a Transparent Community—Differences and Conflict

A church will live its community life in full view of any who engage it. From the time of the New Testament (and certainly before), people of faith have struggled with how to live their faith in community with each other. When writing to his beloved Philippian church, Paul felt it necessary to counsel, "Make my joy complete: be of the same mind, having the same love, being in full accord and of one mind."[7]

No doubt, Paul knew that there would be differing opinions in congregations. However, he invited those followers of Jesus to make those differences a minor premise; the major premise was the love Christ had for each of them that was to be expressed in their love, care, respect, and interaction with each other. With sensitivity to the widespread hunger for community, a church will be wise to be guided by these words in Philippians and live transparently in such a way.

Deeper community

Everything we have mentioned is a good start, but there is also life-enriching community that reaches deeper. Richer friendship and community come when support and presence is offered through a crisis or tragedy. It also happens when people work together on an important task, offer response to a cataclysmic event, or go on a mission trip together. Deep community can develop when a group makes a covenant to gather faithfully and openly share their joys, questions, and concerns together. Community may occur as people go on a spiritual retreat together when there may be time to share deeper convictions as well as perplexing questions and doubts.

Covenant groups, spiritual conversations and retreats, and service opportunities invite a new level of trust. That trust is one way of answering our widespread hunger for community and friendship.

CARE

We are in a new chapter of church and ministry. In our present and future world, there may be a renewed call to be a caring and redemptive presence for God's hurting children. The possibilities I mention may seem overwhelming, particularly when we have acknowledged that many more pastors are becoming part-time in small faith communities with limited resources. A few realities, however, may make this exploration more realistic. First, none of this is the pastor's responsibility alone. It may be helpful to identify this as "community care" rather than "pastoral care." A church may offer training, guidance, and supervision to persons in the congregation to equip and support them in one of these ministries. Second, the church might begin to see itself as a resource center, aware and in touch with available counseling, caring, and healing resources that the community might need.

Reflect with me about opportunities to be a caring presence in your community.

Life-Stage Opportunities

Engagements, pre-wedding and pre-marriage counseling, and weddings have changed! Church connections and pastoral ministry in these areas has decreased. In Chapter 11, we will mention possible ways to be a ministering presence despite these changes.

Births and Caring for Children

The birth of a child is many things all at once. It is a celebration, a spiritual moment of profound co-creation, and a time of re-adjustments, including re-adjustments in life's priorities and schedules. It is also a vulnerable moment where community love and care might be valued. One of my pastor friends and a small church group sent a personal note of congratulation and a small gift to new parents on the birth of a child in their community. There was also an offer to explore a child baptism or child dedication if parents were interested.

Anita and a pastor friend have prepared a book to help families explore religious faith with their children. It is titled *New Directions for Holy Questions: Progressive Christian Theology for Families*.[8] Giving this book to young families may provide important guidance in a new and significant chapter of their lives.

In addition, particularly if the new parents are not close to their own extended family, they might have other needs that a caring community might meet. For example, one new parent recalled being new to parenting and struggling in isolation with questions, insecurities, and fears. She had read of "alloparenting" in other societies. This refers to a community of parents who support each other and love each other's children as their own. She and her husband longed for such mutual support from other parents.[9] Church people could provide that kind of support to isolated and uncertain young parents.

Caring and experienced parents might have much to offer, such as respite care, help in emergencies, and experience in childcare options. Shared wisdom and available support may be welcome throughout the child's life.

Seasons of Loss, Goodbyes, Separation, and Grief

The journey through life also includes endings. Some of these endings are predictable; some are not. But all endings leave holes in our souls! These are times when presence, care, sensitivity, and a listening ear may be needed.

Consider divorce, for example. Divorce brings a variety of different losses, such as the loss of another person, the loss of finances, the loss of a child-rearing partnership, and the loss of mutual friends. After divorce, some people lose their church or their couples' group at church. These losses may persist. The pain of these losses may surface over and over again, especially at times when extended family gathers, for example. One divorced woman reflected with me, "Divorce is a grief time, but the corpse keeps showing up again and again!"

Divorce support groups and even re-married support groups may fill a need.

Frailty, Terminal Illness, Death, and Grief

As life progresses, endings are inevitable. This may be a time when pastoral presence is gratefully needed and received. Even before the final loss, there may be other difficult situations: health issues, terminal illness, and challenging health care decisions. It may be helpful for a failing person and family members to have frank discussions about which treatments are acceptable and which treatments are not. A kind pastor can provide guidance, wisdom, support, and information.

Eventually, the death of family members will come. This loss may be anticipated and come slowly, or it may come suddenly. It may come peacefully or with much anguish. It may come at the hand of another or be self-chosen. Survivors may feel peace or anguish.

Frequently, church people fall short in walking with grieving folks. They offer lavish attention, support, and food through the first few days following a death, but they then might ignore the grievers after that. Sustained community care can sustain those who are grieving by offering assistance through the legal maze, a listening ear, a support group, or a friend to shop with or sit with at public and group events. We will talk more about this in Chapter 9.

Life Hazards

Life stages sometimes contain unpleasant surprises, reverses, and painful experiences in relationships. Beyond that, there are actual hazards that can happen any time in the life journey. These may also be situations where the church as caring community can be responsive and supportive. Let's consider a few of these hazards.

Addiction

In a society where there is free access to a number of "recreational drugs" (for example, alcohol and marijuana), it is a mystery why some people can use these substances without apparent ill effect and why some people become addicted. When addiction happens, life problems multiply. Relationships, employment, and health are all at risk. Persons with this problem may hide it for a while until it can no longer be denied.

In dealing with addiction, a caring church is wise to know of the support, counseling, and healing options in the community. Perhaps the most available and accessible assistance are twelve-step groups such as Alcoholics Anonymous. While the connection to a "higher power" healing source is more generic in these groups than in our churches, these groups are an important and valid ally. A church is wise to know where these groups meet and might even made the church building available as a gathering place.

In my last pastorate, Bill, a new member, took me out to lunch. He told me that he was a recovering alcoholic and attended Alcoholics Anonymous meetings at least four times a week. He also told me that, while he did not want me to share this information widely, he would be willing to help whenever I discovered someone struggling with alcoholism. He offered to be a listening friend, to do an intervention, or to take that person to an Alcoholics Anonymous meeting. In the following years, I called him twice to assist with a person with this problem; both times, Bill's assistance was helpful.

Unemployment and Work Changes

There are often struggles in finding, maintaining, and succeeding in employment. Challengers include finding a job, securing employment, learning good work habits, succeeding and improving in a position, and advancing in a career. From a Christian perspective, our occupation is part of our vocation—an expression of a calling from God.

A church may offer informal one-on-one support to a person struggling with these issues or perhaps develop a support group. Once, in a community where I was pastor, a major corporation faced an emergency and made massive layoffs. Since we had people who were familiar with the process described in Richard Bolles' *What Color Is Your Parachute?* we offered groups to help recently jobless people work on plans and strategies for moving forward.[10] Those who participated in the support group were deeply grateful.

Incarceration

The United States has the highest per capita incarceration rate of any developed country in the world. The rate of incarceration for African Americans is higher than the rate of any other group.[11] I asked my friend Dr. Archie Ivy, a grandfather, retired educator, and pastor, how he counsels youth and young adults in this regard. He responded, "If they are stopped by an officer, I tell them to keep their hands visible and to be respectful." He continued, "If the person stopped has even the smallest amount of marijuana, he will likely wind up in jail. Probably he won't be able to afford bail and must remain in jail. Because of this, he will probably lose his job. Then he will get arrested for lack of child support and get more jail time."[12]

This outcome, of course, would lead to an even more troubled future. Over the course of a lifetime, 28.5 percent of all Black men will spend time in a state or federal prison. That rate is twice the rate for Hispanics (sixteen percent) and six times the rate for white Americans (4.4 percent).[13] A young Black male is more likely to go to prison than to go to college. Even after release, people who have been convicted of a felony will lose many privileges. They cannot vote and, usually, must mention the conviction when applying for a job which makes it difficult to get a job. The incarcerated, formerly incarcerated people, and their family members have many needs. Possible ministry responses might include visits, friendship, caring interest, material support, and advocacy. At least three of the pastors I interviewed and their churches are engaged in this kind of ministry.

Discouragement, Despondency, and Despair

Sometimes people experience life as impossibly sad, whether accompanied by any of the exterior hazards we have mentioned or not. All of us have probably had such experiences. For some, those experiences may be short-lived; for others, the feelings may persist. This pain could be connected to religious crises that we have mentioned earlier, or it could be connected to something else.

A hospitable church community can be helpful. There are at least two possible avenues of care. One is to offer listeners—a simple way for a church to express concern for its community. I once led a congregation in providing a cadre of lay people with listening-caring skills, guided by the training and resources of Stephen Ministries.[14] A simpler way might be to train a group using a single resource such as John Savage's *Listening and Caring Skills: A Guide for Groups and Leaders*.[15]

The other avenue of care provides information about community agencies that offer professional assistance to people who find themselves in difficult times.

Shortly before I wrote this, I learned of a new service called the "Suicide and Crisis Lifeline," Dial 988. A basic way to be responsive to hurting people is to share this number. Churches can remind people that it is normal to feel hurt, and that it is wise to reach out for companionship in times of crisis. These are messages that cannot be repeated too often. C.S. Lewis once noted that "friendship is born at that moment when one person says to another, 'What! You too? I thought I was the only one.'"[16] That "you too" might be an interest, a hobby, or a passion, or it might be an inner pain or life crisis.

A friend of mine was going through a divorce and enrolled in a divorce recovery course. One required activity was to have a conversation with an assigned classmate. Two classmates agreed that they would have their conversation on a walk. The next time I saw my friend, she was smiling more than I had seen for quite a while. Her first words were: "I found one; I have a friend."

Perhaps this quote from the beloved Mother Teresa comes to the core of what I am trying to say in this chapter: "There is a terrible hunger for love. We all experience that in our lives—the pain, the loneliness. We must have the courage to recognize it."[17] And we must be present to each other and respond to each other's hurts and hopes.

FOR CONVERSATION AND REFLECTION

1. From the possibilities I mentioned, what are you and your church already doing? What do you celebrate about your present ministry?

2. What community and care ministries are you offering that I did not mention?

3. What invitations or brainstorms in this chapter stirred your interest or curiosity? As I did my interviews, many were recovering from the isolations and hardships related to the pandemic. As time goes on, how are you and your church doing? What pastoral needs remain? What new ones are emerging?

4. What helpful care and/or counseling agencies in your community have you discovered? Collaborated with? What other discoveries and relationships do you need to explore?

NOTES

[1] Springtide Research Institute, *Belonging, Reconnecting America's Loneliest Generation* (Farmington, MN: Springtide Research Institute, 2020).

[2] Diana Butler Bass, *Christianity After Religion: The End of Church and the Birth of a New Spiritual Awakening* (New York: HarperOne, 2012), 194.

[3] As reported in *Wisconsin State Journal*, David Ahlberg, "Loneliness on the rise as public health threat," 16 July 2023, A1.

[4] Bob Smietana, *Reorganized Religion: The Reshaping of the American Church and Why It Matters* (New York: Hachette Book Group, 2022), 45.

[5] I am describing "Espensa de la Pax (Pantry of Peace)," co-sponsored by Immanuel Baptist Church in Brookfield, Wisconsin. I have described it in more detail in my book *Celebrating the Graying Church: Mutual Ministry Today, Legacies Tomorrow* (Lanham: Rowman & Littlefield, 2020), 167-168.

[6] Ryan Burge, *The Nones: Where They Came From, Who They Are, and Where They Are Going* (Minneapolis: Fortress Press, 2021), 134-5.

[7] Philippians 2:2.

[8] Claire Brown & Anita Peebles. *New Directions for Holy Questions: Progressive Christian Theology for Families* (New York: Morehouse Publishing, 2022).

[9] Michaeleen Doucleff, *Hunt, Gather, Parent: What Ancient Cultures Can Teach Us about the Lost Art of Raising Happy, Helpful Little Humans* (New York: Avid Reader Press/Simon & Schuster, 2021).

[10] Richard N. Bolles, *What Color Is Your Parachute?* (Berkeley: Ten Speed Press, 2022).

[11] Thomas P. Bonczar and Allen J. Beck, "Lifetime Likelihood of Going to State or Federal Prison," Bureau of Justice Statistics, March 1997, Lifetime Likelihood of Going to State or Federal Prison (ojp.gov), accessed 14 August, 2024.

[12] Dr. Archie Ivy, phone conversation, 10 August 2021. I have earlier reported this interview in my book *The Grandparent Vocation: Wisdom, Legacies, and Spiritual Growth* (Lanham: Rowman & Littlefield, 2023), 76-77.

[13] Bonczar and Beck.

[14] Stephen Ministries accessed 13 January 2025.

[15] John Savage, *Listening and Caring Skills: A Guide for Groups and Leaders* (Nashville: Abingdon Press, 1996).

[16] Recalled by Bass, 205.

[17] Recalled by Bass, 206.

CHAPTER 5

Singing God's Praises in a New Key

WORSHIP IN A CHANGING CHURCH AND WORLD

O sing to the LORD a new song,

Sing to the Lord, all the earth.

Psalm 96:1

Near the end of World War II, and near the end of his life, the beloved William Temple, Archbishop of Canterbury, gave a talk on the British Broadcasting Company. He looked out at the conflict and the tragic destruction all around him and concluded that this world could be saved by one thing only—worship. Then he went on to say what he believed worship to be.

To worship is:
- to quicken the conscience by the holiness of God,
- to purge the imagination by the beauty of God,
- to open the heart to the love of God, and
- to devote the will to the purpose of God.[1]

That eighty-year-old description by one of the twentieth century's profound religious thinkers provides us with an excellent foundation for worship. Worship is to be open to the presence of the living and eternal God, and to be encountered and changed by that presence. Because of that encounter, we are enriched and empowered for living in God's service.

That is a good starting place. But how exactly do we do that? How do we plan, lead, and carry out worship that speaks to our times? In this age, when "organized religion" is in decline, worship has a diminished place in the life of many. One study revealed that for those who still attend worship, the average frequency is 1.3 times a month, not weekly as it once was.[2] For those who still worship, at least occasionally, and for those who might be drawn back, what should worship be and how should we plan and lead it today and tomorrow?

MEMORIES, RESISTANCE, AND REGRETS

Some of those who continue in worship have memories that might go back to William Temple's words and even before. They may lovingly remember how it was—and they may miss what worship was like in those days. Diana Butler Bass recalls that in her childhood, "We were white glove Methodists, all dressed up each Sunday and all sitting politely in our pews."[3] "Blue laws," the strict regulations from an earlier time that limited Sunday activities, eliminated distractions for those times. People came to church in their "Sunday best."

Worship often followed a familiar pattern with the singing of a limited number of hymns from well-worn hymnals. The choir had a well-established place in worship and church life. A Bible reading selected by the minister and a sermon followed. After worship, people would linger to visit, talk with neighbors, hear the news, and perhaps gossip a little. Sometimes there was a potluck "dinner." Many faithfully came, one day in seven.

While it may sound quaint and old-fashioned, that kind of regular worship was important. People knew and supported each other. People celebrated each other's good news and reached out with support and help when tragedies and grief struck. Worship renewed our faith in God and called us to remember who and whose we were, what we believed, and for what we stood.

LIVING WITH CHANGE

What used to be assumed in worship has changed. A worship leader's attire has changed from suits, to robes, to robes with stoles of liturgical colors, to informal, to—just about anything. Musical instruments used in worship have changed, as well as the type and style of music. There have been disagreements and even "worship wars" about what is fitting and appropriate in a service of worship. The place of worship has moved from sanctuaries with stationary pews designed to keep the focus on the worship leader—to just about anywhere with moveable chairs arranged for gathering and awareness of each other. Change and variety continues aplenty. With all that change, how can worship continue to be life-giving and restorative in today's church?

Eric Elnes, pastor of Scottsdale (Arizona) Congregational Church, struggled with this question. He had succeeded in engaging youth in Bible study and other worthy activities. However, he felt that worship in his church was not alive or engaging the youth. In a period of introspection about worship one summer while on study leave at a lakeside cottage in Oregon, he sat on the dock pondering, "What is the nature of worship?" As he sat there, the largest bass he had ever seen swam past him leaving a wake of water rippling in its wake. He recalls, "I stood up and gasped as a sense of awe and wonder provoked a surge of adrenaline through my body."

This experience stimulated an insight about the foundation of worship. He thought to himself, "If you can take an hour on Sunday morning and open people to experiencing just the quarter-second of the awe, wonder, and surrender that you just experienced, it is accomplished." The challenge was to offer this without manipulating people's emotions. Rather, he needed to lead them back to their Puritan roots. The Puritans based their faith "on a sense of divine wonder." He suddenly understood that worship was not only for the mind and the intellect but for the whole person, including emotions, will, body, and senses.

This story of Eric Elnes was related by his friend, Diana Butler Bass. Reflecting on that story, she says this:

> Worship is an experience of God, not reflection about God . . . Every act of worship, no matter how private or public, how discreet or elaborate, enacts God's desire for the world. By learning to look for it, by opening ourselves to seeing the awe and wonder of the dance, we might glimpse the ripples of God…Hospitality, beauty, celebration. Awe, wonder, mystery. Communities making merry. For too long, mainline Protestants equated worship with thinking about God. Now, in at least some places, their hearts—the whole capacity of being human—are learning to experience God.[4]

CHANGE IN THE PRESENT

Randy, one of the young pastors with whom I visited, encountered and engaged this issue. He told me that he had been called to a church where "church had become very traditional, very liturgical. There was more scripture and liturgy than I was used to having in worship as well as many hymns, both old and contemporary."

"We were trying to discern how to do ministry there. People would visit the church but not come back. 'Your church is archaic and dead,' some would tell us. We needed to figure out our identity and who we were, particularly on Sunday morning. We thought, 'What if we have two services, one traditional and another something different?' So we started to do that. One worship service was more fluid with different music and an interactive sermon with more discussion and questions, making it possible for people to respond." This began in 2017.

"By the middle of 2018," he continued, "our numbers had almost tripled. On the first week thirty or forty people attended, the second week eighty. This service became a haven for those who came with church hurt. We addressed those feelings and helped them find healing. We offered the two different services up until the pandemic." After the pandemic, they did not restart the traditional service again.

Randy reflects on this approach to worship: "We hungered to have a divine experience, an encounter with God. There is a critique that this worship just plays on your emotions. We didn't do that, but we didn't avoid emotions either. I hunger to be led by the Spirit. Personally, I can't change people, but I bring them to God who can change them." He further reflected, "I would love to get the way of mystics, a contemplative way, into the church. Once in a while, when I feel led, I begin the service with a breath prayer."

Another pastor, Jessica, brought gifts from what enriched her life in her home church: "Growing up we had puppet, dance, and other innovations that still give glory to God. I brought this to the church where I was called. I told them, 'It's okay to do things a little differently, okay to use puppets, praise music, and other things new to people. This may contribute to our having the ability to worship and praise.' I have brought this ability to worship in other ways. Their response? Sometimes, 'Oooh what are you doing?' I say, 'I'm thinking about this; what do you think?' I am careful how I bring my innovations. I do so in a conversational, dialogical way. I am not a bulldozer."

Michael also follows a gentle dialogical approach in leading his church into more meaningful worship. He commented, "I have found that worship is like language. For a church to have its language changed for it by a pastor is not helpful. My aim has always been to increase fluency, rather than to re-work things entirely. The general shape is very similar. One thing I try to do is return to the question: does something continue to have value for us? Is this response what we need to do in worship or is there a more fitting response? I want all of us to feel free to explore what is happening in worship.

It is easier to make changes. I have never wanted to change everything at once. For example, what happens when you have a new music director, very capable but whose skill set lies in a different area? Is this who we are? For a church to try to be someone they are not in worship, it's not going to work out."

On the other hand, Mia, as pastor of a church she founded, is in a different position. She reflects, "In a new church start without a lot of history, heritage, or expectations, we are free to initiate changes, try things, put them in practice if they are helpful or leave them behind if they are not. Our worship has great variety, such as praise and spiritual uplift, silent prayer, guided prayer, scripture, and message. We don't have a paper worship bulletin but project everything on a large screen." Mia invites people to take notes on their phones, to take pictures of various items on the screen in a sermon, and worship in an eclectic, contemporary manner.

A PLANNER'S PERSPECTIVE

Brad Berglund, who has guided many congregations in strengthening and transforming their worship experience, grounds this vision of what worship can be. He begins with some basic assumptions. First, he reminds us that worship is what worshippers do for God. Worship is not a performance, even though many performing and leadership skills can transfer to worship. Rather, worship leaders are to be "skilled mediators of a cosmic drama between Creator and...created." If we are open to God's presence, "worship can transform our lives and relationships and make us more trusting and faithful human beings." Since Jesus calls us to love God with all our heart, soul, mind, and strength, "worship should activate our whole self, including our bodies." We are called to love neighbor as self. Therefore, worship "expands our souls, makes us generous, and sends us into the world to love and serve."[5]

With these visions of what worship can be, there are a variety of means that we can mindfully engage as we plan, prepare, and lead.

LEARNING BY LEADING

Evan helps people discover worship by inviting and training them to lead. He told me: "What we do best is create a variety of spaces for people to participate. We have a great band director and organist. We have many different people leading music, praying, and reading scripture. In the church from which I came, there was a high bar for participation. Here, what we do well is let people use their gifts. We celebrate when they do well, give opportunities and training to help them develop their gifts, and, as leaders, take the fall when they stumble. Shared leadership helps with transparency and overcomes some of young people's distrust of pastors, which in many ways is fair. This also helps to overcome some institutional distrust, and it is also the way of Jesus. We are doing justice work by how we are sharing our power and privilege."

MUSIC

When worshipping with a charismatic congregation, Harvey Cox reports that on one of the drums there was a decal that he could not read from where he was sitting. After the service he walked up to read it. It said, "Music brought me to Jesus." This simple testimony did not surprise him. He noted, "Jazz music and Pentecostalism grew together in startling parallelism."[6] I am not suggesting the use of jazz music for all churches. Rather, the goal is to encourage creativity and flexibility in our engagement of music as one aspect of our experience of God's presence, love, and power as we worship. When Diana Butler Bass observed churches during the pandemic that were doing well even during the downturn in religious interest, she experienced a wide range of musical traditions in the music that energized vital worship in those churches.

It has been noted that, whatever our age, we most love music from the time when we fell in love! That may also be true of religious music; we most love what music accompanied our coming to love the God and the community of our first faith. If our worshipping community is multigenerational, this increases the possibility that a wide range of music will be needed to speak to all of those who worship.

Reflect for a few moments. Think of times when something musical is what most touched you in worship. After that service, the place you were touched, the one thing you most remembered, was that music. I can think of several illustrations of this in my own life. For example, when I was a pastor, I had given music staff information about scripture and theme for each of the upcoming services. Often the pianist, Melody, selected a hymn interpretation, often one arranged by Mark Hayes, for her prelude. As I silently and prayerfully prepared to lead worship and that beautiful hymn interpretation washed over me, I felt that I had worshipped before I even gave the call to worship!

I was at an African American church and a young man sang "His Eye Is on the Sparrow." He sang it with a clear tenor voice and sang with such depth of feeling that the song was his very own witness. I have heard that song and I have sung that song in congregations before and since, but never with such power, never with such a penetration to my very soul.

Recently, I participated in a conference of my denomination. Each evening, worship began with a time of singing led by a choir of volunteers, mostly young adults, music students, ministers of music, and church musicians. They led us in a wide variety of songs, many I had never heard before. It was an enriching time. The varied music was beautiful, but I was even more touched to look upon their faces as they sang—so involved in leading worship, experiencing worship, letting the music speak to their own hearts even as they sang.

Music gives voice and expression to our seeking and finding, to our joy and sorrow, to our loneliness and our community, to our agony and our ecstasy. Through music we speak of our hunger for God's presence and our love for the God who has found us. In worship there needs to be room for all of us in the music we sing and hear.

SILENCE AND PRAYER

Chris Palmer observes that we are most aware of fellow worshippers and most aware of God when the pastor calls on us to confess our sins in silence and then holds that silence for an extended time. He reflects, "Silence makes us acutely aware of the presence of others. It gives room for others to speak. It gives room for God to speak."[7]

Further, he has learned that silence is vital for those who are deeply involved in political and social action. He reflects that this "feels to me like the lifeblood of faithful Christian social practice. Prayer and stillness, in the midst of social movement, offer individual moments of sabbath on the road to justice."[8] Even as he calls us to prayer and silence, he admits that this is a practice that he, in his Presbyterian tradition (and others of us in our traditions), may have ignored or minimized. Silence, invitation, and openness to the mystery of God needs to be taught and practiced as an essential habit to healthy worship.

Silence leads us to prayer in worship. Many earnest Christians confess to distractions and wandering attention when attempting to pray alone. In this regard, I have often been enriched by guided prayer or "bidding" prayer in worship. A leader mentions a concern and asks all to silently pray about that concern and then goes on to kindred concerns—praying alone together. When Jesus' disciples sensed what prayer meant to him, they asked, "teach us to pray." In effective worship, we teach each other to pray, in silence, openness, and listening, as well as in offering our urgent requests.

BIBLE READING, PROCLAMATION, WITNESS, AND TESTIMONY

Bible reading is a central act of worship, but too often it is not done with the attention and care it deserves. Scripture in worship should be given the best possible oral interpretation. I recall that when the Rev. Dr. Bill Herzog would preach at the church where I was pastor, he would request that *he* read the Bible passage on which he would preach. He would say that his reading was the "first interpretation of the text" which his sermon would explore further.

As worship continues, the Bible passage is explored and interpreted. Guidance on living its truth is offered. This may be called a sermon, a homily, or perhaps simply a teaching. Even after worshipping for many, many, years, this is a moment in worship that I highly anticipate. I hope there will be a word that helps me hear something from the Bible I hadn't noticed before, understand something in a new way, open the door to new hopefulness, or call me to new repentance, commitment, or action.

During my years serving as pastor of a church, I studied, reflected, and prepared, hoping each week that the sermon would be a meaningful worship experience for those gathered. I asked that same thing of others when they preached. Of course, many persons in a congregation may have such gifts to offer, not only sermons and Bible studies, but also reflections, testimonies, and calls to prayer or giving. A wise church encourages the sharing and hearing of wisdom from everyone in the gathered church to the enrichment of their worship life together.

ACTIONS, SACRAMENTS, AND ORDINANCES

There are also rich opportunities in worship through things we do and actions we take. Let's consider several of these.

The Table

In various ways, Christians engage in a ritual that includes eating (leavened or unleavened) bread and drinking (fermented or unfermented) juice. They do this in response to an invitation, and they do so in the company of people who share the same hungers, searchings, failings, and aspirations. This event is to remember Jesus' many meals with his followers and, in particular, a meal and an invitation Jesus gave on the last evening of his life on earth. Christians have sensed that this is something Jesus has asked them to do, and it must have been for a reason. Indeed, in countless ways, this community sharing adds possibilities to worship that words and silence alone do not seem to provide. It gives worshippers a chance to express a hunger for and a willingness to receive God's transforming presence.

Even reaching out to receive the bread and the cup is significant. Nora Gallagher notes, "If we did nothing else, if nothing was placed in our hands, we would have done two-thirds of what needed to be done, which is to admit that we simply do not have all the answers; we simply do not have all the power. It is, as the saying goes, 'out of our hands.'"[9]

Sometimes this experience is quiet and little noticed. Sometimes it is dramatic. For example, Sara Miles was well into midlife, with a background in a secular home and little or no interest in religion. She knew practically nothing of the Bible and had never prayed the Lord's Prayer. But at a San Francisco Episcopal church, someone invited Sara to the table.

She relates, "And then something outrageous and terrifying happened. Jesus happened to me." It was an overwhelming experience. Sara reflects, "I couldn't reconcile the experience with anything I knew. But neither could I go away. For some inexplicable reason, I wanted that bread again." It was a persisting feeling as acute as physical hunger.

Out of that initial invitation, encounter, and continuing participation, she converted to Christianity. Not only that, but she also devoted herself to create a massive food pantry where the despised and outcasts of every type are honored, welcomed, and fed.[10] We might think of the table as a place for committed Christians. Some denominations demand confirmation and strict doctrinal conformity in order to receive the elements. However, Sara's story reminds us that the table is for any seeker, and seekers come at their own risk!

Some years ago, I heard psychiatrist Scott Peck (author of the bestselling book, *The Road Less Travelled*) speak of his experience. He had become a Christian later in life, well into his lively career. He related that he had been hired as a consultant for a community of nuns. During the time he met and worked with them, the nuns obtained permission from their bishop to invite and include him when they received the Eucharist. He related that without that hospitality and that experience, he probably would not have become a Christian.

Worship around the table has the potential for welcoming love and transforming encounter! Further, at least three of the pastors with whom I visited were adding meals to at least some of their worship times. Their purposes for this combination of meal and worship differed; only one specifically connected it to the Lord's Supper.

Randy

"One thing I am really excited about is that on the first Sunday of every month, we have a love feast. We take a potluck meal and worship and throw the two together. We took a couple classrooms, arranged tables for fellowship time to eat together, and experience the community aspect of faith. There is time to talk together and then a time of music, prayer, and a short message that connects with kids, intergenerationally. Then we go into communion. On the last song, we stand up and make a circle, hold hands, and sing together. Such a good time. Something about which we are learning and making our adjustments. I would love to get rid of the pews and replace them with tables and chairs, so that people would linger. Around tables, we get to worship, learn from God, be informal, and talk about our questions."

Joanna

"We are starting a Sunday evening service with a meal. We don't have a capacity for a separate program with kids. We love having the kids here, and this will be a time for children and adults to participate together. We may have a Bible story presentation, or story, sitting in a circle, in a more active way, or we might have various activity stations, connected to peace making or creation care. We will do it instead of morning service and just have the evening worship. Part of that is related to our capacity and volunteers. We are trying not to burn people out."

Mia

"Once a month we have Dinner Church. We simply invite people to dinner to eat, talk, and get to know each other. This draws some economically challenged folks and some persons who have been incarcerated. It is a way to relate to some people who will not be likely to come at 11:00 on Sunday morning. Dinner Church meets about twenty minutes away from our building in the facilities of another church in a less economically prosperous area."

For each of these, welcome, shared food, worship, and hospitality come together in life-giving ways.

The Basin

There is another activity in which Jesus engaged near the end of his life. He washed the feet of each of his disciples and told them to do for each other as he had done for them (John 13:1-20). This instruction is remembered and practiced by some Christian believers, but not nearly as often as the table celebration. I was touched by the experiences of two people who did take part in this act.

Yolanda Pierce, a distinguished theological leader, grew up in a small charismatic church in Brooklyn, where foot washing services were frequent. She recalls that on the night before she left for college, in response to her devout grandmother's request, she reluctantly went to one more foot washing service. She had washed feet many times, but she had never had her feet washed. That night her grandma guided her to a place to sit, knelt before her, and washed her feet! She recalls, "My sense of unworthiness brought tears to my eyes and a spirit of repentance touched the very core of my being." Later, her grandmother and her other "church mothers" anointed her forehead with oil in the sign of the cross. She remembers, "They were preparing to send me away to college and away from their influence. They were calling on God to protect me from the crown of my head to the soles of my feet." She would always remember "cool water pouring over my bare feet…and then the loving hands patting my feet dry."[11] Her grandmother, whose prayers sustained Yolanda both before and after that moment, engaged her faith practices to help them move through this transition in both of their lives with trust and hope.

Barbara Brown Taylor recalls a quite different experience of the basin. She had been co-teacher of a weeklong seminary class on Christian practices. Forty persons had gathered to discuss and experience various Christian practices, such as pilgrimages and labyrinths. During the week, the teachers announced that the last session would be foot washing, with the concession that people could do hand anointing if they preferred. This was met with immediate resistance and rebellion. Many objections and criticisms were raised. But the teachers stood firm. The class participants were not required to do this practice, but at least they needed to come to the chapel and remain throughout the evening.

When that time came, Liz, her co-teacher, had transformed the chapel into "a sacred spa." Chairs were arranged in a circle around the Communion table and four pairs of chairs faced each other with empty basins and pitchers of water by each. A variety of candles flickered, and various lotions were available. When the class members had reluctantly gathered, Liz slowly looked around at each person, smiling and taking her time. Then she spoke, "Everything is here. There is no right way to do this, which means you can't do it wrong. The Spirit is here. All are invited to come."

Barbara had her hands rubbed with ginger lotion by a woman the same age as her mother. Gradually, pairs came to wash or anoint each other—two men who had hardly touched all week long—a woman, whose son had killed himself, washing the feet of another woman who had been sexually abused as a child. When the wife of a married couple, who had been quietly fighting all week, took her husband's foot in her hands, she did it so tenderly that he began to cry. She wept also, bathing his foot with her tears. Then he took all her rings from her hands, lovingly massaged her hands with lotions, and put the rings back on.

When it was over, no one had much to say. They blessed each other, said goodbye, and left. As Barbara reflected, she said, "You don't have to understand this at all, you just need one other person, a bowl, a towel, and water. Bend over it for any reason at all—to cleanse, to heal, to refresh, to forgive—and you too can hear the wind of God sweeping over the face of the waters...again and again, wherever two or three are willing to get wet."[12]

FACING, ATTEMPTING, AND EXPERIENCING THE IMPOSSIBLE IN WORSHIP

Peter A

As with my other interviews, I visited with Peter A about many things. When I asked about worship, he became animated. I learned that he and his wife, Grace, have a ministry to provide resources for creative and powerful worship. He told me, "Arts and music ministry are what my wife and I do. Word, art, and song: these are three avenues through which God communicates, and we work in these realms quite a bit."

"The universe came into existence by a word. We wanted to give a more wholistic way of offering approach. The church's past approach has been very anemic. Stories communicate something powerful. C.S. Lewis spoke of dragons that guard our heart. Stories help us past those dragons. We also offer art for God's revelation to be offered through the eye. As of now, art seems to be relegated to the background or to the color of paint on the wall. We are helping to bring art back. Music is complex; it is beautiful and transcendent. Why do we have worship wars? Because music matters. In all of these things, we are trying to reach out to God and each other in different ways."[13]

NUDGING THE CULTURE OF WORSHIP

In the church where I worship remotely, Tim was called as pastor during the pandemic. He led the church in refining its worship practices during and coming out of the pandemic. He told me, "I used to think of worship as being what we do when we come together. The new generation is more drawn to living in the community and living out their values. We need to recognize that as a form of worship as well. The growth of the nones and dones has changed the way we do ministry. The pandemic has forced churches to make some changes. Streaming has brought folks within our reach."

"As we made transitions, we agreed there are things we need to continue, and, with others, we can't go back to normal. There are some things we stopped doing. We stopped passing the offering plates in services. This is a most awkward place in service, a highly visible time where people feel some pressure. We intentionally did not bring it back. In so doing, we sent two messages, giving visibly and money isn't everything. You can give in many ways. You should never give if it means you can't pay rent. Give out of your abundance. Serving on boards or doing volunteer work are also ways to give back."

In his welcome at the beginning of worship, Tim invites freedom in the way they worship, such as sitting, standing, moving, dancing, or lighting a candle. I asked about this. He responded, "My goal is to change the culture. At the beginning of the service, there are forty or so candles, and by the end of the service almost all the candles are lit. One of our members has started to dance. She feels our services are so restrictive. She has become more comfortable with that. It makes some others uncomfortable. We need for people to come as they are. It's worth a conversation: why does dancing in the aisles make them uncomfortable?"

Another aspect of offering cultural change is in the varied art on the weekly folder. Tim told me, "In the beginning, I resisted putting artwork on the bulletin cover. I thought it took away people's ability to imagine. However, there was feedback from people who missed it. We had a long discussion. If we are going to use art, we try to draw on a variety of sources, such as images of Jesus in their own cultural context. That, in and of itself, has been valuable. African American people feel more involved. There was a week where we had a worship cover by a Native American artist. These are exposing people to different things, offering the possibility of differing interpretations. And so, the changing of culture goes on."

AND SO

Clearly, there is variety in how the pastors with whom I visited view and experience worship. I was enriched to experience their involved searching and exploring as they rethink and experience worship in these changing times. While we spoke of many aspects of worship, we did not touch on everything.

There are other actions that we do in worship. For example, the dedication or baptism of infants and their parents, believers' baptism or confirmation, welcoming new members or saying farewell to members who are leaving (including pastors sometimes), and blessing short-term or long-term participants in a mission. Each of these worship actions are full of God's presence and grace that may in turn grace the worshippers.

FOR CONVERSATION AND REFLECTION

1. What is your greatest delight in worship as you experience or lead it? What is most enriching for your life and faith journey?

2. What is your greatest longing for the worship you are experiencing or leading?

3. What, if any, of the thoughts-suggestions in this chapter might enhance worship for you and your community?

4. What are some ways you have found to enrich worship that are not mentioned in this chapter?

NOTES

[1] William Temple, 1944 BBC Broadcast.
[2] Bob Smietana. *Reorganized Religion: The Reshaping of the American Church and Why it Matters* (Nashville: Worthy Books, 2022) 147.
[3] Diana Butler Bass, *Christianity for the Rest of Us* (New York: Harper Collins, 2006), 252.
[4] Ibid., 173, 176, 178.
[5] Brad Berglund, *Reinventing Sunday: Breakthrough Ideas for Transforming Worship* (Valley Forge: Judson Press, 2001), xvii-xviii.
[6] Harvey Cox, *Fire From Heaven* (Reading, MA: Addison-Wesley Publishing Company, 1995), 139, 146-7.
[7] Chris Palmer, "Bodies in Silence: A worship practice Zoom can't replicate," *Christian Century*, 12 January 2022, 13.
[8] Ibid., 12.
[9] Nora Gallagher, *The Sacred Meal* (Nashville: Thomas Nelson, 2009), 45, 46, as quoted in Rachel Held Evans, *Searching for Sunday: Loving, Leaving, and Finding the Church* (Nashville: Thomas Nelson Books, 2015), 143.
[10] Sara Miles, *Take This Bread* (New York: Ballantine Books, 2008), 58-60, as quoted and described in Rachel Held Evans, 146-7.
[11] Yolanda Pierce, *In My Grandmother's House: Black Women, Faith, and the Stories We Inherit* (Minneapolis: Broadleaf Press, 2021), 132-135.
[12] Barbara Brown Taylor, *Always a Guest: Speaking of Faith Far From Home* (Louisville: Westminster John Knox Press, 2020), 148-153.
[13] There is more information and access to their varied resources at their website, "Poems of Grace." https://www.poemsofgrace.com/ accessed 4 January 2024.

CHAPTER 6

An Alternative to Illiterate Proof Texting[1]

How sweet are your words to my taste,
sweeter than honey to my mouth!
Your word is a lamp to my feet
and a light to my path.
Psalm 119:103, 105

The Bible...is a story—a story of God's people in their long, diverse, up-and-down, spiritual journey, a story written by different people, under different circumstances, for different reasons, spanning more than a thousand years. It was written during times of peace and war, in safety and exile, in Israel's youth and chastened adulthood. Its writers were priests, scribes, and kings, separated by time and geography, not to mention Myers-Briggs personality types.—Peter Enns[2]

These strange and difficult times of being church and doing ministry have many aspects. One of these is the widespread ignorance about the Bible and the sometime frequent misuse of it.

Today, people inside and outside of the church are spiritually hungry, exploring, evaluating, experimenting, and searching. Throughout history, one place for spiritual discovery and renewal was a rediscovery of the Bible or a key teaching within it. That does not seem to happen very often today. Biblical knowledge and biblical literacy seem to be shrinking.

Here are some questions we need to consider: How can we address this widespread biblical illiteracy? In what ways can we lead people toward authentic listening to, studying, and learning from the Bible? What conversations about interpreting the Bible are needed? How can we hear each other across our differences in how we see the Bible?

I will share reflections on some work I have done on these topics and what the pastors I interviewed told me about their experiences.

WHY IS THE BIBLE NOT BETTER KNOWN?

Why are spiritual hunger and biblical illiteracy happening at the same time? Probably for many reasons.

First, people are not reading much of anything today; at least, people are not reading as much as in the past. Today's media revolution is leading to significant changes in our brains and in our reading habits. Most often, computers and phones with brief texts, catchy slogans, and vivid images are our sources of information—or misinformation. Our brains are being re-wired, and part of this re-wiring diminishes extensive reading. The younger we are, the more this is likely to be true; the youngest among us are most at home in the various media and less involved with book reading.

Further, people may not understand characteristics of the Bible itself. For example, what really is the Bible? One way to answer that question is to understand that the word "Bible" itself comes from the root "biblia" which means "books." Therefore, "The Bible" really means "the books" and, thus, "the library."

This awareness can help us understand how to approach the Bible. When we pick up a single book, we might start at the beginning and read to the end. When we come to a library, however, we might ask a librarian to help us find a book or even a place within a book that will help us answer a question or reach some understanding.

This Bible, this library, has huge sections—genealogies and law codes among them—that are impossible reading and not meant to be read in a way that we might read other books. Furthermore, within this library there are many different kinds of literature. There are books of poetry and hymns, wisdom, advice, collections of speeches and sermons, dramas, novels, short stories, histories, biographies, letters, and so much more.

Therefore, a wise first step is to identify what we would like to know or experience from this library and ask a guide to help us start our search. As we well know from our contemporary reading, different kinds of literature call for different kinds of understanding and interpretation. We read a poem differently than we might read a news article. The same thing is true with the variety of types of literature in the Bible.

The Bible is, in the words of Bible scholar Peter Enns, "ancient, ambiguous, and diverse."[3] The "ancient" covers a vast expanse of time, perhaps two thousand years from the time of our fore-parents, Abraham and Sarah, to the last of the letters in the New Testament, close to a century after the life of Jesus. As the people of the Bible lived through those centuries, they experienced varying circumstances, such as being nomads, living in captivity, having their own kingdom and king, exile, and more. In this Bible, as subsequent generations asked the enduring questions of faithfulness and obedience, different circumstances led to different answers and, thus, apparent "contradictions." (Enns would say rather that these are "developments" and, therefore, "wisdom.") As we will note later, this process of seeking and re-thinking guidance for living occurs not only within the Bible but for us as we walk with these scriptures into our radically different modern age.

While the Bible describes events over a long period of time, it is all ancient from our perspective. There has been nearly another two thousand years of history since the last part of the Bible was written. The world of the Bible is in the distant past. Both the events of the Bible and the writing of the story happened before many bodies of knowledge and thinking were developed. For example, the scientific disciplines of physics, chemistry, electronics, geography, and astronomy have developed since then. The Bible and science do not contradict each other; they speak in different times and stages, and to different issues and frameworks.

Scholars are discovering more about ancient cultures, including those described in the Bible, and making that knowledge available to us. Two resources that offer this information and perspective are Bruce Malina, *The New Testament World: Insights from Cultural Anthropology*,[4] and John Pilch, *The Cultural Dictionary of the Bible*.[5]

It is important to understand how the scriptures came to us. This includes learning about how the various parts of the Bible were written, edited, and revised. Some of those writings were selected to be part of the "canon,"[6] and some writings were excluded. The canon includes both the Hebrew Bible/Old Testament and the New Testament. (Catholics and Protestants have reached somewhat different conclusions about the books that are included.)

Further, there is the study of how the Bible was transmitted and copied by hand (one copy at a time) for centuries, resulting in large numbers of surviving manuscripts. It is also important to understand the process of translating the Bible from the original Hebrew, Aramaic, and Greek into various languages, including English. (Any person who has knowledge of two languages knows that exact translation is impossible.) There are many versions and translations of scripture, each offering something special in the attempt to communicate from one language to another.

Roger Wolsey explains that all of these steps comprise what is called the "*historical-critical*" approach to scripture. (That word "critical" is often misunderstood. It simply means trying to discern what is accurate.) This process involves "giving great consideration to the best scholarship available seeking to understand the context in which a given text was written, by whom, for whom, when, where, and why. This approach seeks to discern what issue or problem of the day it was responding to and how the original audience likely interpreted it."[7]

This study and the insights gained from it may be upsetting to some people. However, it might be helpful to others who are searching and perplexed by the strangeness and diversity of what they read in various parts of the Bible.

Persons also need to understand that they bring themselves to the study of the Bible! While we might tend to believe that we are simply listening to what we hear in the reading, that listening is shaped by our life experiences, our culture, our political involvement, our traumas, our joys, and our sorrows. Our own personal background impacts what we look for, what we hear, and, perhaps, what we are willing to accept from the Bible portion we are reading. How are my life and experiences influencing what I hear when I read?

This is a lot to understand for people who don't read much anymore!

HOW TO ALLOW SCRIPTURE TO BE HEARD AFRESH AND ANEW

From all that history, we have this volume, this collection, this library, which we believe is inspired—inbreathed—by God. The Bible is, contains, and becomes the Word of God as the people of God read, explore, discuss, and live by what they have read. This happens as we read and study the Bible reverently, expectantly, inquisitively, and openly. We might carry on this study individually and privately or we might study in groups. Then, those who lead worship share what they have discovered in their study of scripture.

But how does that happen when there is biblical illiteracy, misunderstanding, and misinterpretation? Several strategies will assist in this task. It is my hope that we will embrace Bible study and teaching with new depth and urgency so that we might hear a living word for our changing times.

Group and Individual Study

There may be persons who want the broad and basic understanding of the story of the Bible that I have just briefly described. There are many who want to understand what the Bible is and how was it created, selected, and passed down over the centuries. When I was a pastor, I enjoyed exploring these matters with a dedicated and interested group of people. The resources that provided the basis for this study were from the Kerygma Bible Study Series.[8] A recent, briefer overview of what the Bible is and how it was formed can be found in the Bible Projects video series, "How to Read the Bible."[9]

Other people may not be interested in those matters, but they might still want to experience basic encounters with what scripture teaches. For all its vastness, the Bible contains many small pieces that can be explored to our benefit. An individual psalm or hymn, a parable or a story, an encounter, a journey, a teaching on a particular topic—any of these small portions of scripture can be an opportunity for fruitful study, conversation, and encounter.

Anew, we invite people to gather, read, and explore scripture with us. We promise, and we keep the promise, to make this a "user-friendly" time. All questions are honored and responded to. Steve Jacobsen, a California pastor, serves a church with wide diversity. He sees this diversity as a gift for growth and discovery. He reflects, "We believe that when we do a scripture reading that everybody has a piece of the puzzle. When we all come to the end, we are blessed by the encounter. To me that is when I feel God's presence."[10] May those sorts of experiences multiply!

EXAMPLES FROM GEN X AND MILLENNIAL PASTORS

Several of the pastors with whom I visited found ways for these sorts of Bible study groups and conversations to happen.

Cindy guided her church in reading through the New Testament one year, and the Hebrew Bible/Old Testament the next year. Worship, small group discussions, and church life revolved around the congregation's reading focus at the time.

James was surprised and pleased to discover that there was hunger and openness to focused Bible study. While he had never thought of himself as a Bible scholar, this was a rewarding time for him as well. He reflects, "It has been refreshing for me. I may not have a more favorite time in ministry than leading a group of a dozen people exploring some Bible book or theme. It might be a study of a book of scripture, or a theme such as prayer or worship, or a general overview survey of scripture." They have a planned focus and a commitment to a six-to-ten-week study time. Then they take a break before starting another series.

Edris found a small group willing to come together once a week to watch and discuss an episode of the TV series, *The Chosen*.[11] This is a multi-year series of episodes about Jesus produced by filmmaker Dallas Jenkins. A reviewer of this series noted, "With the intention of differing from previous portrayals of Jesus, [Jenkins] crafted a story arc which focused more on the people who encountered Jesus and viewing him through their eyes. He has stated in interviews that he sought to present Jesus in a way that was more 'personal, intimate, [and] immediate.'"[12] Edris noted that for her little group, viewing and discussing these episodes "brought them closer to understanding God and the humanity of Christ. I have gained many inspirational thoughts from it."

Children and Youth

Kathy is working on Bible engagement and knowledge with the children and youth with whom she works. At a retreat with her confirmation class, the leaders designed and played a game like "Jeopardy" with them. One of the questions was "Name two of the Ten Commandments." When no one could do that, she realized, "We have a couple things to cover." She thought it likely that Covid had made these knowledge gaps even worse. Therefore, she and the church where she serves are attempting more comprehensive training. When children enter the third grade, they are given a Bible. Classes and activities for the children are based on the seasons of the church year and the lectionary passages that guide the church's worship.

Evan had an equally perplexing time with education of children and youth from the other end. Meeting with a group of nine-and-ten-year-olds, he asked for their questions. Two themes emerged from the responses of these children: "Where did God come from?" (The pre-existence of God) and "Who is Jesus?" (the divinity of Christ). Here were nine-and-ten-year-olds trying to grasp the profound basics of their faith. He saw them asking, "Who is Jesus?" while trying to find answers by synthesizing what they were hearing in church with the superhero stories they were viewing. Evan confessed, "I don't always know how to answer big questions either. In fact, sometimes we can't answer them."

Ways Into Scripture Encounter

There are many ways to stimulate these conversations. For example, a pastor might invite interested people to meet together a week or days ahead of next Sunday's worship to read and explore together the scripture passage that will be the subject of the sermon for the following Sunday. Participants can bring their observations, questions, struggles, and take-aways from the text. Then the pastor can reflect on this conversation and preach the group's sermon out of the shared insights.

Or a small group might gather to encounter scripture and each other for their personal and mutual growth. Wolsey suggests that using the insights of the various Bible scholarship we have mentioned, the individual or group can approach a passage of scripture "sacramentally," as a means of grace and as a way of encountering the divine.[13]

One way to do this is through the ancient spiritual practice of "Lectio Divina" established by Benedicto of Nursia in the sixth century, with the four steps in the practice identified by another monk, Guigo II, during the twelfth century. In this practice, a brief scripture passage, perhaps six to fifteen verses, is read aloud four times with a different focus each time. (If you would like to try this with a scripture passage, you might read Mark 2:13-17). Let's visualize this as a small group exercise. Each of the four times, a different person will read the passage aloud with a different focus. There will be some silence after each reading, and then the next reader will read the same passage. If persons read the passage from different versions of the Bible, all the better. Each reading will have a different focus:

1. Sense. "What do I observe with my senses when hearing this text? What do I 'see'? What 'sounds' do I hear? What do I 'smell'? What do I 'taste'? What do I sense with my skin?"

2. Notice. "What word or phrase within this text calls or speaks to me?"

3. Feel. "What emotion(s) do I feel upon hearing this passage?"

4. Discern. "What might this passage be inviting me to do?"[14]

After some silence following the fourth reader, the leader may ask any participants to share what they experienced on each reading in turn, making sure that the quieter persons get a chance. It is wise to listen to the shared thoughts without questioning or critiquing the comments and reflections. Each person may share some insight from the experience, but nobody should be forced to share.

These are just a couple of examples of Bible study group possibilities. There are many more.

Public Worship and Proclamation

When the community gathers for worship, the pastor has an opportunity to invite a deep dialogue with the scripture passage of the day. I recall what Dr. Wallace Hartsfield, Professor of Hebrew Bible and Preaching at the seminary where I once taught, would tell us. He said that when the scripture text for the day has been read, the preacher has two responsibilities: first, to name the claim the text made on its first hearers; second, to name the claim the text makes on the present hearers, including the preacher! Until the preacher completes those two tasks, he reminded us, the preacher has not really preached!

Persons who are not likely to come to a Bible study group do come to a worship service from time to time. In that setting, the pastor has the opportunity to lead the gathered group into an encounter with the God who spoke to those who gave us our Bible and will speak to us again. Often this is done by helping the congregation hear and ponder what the scripture of the day may be saying to them. This may be exactly what people are seeking. Too often, they go away disappointed!

The Gen X and Millennial pastors I interviewed had found many ways to accomplish this holy task.

Joanna shares, "We have been using the Narrative lectionary.[15] This is a four-year cycle that goes through mostly narrative passages in scripture through the school year. It guides us through Hebrew scriptures (mostly narrative) before Christmas. After Christmas there are four New Testament cycles, one on each of the four gospels. There are a lot of stories people know but don't understand how they fit in the larger contexts. We fill in the gaps between episodes with brief summaries in worship or videos, three to four minutes long, explaining what happened in between."

Another way she has also found to stimulate intensive Bible study is to assign a lay person to preach on a given text! Since she is a part-time minister, other preachers are needed on the Sundays she will be absent. Giving a person that opportunity and then guiding them to study tools and resources can stimulate much personal growth and biblical awareness.

Jonathan, whose degree is in biblical linguistics notes, "My sense is that people are biblically illiterate in two senses, lack of understanding of what Bible actually says, and what that implies in their lives." He uses his training to help people overcome these barriers to hearing the Bible accurately and clearly. Whether preaching or leading a small group, he shows them the work he is doing to understand the Bible passage under consideration. Among other things, he looks at the Bible verses in their context, precedents, meanings of what is said, and parallel passages. He removes the mystery of how he learns what he shares and helps others discover how they can also hear the Bible more clearly and study purposefully.

Evan is also using worship and preaching to increase Bible engagement. He recalls that a few years ago, when he was on the staff of a Texas church, they were going to do a series of sermons on Daniel. In preparation, they took an informal poll to see how many knew the stories of Daniel. The poll revealed that less than half of the congregation did! In the Bible belt! He concludes, "Congregations may be smarter than you think, but often they know less about scripture than we assume."

Evan further reflects, "This has influenced my preaching ever since." He is aware that "people don't know the Bible; they probably haven't read it much. They may see it as complex, difficult, and mysterious." In the face of these struggles, Evan explains, "I am trying to communicate about the Bible in a way that is accessible."

Worship leaders have other opportunities for the Bible to be experienced as well. For example, there can be communication through the various media that engage modern and changing minds. Whether in print pieces, a worship bulletin or newsletter, or with projected images during worship, vivid and searching images can probe through our consciousness and lead or invite us into deeper encounters. One of the most encyclopedic of visual resources is Google Images. As a matter of fact, Google Images is self-described as "the most comprehensive image search on the web."[16] David May notes that when searching any religious subject, one can also add "stained glass" to the search. This will often provide visual images with vivid color, so helpful for this purpose.

One's voice can communicate as well. As I recalled earlier, Dr. Bill Herzog, when he preached for my congregation, would always ask to read the scripture passage on which he would preach. His reading of the text would be his "first interpretation of the text," he said. And it was! Whether it is the preacher or someone else with reading and dramatic skills, reading the scripture can make the passage live for all who hear. If the Bible passage has more than one person's voice within it, a group of voices can communicate those dimensions in a voice choir interpretation.

Our goal is to allow the Bible to be heard afresh with new understanding and to communicate its invitation to live its truth.

CAN DIFFERENCES IN INTERPRETING THE BIBLE BE CREATIVE?

We seek a renewed acquaintance, literacy, and encounter with scriptures. I recall hearing about the encouragement of Pastor John Robinson when he addressed the pilgrims departing from the Netherlands in the seventeenth century: "There is yet more light and truth to break forth from God's Holy Word." Believers have always claimed this promise and found it to be true. Occasions of renewal and calls to new forms of ministry have happened when people encountered the scriptures and heard them speaking anew to a different age. At the same time, there is a parallel question. Is it also true, as well, that God has more light and truth to break forth in other ways than scripture for the problems and dilemmas of our day? Scripture bears witness to God's speaking to us out of history, both the history of the times and our personal history. I remember a beloved Professor of Bible, Dr. Harrell Beck, who told his students that the only trouble with the New Testament was that it had a back cover! The revelation, guidance, and renewal continue, century after century, generation after generation.

Still, people have different ways of interpreting scripture as it speaks to modern issues and moral decisions. I recall Virginia Ramey Mollenkott suggesting that some Bible teachings are for an age and some for all ages.[17]

At least four current and historical issues highlight the reality of differences in interpretation about what the Bible teaches: slavery, divorce and remarriage, women serving in ministry and leadership, and issues related to gender and sexual identity.

Tim has engaged in many conversations about Bible interpretation. He told me, "I never tell people that this is the one true interpretation. Rather, we discuss different ways to look at things. How do we interpret scripture in the light of the life experience we bring to it? Sometimes, those who are most sure of their interpretation do the most harm with their interpretation."

He further reflects, "The hard question is, what is the line between allowing people their own interpretation but also protecting people from harm? I might say your interpretation is harming someone else. This is true for gay issues and women's leadership in the church. The Bible was written over hundreds of years with different authors and in different genres. The Bible doesn't always agree with itself. If the Bible has different interpretations, we should be able to do that, too."

Peter A also works hard at this issue. He reflects, "My role is to help to interpret what the Bible means. A Bible without tools for interpretation is about as dangerous as a gun without instructions on how to handle it."

He engages three helpful guidelines:

1. Contextually. What does this Bible passage mean historically? We need to consider the author and the situation. And we need to pay attention to the place where we enter the conversation.

2. Harmonically. We can't extrapolate one thing from the Bible that clashes with the rest of the Bible. How do the passages harmonize with each other?

3. Humility. The Bible is perfect, but I may not be. There is a possibility that my interpretation may not be right.

Good News! (Good Bible Study Aids Are Close at Hand—and Some Are Free!)

We have been talking about an important part of the role of pastor and church leader in this changing world. To be sure, helping others understand the Bible is a demanding and important part of pastoral leadership. The good news is that there are valuable and helpful resources close at hand. There are many aids to Bible study on the internet. Many of them are free. Here are a few examples:

- The Revised Common Lectionary (vanderbilt.edu) https://lectionary.library.vanderbilt.edu/ This site provides support for those who plan their worship around the three-year lectionary engaged by many Christian denominations. It offers a variety of resources, the weekly texts in different versions of the Bible, prayers, hymns, art, and more.
- The Text This Week: Lectionary, Scripture Study, Worship Links, and Resources. http://www.textweek.com/ This site includes a wide range of sermons and Bible study literature, arranged both by weekly lectionary text and Bible passages.

The following items were mentioned by Dr. May in response to my query.

- STEP. STEP is a website created by Tyndale House in England. It is especially helpful for those who are interested in different translations and the meaning of different Bible words. This tool can function either as a simple concordance or as an advanced concordance. https://www.stepbible.org/
- Bible Odyssey. This website is produced by the Society of Biblical Literature and by the National Endowment for the Humanities. It has short introductory articles on a host of biblical issues and passages. It also has short videos on topics. Among other resources, it provides access to the entire *Harper Collins Bible Dictionary*. https://www.bibleodyssey.org/
- Logos. Logos is a company that specializes in selling books and Bible studies. They do have some free and accessible materials. https://www.logos.com/grow/category/bible-study/
- Bible Project. I mentioned their videos in an earlier section. One small example of their many brief videos of Bible study: Study the Story of the Bible With Free Tools (bibleproject.com).
- NT Wright Online, Renewing Minds Through Biblical Teaching. Highly regarded Bible scholar Wright offers a wide variety of Bible studies. These have a cost. https://www.ntwrightonline.org/blog/ Dr. Wright also has a complete set of commentaries titled *The New Testament for Everyone*. These are helpful for the inexperienced reader.

AND SO

I have been speaking of a never-ending need and a never-ending process! Still, for ages, pastors have been called to invite and guide others into hearing and understanding the scriptures afresh. That remains the task of pastors today! The experiences and resources I have described here offer some possibilities for this sacred task.

FOR REFLECTION AND CONVERSATION

1. Where does your experience regarding biblical illiteracy coincide with what I describe in this chapter? Where does your experience differ?

2. What strategies have you employed to address the need for greater biblical awareness and knowledge? Have you used some methods not mentioned here? What are they? Which strategies worked? And which strategies did not work?

3. What is your experience with regard to different interpretations and opinions about scripture? How do you deal with those differences?

4. What have been the most enriching and rewarding times of scripture exploration and growth in your leadership?

5. What did I miss? What more needs to be said about helping people grow morally and spiritually through encounters with scripture?

NOTES

[1] I am grateful to Dr. David May, a wise and experienced Professor of New Testament, for generously responding to my many questions in phone conversations and in correspondence.

[2] Peter Enns, *The Bible Tells Me So: Why Defending Scripture Has Made Us Unable to Read It* (New York: HarperOne, 2014), 136.

[3] Peter Enns, *How the Bible Actually Works* (San Francisco: HarperOne, 2019), 5.

[4] Bruce Malina, *The New Testament World: Insights from Cultural Anthropology*, 3rd ed. (Louisville: Westminster John Knox, 2001).

[5] John Pilch, *The Cultural Dictionary of the Bible* (Collegeville, MN: Liturgical Press, 1999).

[6] The canon is the "collection of books which form the original and authoritative written rule of the faith and practice of the Christian Church, i.e. the Old and New Testaments. The word *canon*, in classical Greek, is properly a *straight rod*, 'a rule' in the widest sense, and especially in the phrases 'the rule of the Church,' 'the rule of faith,' and 'the rule of truth.'" https://www.biblestudytools.com/dictionary/canon-of-scripture-the/#:~:text=Canon%20of%20Scripture%2C%20The%2C%20may%20be%20generally%20described,Christian%20Church%2C%22%20i.e.%20the%20Old%20and%20New%20Testaments.

[7] Roger Wolsey, "Sensing the Sacred—Lectio Divina—a Spiritual Experience of Scripture," Accessed 27 August 2024.(patheos.com) This and what I will further summarize is also part of his book, *Discovering Fire: Spiritual Practices That Transform Lives*, independently published, April 2023.

[8] Kerygma Bible Study Resources for Groups—The Kerygma Program. https://kerygma.com/

[9] https://bibleproject.com/explore/how-to-read-the-bible/ accessed 4 April 2023.

[10] Cited in Diana Butler Bass, *Christianity for the Rest of Us*. San Francisco: Harper Collins, 2006), 146.

[11] https://new.thechosen.tv/

[12] https://en.wikipedia.org/wiki/The_Chosen_(TV_series)#Episodes

[13] Wolsey, "Sensing the Sacred."

[14] https://www.workingpreacher.org/narrative-faq

[15] Home—Narrative Lectionary—Working Preacher from Luther Seminary accessed 6 January 2025.

[16] https://images.google.com/?hl=xx-elmer&gws_rd=ssl. accessed 4 April 2023.

[17] Virginia Ramey Mollenkott, *Women, Men, and the Bible* (Nashville: Abingdon, 1977).

CHAPTER 7

Flourishing in the Wilderness; Renewing in the Exile

Even youths will faint and be weary, and the young will fall exhausted,
but those who wait for the LORD shall renew their strength;
they shall mount up with wings like eagles;
they shall run and not be weary; they shall walk and not faint.

Isaiah 40:30-31

As scholars have looked for ways to understand the present day for the church and Christianity, two biblical images have shaped the conversation. These two images both convey truth and provide insight as we seek to survive and thrive in ministry today. These two images are the wilderness and the exile.

WILDERNESS

Wilderness was the experience of the children of Israel when Moses delivered them out of their Egyptian bondage through the Red/Reed Sea and into the barren territory beyond. Many experiences from that time are reported in the books of Exodus through Deuteronomy. The wilderness wandering was a time when God's people were lacking in food and water. Their food sometimes included manna and quail. This was a time of deprivation and hardship. This was also a time of great danger as God's people contended with and fought other peoples.

Not surprisingly, this was also a time of complaints, conflict, and even rebellion. Some people even stated that they would prefer to go back to Egypt to the better diet they had there, a diet that included fish, cucumbers, melons, onions and garlic. Of course, there was also slavery back in Egypt, in contrast to freedom in the desert! (Numbers 11:4-6)

As Bernhard Anderson noted, this time of testing was necessary. These people did not become "a stable unified community overnight." They were drawn together by "a powerful centripetal force, the liberating action of Yahweh [God]." But there were also "powerful centrifugal forces" that pulled the people apart "such as tribal rivalry, power struggles for leadership, hunger and thirst, and the human incapacity for faith."[1] This was a time of testing, learning, growing, and maturing.

God's people also experienced gifts in the wilderness, for this was where God, Moses, and the children of Israel entered into covenant with each other. Through chosen leader Moses, the God who had delivered them spoke to the people of Israel and gave them the Ten Commandments and the Torah (Exodus 20:1-17). The people promised to obey God's commands, and they learned how to live their faith in the wilderness. This wilderness was also a place of spiritual awakening, deepening, and empowering.

The biblical accounts say that this wilderness time lasted forty years, which is an expression for a whole generation, or simply an expression for a good long time. As the account proceeds, we learn that no one from the generation that left Egypt lived until the time when the children of Israel entered the new land they would eventually conquer and occupy.

In a speech near the end of this time, Moses spoke of the reason for this time in the wilderness: "Remember the long way that the LORD your God has led you these forty years in the wilderness, in order to humble you, testing you to know what was in your heart, whether or not you would keep his commandments. He humbled you by letting you hunger, then by feeding you with manna, with which neither you nor your ancestors were acquainted..." (Deuteronomy 8:2-3).

When we think of wilderness, we also remember the forty-day experience Jesus underwent following his baptism. (Matthew 4:1-11, Mark 1:12-13, Luke 4:1-13). This was also a time of testing and temptation that guided Jesus into his role and mission. He launched his public ministry following that wilderness experience.

EXILE

The Exile is another experience described in the Bible that provides an image and food for thought about life, ministry, and faith today. The exile happened after the reigns of Saul, David, and Solomon, after the divided kingdom, and after the fall of the northern kingdom.

In 597 and 587 BCE, Jerusalem was conquered and ravaged, and the temple was destroyed. There were large—though not total—deportations of its people to Babylon. As Anderson notes, "Only the cream of Jewish leadership was taken, and the poorer elements of the population were left behind to harvest the crops."² This strategy prevented any hope of a national revival. Many of the leadership classes of Israel were taken far away—away from their Jerusalem and away from their religion that was grounded in the festivals and sacrifices in their now destroyed temple. This was a crisis-filled time of grief and tears.

As a Psalm vividly recalls:

By the rivers of Babylon –
>   there we sat down, and there we wept
>   when we remembered Zion [Jerusalem, the city of David].
On the willows there
>   we hung up our harps…
How could we sing the LORD's song
>   in a foreign land? (Psalm 137:1-2, 4)

After the early years of loneliness, the people adjusted to their new surroundings and situation; Anderson notes, "things were not going too badly for the exiles in Babylon." These Jewish exiles experienced a degree of social freedom and economic opportunity. Within the century, they were owners of economic enterprises. There was not anti-Semitism, at least not to the extent it would be experienced in later centuries. According to Anderson, "Babylonian Jews were permitted to move about freely, to live in their communities within or near the great cities, and to carry on their way of life."³

However, there was one big problem—religion. Their faith had been founded and built around God's blessing them and giving them a land. Their devotion was centered in the Temple in Jerusalem. It was there that the unifying experiences of their faith had happened—great festivals with sacrifices to God, as well as priestly leadership and guidance. Now that was gone, and the people were surrounded by a sophisticated and powerful Babylonian culture, including its religion. Would they be swallowed up in it? Would they be absorbed into it? The prophet Ezekiel pondered, "Can these bones live?" (Ezekiel 37:3)

Faced with these hard realities, their faith not only survived but also changed and adapted. Indeed, their faith was deepened and enriched. Alban Institute founder Loren Mead looked to this experience for hope and guidance for today's church. He pointed out that when the people lost all the former supports for their faith and community, they gradually found a new way.

Lacking a temple, they created a community where people could come together, recall their faith story, reflect on it, learn from it, and pray. Over time, those communities became known as synagogues. This pattern continued over the years and was eventually adapted by early Christians for their churches. Lacking priests, they created the role of the teacher, who would study deeply and teach others. The role of rabbi became an important ingredient in their survival.

Out of their life together, they pondered their stories and wrote much. This writing included many Psalms and other writings that came to be part of what is now our Bible. Even more, they discovered that their faith did not depend on the temple. Their faith heritage could be passed from generation to generation through the teaching and witness of the family. The great events of their history were remembered in family celebrations and rituals. By the end of the exile (when some, but not all, returned to Israel), the people had reformulated their faith and practice in a way that allowed them to survive and thrive for generations to come.

As Mead pondered the exile from the perspective of researching the church in decline (this was during the 1990s), he also reminded us that the exile was seventy years long. It may feel to us today that we are in a season of exile. If that's true, our exile may last for a long time. Our exile may last for generations. As we experience and adapt to our new world, Mead reminds us that we have much to learn from that time when God's people were in exile.[4]

FLOURISHING AND FLOUNDERING

Ministry can be a difficult profession. Even worse, in our present time of wilderness and exile, it seems to be getting harder. For each of the last two years, the Barna group has surveyed hundreds of Protestant senior pastors. In their latest survey, the Barna group discovered that forty-two percent of full-time pastors have considered quitting. The previous year that figure was twenty-nine percent. Why were these pastors considering leaving? Three main reasons surfaced in the surveys: "the immense stress of the job" (fifty-six percent); "I feel lonely and isolated" (forty-three percent); and "current political divisions" (thirty-eight percent).[5] These pastors probably felt that they were either in a time of wilderness wandering or in exile!

As I visited with younger pastors, I also heard stories of those who strongly considered leaving or had already left local church ministry—temporarily or for a longer time. (For this chapter, I use pseudonyms for the pastors whose stories I tell, except when they asked me not to do so. I do this out of respect for confidentiality and the vulnerability with which these pastors spoke with me.)

"Donald"
"The church I served closed and terminated my services. It was a time of discouragement. I thought of looking for a teaching position or pursuing doctoral studies. There were moments when I thought about putting ministry on hold. I came back to the truth that I have done the hard work of getting to ordained ministry. I returned to waiting for hearing that call to another pastorate, when that connection would be made, instead of thinking there would not be one."

Cindy
"I was in a car accident with a head injury. I told people if my issues got in the way of ministry, I wanted the church to move ahead and I would be willing to step aside."

"Jack"
"Prior to going on sabbatical, I had considered resigning and finding a new career. My undergrad was education. I could have gotten a job."

"Jerry"
"A short time into my present pastorate I had the strong feeling that this is my 'last rodeo.' I didn't feel accepted. There were about twenty-five people coming to worship, and I wondered why I would drive two hours to lead worship with twenty-five people, half of whom didn't like me."

Jennifer
"I am resigning and moving to a different state because of legal hostility to my child's gender identity. I need time to heal. I will withdraw from active ministry for a while, seeking and continuing therapy."

"Patrick"

"I was on the staff of three different churches, and now I teach high school. Why? For many reasons including power dynamics and conflict mismanagement. In the first setting, the church grew, and the lead pastor faced the challenge of how to keep being pastor when it conflicts with being CEO. I saw him enjoying the fame of being more and more known, associating with big pastors. In the second church there was more money involved. People with wealth had a lot of say. There was always the concern, 'If we lose that family, we would lose a lot of income.' Was this pastor afraid about that family leaving? How do you treat your leaders? There was fear of conflict, sometimes when conflict was needed. The third church was really afraid of conflict. I was there when Covid happened. I wasn't caught in the conflict, but it was easier to let go. I am now a member and a lay leader in the church I chose."

"Philip"

During an inspiring trip to the Holy Land, Philip strangely sensed God inviting him to step away from ministry. "I was dreading a return to business-as-usual, where I essentially found myself pimping out my relationship with Jesus in order to sustain what we've come to know as 'church.'"

There is much to learn and reflect on as we ponder church and ministry in the light of these eras of history—the Bible eras and our own. For now, let's consider what we might discover about flourishing in such times. What steps can we take to be strong, renewed, winsome, inviting, and relevant even as we live in our twenty-first century versions of wilderness and exile?

How are pastors flourishing in these challenging times? I heard a few stories, including responses to the crises we earlier mentioned. Here are a few of those experiences:

"Donald" (on his practices after the church closed and terminated him): "Reading…listening to a lot of music…being outside…riding my bike…seeing all nature had to offer…meditation…finding ways to ease my mind, as much as I could. I am now in a transitional ministry, and it is going well. I think and reflect about ways to become a better and more effective minister, so I don't get burned out early on. I have become more mindful about the rest that is allotted to me such as taking the vacation granted me."

"Jack" had spoken of a sabbatical restoring his love of ministry. I asked him what he did on his sabbatical. He responded: "I had stopped reading theology for fun. Part of my sabbatical was flexing my theological muscles. I bought and read books I hadn't read. I took a class on interim ministry. My family and in-laws took a three-week road trip out east, places my father grew up. We visited family we haven't seen in decades. Our last part of sabbatical was getting our too small home ready to sell and move into a spacious adequate home we had purchased." He found the combination of activities that restored him and his love of ministry.

"Philip" (on his continued growth and healing after resigning from his pastorate): "I am learning to live and speak and create out of an overflow of my life with God." "Philip" has since returned to ministry.

"Judy" was reluctantly called to a part-time ministry by a church that wasn't sure they wanted a woman pastor. But she came, found worthwhile work to supplement her income, and lived into a life of caring and relationship building. She reflected, "This is my role now to be pastor to people who are hurting. My congregation appreciates me. They will say, 'Ok pastor "Judy," have you had a break?' They make sure I have a vacation, and they sent me to my denomination's biennial in Puerto Rico. They are very aware of how stressful ministry can be. Some of my deacons will take it off my plate and do some of the visiting. I am invited to family anniversaries and other parties. We care for each other."

I also visited with two pastors who did not speak specifically of self-care strategies but who worked in difficult situations, and I found myself asking them, "What keeps you going?"

Seth serves an elderly congregation of persons of an ethnic group other than his, and has, among other things, helped them secure their hold on their building. He responded to my question this way: "I have a strong sense of justice and want to see justice happening, love, equality, inviting people to sacrificial relationships that we see in the life of Christ. I want to continue serving them. I support them in what they are good at, being a faith place for each other, in their mother tongue, respectful of culture, in their honor seeking society."

"Dorie" works with a congregation with special needs, which she shares. She has been a part of this kind of ministry all her life and has worked with these congregations for years. She responds, "I believe even more basically, it is my calling. It is the work of the Holy Spirit. Otherwise, I think I would be totally and utterly out of commission—if I didn't have the work of the Holy Spirit in me, working me, pushing, driving, encouraging, calming, putting a fire under me. As Christ said, the Holy Spirit is a gift, and, boy, is it."

In widely varying ways, these ministers responded to my inquiries by bearing witness to a variety of practices, experiences, and convictions that have sustained them in the work they are doing.

OTHER POSSIBILITIES

There are some helpful strategies that echo the reflections of these young pastors and point to new possibilities. The term often used for these strategies is "self-care." However, this term has sometimes been criticized. To some people, "self-care" sounds self-centered and self-serving. To these ears, the term sounds contradictory to the all-encompassing servanthood of a true pastor. Others suggest that "self-care" tends to focus on the effort to do something by oneself when in truth this requires the support and participation of a whole community. Some feel that "self-care" appears to leave that community out of the loop.

Matt Bloom offers an alternative image: "ecosystems of wellbeing." He notes, "The people we live and work with are part of our ecosystem, but so, too, are the groups and organizations that create and shape the environments in which we live and work."[6] Clearly, the entire community can contribute to the health and well-being of its leaders.

We need to be clear. Self-care is not only for the individual's comfort; it is a means to being renewed for the claims of ministry. Years ago, Elton Trueblood spoke of "the principle of alternation." He was primarily referring to the example of Jesus and his disciples stepping away to rest from their demanding ministry to be prepared and strengthened for the next episode of serving. Likewise, we relax, rest, or engage in self-care to alternate back into committed serving.

Further, whatever we need for our own renewal, we should desire for the whole community we serve. Granted, sometimes the care we seek may have a unique form. For example, I was once granted a three-month sabbatical and spent it making friends and learning from others in another part of the world. I was able to teach pastoral care in seminaries, and I led pastors' retreats in Southeast Asia. (This was one sabbatical in over forty years of ministry—I probably would have been a better minister if I had had more sabbaticals, wisely planned and used.) There were a few persons who commented that they had never had a sabbatical, and that it would be nice to have one. It would have behooved me as their pastor to help them find what renewing event (even if it wasn't a three-month sabbatical) might have enriched them in a similar way. At the same time, I came back so invigorated that church leaders joked that they wished they had sent me sooner!

Clues

How do we discover and plan this strategy? In our biblical examples, the people found helpful opportunities even in difficult times. For example, in the wilderness, the Israelites didn't have the diet they once had, true. But they also had opportunities for spiritual renewal they didn't have before. They had the cloud by day and the pillar of fire by night revealing God's guidance and care. They had their fellow Israelites with whom to relate in a new way. In time, they had the mighty revelation of God, calling them to covenant and relationship. There were indeed opportunities for renewal within their difficult journey that they did not have before.

And for those in exile? After they dried their tears and realized that even though there was no temple, no glorious festivals, and no animal sacrifices to restore right relationship with God, there were new opportunities. They came to see that renewal was possible even within the exile. In time they discovered each other. Eventually, their conversations and community evolved into their synagogue. In that setting, some were more able to teach and guide. Over time, some of these teachers became their rabbis. As they pondered the stories of faith, they sang the psalms and created new ones. There were rich renewal possibilities within the exile.

Friendship and Relationships

In an earlier chapter, I spoke of the widespread loneliness and the need for loving friendship and community. Ministers and church leaders have a similar need! Ministry and church leadership can involve lonely tasks and roles. Certainly, we need to be present with people in their struggles and griefs. But we also need people who are present in ours. An important part of our "ecosystem of wellbeing" needs to be relationships that are tended and nourished. As Diana Butler Bass comments, "We make friends, join a group, or enter into a romance because it is this person or these people who make our hearts lighter, bring joy and comfort, and make the world more interesting and bearable."[7] Whoever those people are, mutual support and care deserve attention and effort.

- For those of us who are married or partnered, this may start with that partner and with any children and other members of the household.

- It can extend to professional friendships, perhaps a regular gathering with those of our denomination, or an inter-denominational or inter-faith group. Or perhaps friendships with persons in kindred occupations—counselors, social workers, hospice staff, and chaplains—would be enriching.

- There may be "doing together" groups or individuals—those who share engaging in sports, playing and singing music, sharing a craft or artistry, or cooking together. Others may be enriched joining together on a mission trip, a Habitat for Humanity project, or some other service.

- And there are, for lack of a better term, just good friends. They may come from way back—high school, college, military service—or they may happen along the way. As Sam Keen noted, this kind of friendship "is based on the simplest of the heart's syllogisms: I like you, you like me; therefore, we are friends. And while we can imagine a satisfying life without the juicy overflow of sexual love or the sweet burdens of family, we know intuitively that without a friend, the best of lives would be too lonely to bear."[8]

It is wise to ask ourselves if we have friends like that. If not, who might be a possible friend? Are we nourishing our friendships? What can be done to make our relationships mutually enriching and renewing?

Mind, Heart, and Spirit

Matt Bloom reports consistent research support for the longtime wisdom that we are beings who search for meaning. Indeed, "Research studies show that a sense of meaning and purpose are fundamental elements of well-being. Meaning arises from having core life values and beliefs that give direction to our lives and set ideals for the kind of person we should strive to become."[9]

Certainly, ministers and church leaders should have a rich sense of meaning and purpose. We explore and share the meaning of faith, belief, and the purpose for which we exist on this planet. We explore sacred writings and interpret them with others. We are present with people in their important life passages and in the joys, triumphs, sufferings, and sorrows of their lives. We are among those speaking for God's justice in the life of our nation and world.

At the same time, all of this takes a toll. Our life patterns need a balance where we are renewed to offer what is asked and needed of us. As church leaders, we are concerned about our community's doubts, struggles, questions, and spiritual needs. We also need to be sensitive to our own. What will keep us spiritually aware and on the growing edge? Might we need a spiritual director or peer? Do we need time alone, time in community, or time at a spiritual retreat? Might we be helped by a deep dive into a new spiritual school of thought—Celtic spirituality, for example?

And what intellectual learning and growing do we need to do? How can this be best accomplished? Personally, I resonate with the Torah scholar who wrote, "When I pray, I talk to God. When I study, God talks to me." What study do I need to be equal to the ministry before me, and what is the best means and medium for me to do this learning? Where do I need to hear God talk to me in a new voice?

Wise is the person who does some "preventive maintenance" on the heart, soul, and mind. Embracing that important task will assure that we are resourced and ready for the facing and serving of this day.

Physical Self-Care

When the demands of work are highest and when crisis after crisis seems to come, what we are most likely to give up in order to respond is our care for our bodies. We might eat unhealthy "fast food" too much or simply eat too little. Our exercise regimens might get crowded out. If we happen to use tobacco or alcohol, that use may expand. If these changes continue, our health will suffer. And our bodies will deteriorate.

In high school and college, I participated in competitive sports. In later years, I continued to play at least a little pick-up basketball and take up new activities such as jogging, swimming and tennis. Through those years I was able to claim something I experienced in my more competitive sports days—that extra burst of energy, the second wind, the runners' high. Because I had stayed reasonably healthy, I still had that extra burst available for ministry demands. When an emergency happened, when deaths came one after another, and when there was a tragedy (all in a busy church season), I could claim that needed additional energy to do and to be more. My body had a reserve that I could claim whenever I needed it.

Then there came a time in my ministry history when I had a health crisis of my own. There was blockage in an artery that led to angioplasty, physical therapy, cardiac rehab, and many doctor's appointments. At that point, I no longer had that extra reserve. It was time for me to adjust to some form of ministry that was less demanding.

Our high calling deserves our attention to wise health practices. We need to give attention to diet, to our weight, to getting enough sleep, and to establishing and maintaining at least a modest exercise schedule. No one does this perfectly. Our goal is "good enough" practices and health. We need to do these things enough to make possible our sense of well-being and energy for the ministry opportunities of the day.

Play and Laughter

Laughter and play also renew and empower us. We can learn from the wisdom of Susan Sparks who has at least two parallel careers: parish minister and stand-up comedian. She brings these together in her helpful—and hilarious—book, *Laugh Your Way to Grace: Reclaiming the Spiritual Power of Humor*.[10] Here is one of her insights:

Laughter is the GPS system for the soul. Humor offers a revolutionary, yet simple, spiritual paradigm: If you can laugh at yourself, you can forgive yourself. And if you can forgive yourself, you can forgive others. Laughter heals. It grounds us in a place of hope.[11]

Susan has another book that relates humor to our pastoral work of preaching: *Preaching Punchlines: The Ten Commandments of Comedy*.[12] Yes, indeed! Laughter, playfulness, and humor are not only enjoyable; they are also wonderful sources of restoration and renewal in a busy and demanding life. And they are spiritually renewing! These are good questions to ask: Where do I find playfulness, play, laughter, and humor? And how can I engage these sources more regularly?

We might find laughter listening to standup comics or watching various entertainers. Laughter may be discovered in various books and magazines. If our humor favorites go back a long way, we can find old comedy sketches stored away in archives and available through a computer search. Those of us who have friends or family to enjoy and laugh together are fortunate. I fondly recall such a friend. His name was Lee. If we were together for a few days, at some point we would laugh ourselves into helplessness, our knees buckling under us. If you have such friends, search them out, share your chuckles with them, and ask to hear theirs.

There is also laughter without jokes. Indian physician Madan Kataria developed and promoted what he calls "laughter yoga." It began with a small group of friends gathering each morning for a few moments of jokes and laughter. Soon they discovered they didn't need the jokes; they could just gather and laugh together. This has now grown to thousands of laughter clubs in at least seventy-five countries. His "Ted Talk" describes and demonstrates this practice.[13]

I am convinced that engaging laughter and humor can be a spiritual practice. Susan Sparks underscores this by speaking of the Celtic Concept of "thin places"—those persons, experiences, or places where we feel very close to the presence of God. She suggests, "Another thin place we don't often think of is laughter. It clears our hearts of insecurity, neediness, and stale expressions. It opens our hearts anew for the words or songs or silence we were meant to receive. With laughter, our hearts are laid bare before God."[14]

Playfulness can be restoring for us. It is wise to reflect on what brings out our playfulness. Perhaps this will happen as we spend time with a child or a group of children, as we enjoy a pet, or relish a walk in the woods. For example, I recall taking grandchildren to a public swimming pool with slides. How much fun we had, going down those slides, one after the other! Another memory involves backyard whiffleball baseball games filled with afternoons of triumphs, fun, and delight.

Still another way of engaging this self-care is what some might call a hobby, but which Notre Dame's Flourishing in Ministry Project call a "restorative niche." There are innumerable possible "restorative niches." A "restorative niche" should have two qualities: first, it is something we do well and something for which we can achieve a degree of mastery; second, it is something we do simply for the joy of the activity itself. In their study, researchers found that only about one in four ministers had such an activity. Further, they discovered that even fewer engaged in their "restorative niche" regularly, at least weekly. However, those who did so were among those most flourishing in ministry.[15]

Through Highs and Lows

Being attentive to our needs helps us function effectively. Matt Bloom explains that flourishing builds on "high levels of *daily* wellbeing, resilience, authenticity, and thriving."[16] Wellbeing should be a conscious way of life. It requires frequent attention, good habits, and course corrections when needed.

Of course, seasons of wellbeing will often be interrupted with what Thomas M. Skovholt and Michelle Trotter-Mathison describe as "those disequilibrium periods, those times of exhaustion, pain, despair and quiet." What then? Those who study such dynamics acknowledge that they have only a few things to suggest. They summarize: "A short answer to a difficult question is that we must continue self-care but do so at an accelerated rate."[17] At the very least, this means providing for ourselves the care, understanding, and compassion that we would offer another person going through such trying times.

AND SO

Granted, this is merely a small introduction to a much larger topic. Volumes can be written on this subject. Some years ago, I led a team of colleagues in writing one of those volumes. For years, I offered a course to seminary students on stress-management and self-care. In more recent years, I co-taught that course with my colleague, the Rev. Dr. Ruth Rosell. We also recruited two of our Doctor of Ministry candidates who did their D. Min. projects on self-care topics: Nathan S. Marsh and Angela Barker Jackson. Our book is titled *A Guide to Ministry Self-Care: Negotiating Today's Challenges with Resilience and Grace*.[18] In this book we examine the challenges of burnout, compassion fatigue, stress, and several more dimensions of self-care.

Another approach, quite different from ours, but wise and insightful, is that of the Flourishing in Ministry Project at Notre Dame University. Matt Bloom leads that effort, and in this chapter I have provided insights from his work. I have also offered citations of their investigations and his book in the end notes.

Perhaps more help than a book is needed. In their extensive study *Caring for Clergy: Understanding a Disconnected Network of Providers*, Thad S. Austin and Katie R. Comeau do a survey of the wide variety of clergy care providers, how they came into being, and what they offer. They explore five types of support:

- Denominations, Networks, and Associations,

- Granting Organizations and Funders,

- Pension Benefit Providers and Insurance Providers,

- Frontline Providers (including counselors, spiritual directors, career assessment providers, and more), and

- Continuing Education Providers (including Doctor of Ministry programs).[19]

One of their key discoveries is how separate and disconnected these various clergy caregivers are from each other. They call for greater communication, coordination, and networking. Beyond that need, however, is the key message that there is professional help to heal and to thrive, though it may take some sleuthing to find it.

Working for mutual and self-care is, beyond question, essential for lives of ministry marked by resilience, hopefulness, and joy. It is equally needed for the communities and those who lead. There is hope, strength, and renewal within these possibilities!

FOR REFLECTION AND CONVERSATION

1. In what ways, if any, do the biblical images of wilderness and exile connect to your experience of church and leadership of a church?

2. What are the biggest challenges or difficulties you encounter in ministry and church leadership?

3. Have you considered resigning and finding other work? If so, what sustains you in what you are doing?

4. What self-care activities are most renewing and helpful for you?

5. What self-care activities are you feeling a need to begin? What can help you get started?

6. Do you have a "restorative niche" as described above? If so, how are you doing at engaging it regularly?

7. What individuals, agencies, and organizations are most helpful to you in your being healthy and strong in your life and work?

8. Have you been able to overcome the loneliness in ministry that some experience? If so, how have you done it, and where have you found community, friendship, and support? If not, where might you start?

NOTES

[1] Bernhard W. Anderson, *Understanding the Old Testament*, 4th ed. (Englewood Cliffs: Prentice-Hall, 1986), 115.

[2] Ibid., 446.

[3] Ibid., 447.

[4] Loren Mead, *The Once and Future Church Collection* (Herndon, VA: The Alban Institute, 2001), 362-366. This portion of his anthology was originally in *Five Challenges for the Once and Future Church* (1996).

[5] https://www.barna.com/research/pastors-quitting-ministry. accessed 27 February 2023.

[6] Matt Bloom, *Flourishing in Ministry: How to Cultivate Clergy Wellbeing* (Lanham: Rowman & Littlefield, 2019), 3.

[7] Diana Butler Bass, *Christianity After Religion: The End of Church and the Birth of a New Spiritual Awakening* (New York: HarperOne, 2012), 205.

[8] Sam Keen, *Fire in the Belly: On Being a Man* (New York: Bantam Books, 1991), 173.

[9] Bloom, 44.

[10] Susan Sparks, *Laugh Your Way to Grace: Reclaiming the Spiritual Power of Humor* (Woodstock, VT: Skylight Paths, 2010).

[11] Ibid., *Laugh*, 6-7.

[12] Susan Sparks, *Preaching Punchlines: The Ten Commandments of Comedy* (Macon, GA: Smyth & Helwys, 2019).

[13] Madan Kataria, TED Talk, accessed 26 October 2017, https://www.youtube.com/watch?v=5hf2umYCKr8.

[14] Sparks, *Laugh*, 124.

[15] The Flourishing in Ministry Project, *Flourishing in Ministry: Emerging Research Insights on the Well-Being of Pastors* (Notre Dame, IN: University of Notre Dame, 2013), 20, 50.

[16] Bloom, 53, italics mine.

[17] Thomas M. Skovholt and Michelle Trotter-Mathison, *The Resilient Practitioner: Burnout and Compassion Fatigue Prevention and Self-Care Strategies for the Helping Professional*, 3rd ed. (London: Routledge, 2016), 131.

[18] Richard Olson, Ruth Rosell, Nathan Marsh, and Angela Jackson, *A Guide to Ministry Self-Care* (Lanham: Rowman & Littlefield, 2018).

[19] Thad S. Austin and Katie R. Comeau, *Caring for Clergy: Understanding a Disconnected Network of Providers* (Eugene, Oregon: Cascade Books, 2022), 11.

CHAPTER 8

Seeking Racial Shalom in a Changing Nation

"I truly understand that God shows no partiality, but in every nation anyone who fears God and does what is right is acceptable to God."

Acts 10:34 (An Inclusive Version)

In 1960 (the year I graduated from seminary and began serving as a pastor), according to census reports, nearly eighty-nine percent of Americans were white. Just over ten percent were Black. Americans of other ethnic groups made up the remaining one percent.

By 2060, according to Census Bureau projections, only forty-three percent of Americans will be white. By then, twenty-eight percent will be Hispanic, fifteen percent will be Black, nine percent will be Asian American, and six percent will come from two or more ethnic backgrounds.[1] Presently there are about 6.79 million Native Americans, about 2.9 percent of the United States population. I have not seen projections about future percentages for this group.

Bob Smietana, national reporter for the Religious News Service, addresses the implications of this present and projected change: "The reality is this: it is no longer viable to build a sustainable religious institution in the United States with a supply chain of primarily white Christians."[2] For survival reasons alone, churches must become more diverse. As his Religious News Service colleague Mark Silk puts it, "The future of religion in America belongs to the Nones and the 'Nons'—Christians who are not white."[3]

Of course, there are also many other good reasons to become more diverse and engaged inter-ethnically. There are theological reasons. Our Bible makes clear that every person in God's diverse creation is created in God's image. The Apostle Paul affirmed in the book of Galatians: "There is no longer Jew or Greek; there is no longer slave or free; there is no longer male and female, for all of you are one in Christ Jesus." (Galatians 3:28)

Further, there are many reasons that people, through no fault of their own, are displaced from their homes—wars, persecution, danger, climate change, drought, famine, crime, unemployment, and hunger, to name a few. In the face of this, there are the haunting words from Jesus' own lips, "I was a stranger and you welcomed me…I was a stranger and you did not welcome me." (Matthew 25:35b, 43). Further still, we are called to seek justice for all of God's children, something we do better when in communication and relationship with our sisters and brothers of various ethnic and racial groups.

In addition to these reasons for care and welcome, there is another. That is the personal enrichment and inner joy that comes when we meet another person and become friends across all those barriers that would tear us apart.

It appears that this kind of relational community is beginning to blossom, although slowly and in limited ways. A Faith Communities Today Survey notes that presently one in four congregations is multi-ethnic, defined as a congregation in which twenty percent of the participants in the church are not part of the dominant racial group in the community. According to their studies, this is up from twelve percent in 2000. That is growth to be celebrated. However, these scholars also note that this racial and ethnic diversification is occurring mostly along a one-way street. That one way is from various ethnic and racial groups to predominantly white congregations, with very little movement in the other direction.[4]

The congregations I served found our way to at least some growth in friendship, cooperation, and deeper inter-racial and inter-ethnic relationships. We did this in a variety of ways. So have the younger pastors with whom I spoke, and they also have done so in various settings and in different ways. In the following pages, I will speak of what they and I experienced and heard. This chapter will be a report and a reflection on these experiences and possibilities.

BUILD ON RELATIONSHIPS ALREADY IN PLACE

I am privileged to be part of a denomination and a regional family of churches that have a variety of congregations from different ethnicities. The coming reality of no majority ethnic group in our nation is already true in my denomination. We see this as something to celebrate, to enjoy, and to learn from. Recently I heard the Wisconsin region executive minister of my denomination, the Rev. Mindi Welton-Mitchell, describe our Wisconsin Baptist regional family:

The American Baptist Churches of Wisconsin are the most diverse denominational body in this state. We are currently about one-third historically Euro-American churches, one-third African American, and one-third Asian (including Chinese and members of the Burma Diaspora), Latino, and Native American. Two of our congregations are Welcoming and Affirming, and two of our Euro congregations are pastored by ministers of color. We also have one congregation that is intentionally intercultural with all four congregations—Euro, Hispanic, Burmese, and Indian Language (Telugu) meeting together for worship on Sunday mornings. There is no other denominational body like ours in the state.[5]

Whatever one's location and denomination, a starting place may be to reach out with friendship, openness, curiosity, and eagerness for shared projects among those with whom one already has a structural relationship.

EXPAND NEIGHBORHOOD OPENNESS AND FRIENDLINESS

A few pastors with whom I visited find themselves in increasingly diverse communities, and their churches are striving to embrace that reality.

David
David recalls that in a church he recently served, "There were members from Russia, Haiti, and various countries on the African continent. All had a part to help us take a broader global perspective. This helped us to be intentional in justice work and to do mission work in interethnic ways. Church is much more when we are multicultural and inter-ethnic, fully embracing what the church is called to be."

David also recalls how their relationship with a Korean church renewed and enhanced their worship. He recalls, "We did occasional interactive worship with the Korean church with whom we shared our building. This Korean congregation had a lot more energy and interactive aspects of worship. This was something that was always appreciated when we had opportunity to worship and pray together in English and Korean. We also shared fellowship over food. Everyone loves Korean food! The times around table, sharing stories and experiences, were so special. This is something that people who share buildings might take for granted. But it was something I really appreciated. We were there for each other in good times and hard times."

Anita

Anita reflects on the church whose ministry she joined and guides: "We are eighty to eighty-five percent European American, but our membership includes Asian, Central American, persons from India, all sorts of folks from all over the world. Racial justice has been on the radar of the congregation for a long time. Protests after George Floyd spurred our thoughts. We are non-racist, but are we anti-racist? As a leader, a young white woman, I am doing my own work, trying to meet the congregation where they are. This is my church community, but I am hurting over where my church is on racism. The journey to antiracism is a long journey. There will never be a time when we have eliminated racism from among us."

She further reflected on their history in this regard: "Our congregation has a couple Filipino families who been in church forty or fifty years. This congregation has welcomed immigrants as far back as I know. The last twenty years have seen a lot of growth. It does represent changes in Seattle. The growth in large locally headquartered corporations—Amazon, Microsoft, Boeing, for example—has brought an even more international group to the city and our church."

Kathy

Kathy is on the staff of a church in a suburb/separate community in the Kansas City area. "We are still mostly white. There are a few members of other ethnicities—a couple from Fiji, a Kenyan family, and a Korean family. I think our community gets excited when this happens. We are anxious to welcome them but are not sure how to be more welcoming. We do build space for families to connect with each other in different cultural histories and traditions. Some of the folks who come went to a Methodist church in other parts of world, and so coming to a Methodist church here is a connection for them. We are a growing diverse community. That is on our radar to build that aspect of our program more."

Seth

Seth finds himself in a different place. He is a non-Laotian serving as part-time pastor with an old and traditional Laotian congregation. An effort he co-led to combine with another congregation of different ethnic heritage was resisted and rebuffed.

He also offers part-time pastoral presence and ministerial leadership with Border Church, the gathering and worship community on the California-Mexico border. He has often invited members to join him on Sunday afternoons as he joins cause with Border Church. Virtually no one has accepted. Seth has devoted himself to a ministry of racial reconciliation and justice, so far with very little encouragement or support.

Evan

Fairly recently, Evan came to serve as pastor in Philadelphia. This church has a small inter-ethnic membership. However, one form of their commitment has been a twenty-year connection with an African American church. He notes, "That has kind of waned. We are rebuilding that now." He sees this congregation growing in commitment to racial justice. Part of the form this takes for them is in partnership with churches that have other ethnic makeups. Steps taken have involved shared services such as a Juneteenth ecumenical celebration and a multi-congregation Justice book club, reading and studying together with these other churches. They are making a start, he notes.

Evan's response and struggles struck a responsive chord with me. I also recall a very intentional effort to build a relationship with an inner city African American church of my denomination and its pastor. It was slow going, but over time, we had a series of pulpit and choir exchanges, joint services, and conversation times. The response from both congregations was scattered, but for those who took a risk and entered in, growth in relationships and understanding slowly happened.

Mia

Mia has a unique but formative experience for us to consider. She is the founding pastor of "NextGen Church." When I asked her to tell me about the church and its name, she recalled, "I came as a child in an immigrant family from Korea. We were not particularly religious before we came, but we became part of a first-generation Korean church. Though I appreciated it, I felt I was always treated like a child and not allowed/invited into leadership. And so Next Gen church was founded to help me and subsequent generations give leadership to the church, to engage, and to reach out. It is a multicultural church. I visualized it as a pan-Asian church, but as we reach out and engage the community, we have related to other culture groups. The church doesn't look like a church. It is in a strip mall, not far from a synagogue, and it was a former children's play area. It is not a large building. We have space for a hundred or so worshippers. Its focus is outward and service to its community and its world."

Mia was just back from Rwanda. I asked her about that. She said that this is one of the African countries where a personal connection led to involvement. This started when a Nigerian pastor joined NextGen church. Working with him and his connections, they founded a school in Nigeria. They also have involvement in Kenya, and they are now starting work in Rwanda.

WELCOMING A REFUGEE INDIVIDUAL, FAMILY, OR CONGREGATION

Another way to become more diverse is for a congregation to welcome a person, family, and/or another congregation, perhaps a congregation of immigrants, into their building. I was once pastor in a congregation where this was happening. It began before I arrived. A small group of Spanish-speaking Christians gathered for worship in the chapel at the same time the English-speaking congregation was worshipping in the sanctuary. This small band of Spanish speakers came from several Latin American countries and the southwest United States, and so they had several cultures to negotiate in their life together. With their small numbers, their children might stay with their parents or come to English-speaking Sunday School. The youth group was fully integrated from the two congregations.

Occasionally we also would worship together in a bilingual service and have dinner afterwards, sitting down together, sampling each other's special dishes. Those shared language worship times and meals were days when it felt as if we were a bit more of what God wanted the church to be. The best job of building deep community was done by a combined women's group, where they would learn a bit of the other's language, have conversations about mutual concerns, enjoy each other, offer support for each other, and develop friendships.

I also recall another church where I served in the late twentieth century. A congregation came into being from the refugees we sponsored. This process started before I arrived. The church mission board had actively applied to sponsor a refugee family. After much waiting and some false starts, a family of Lowland Lao finally arrived. The father had been a translator for the United States military. The church welcomed them, provided a place for the family to live, and helped the father find his initial employment.

In time, this family knew of another family that wanted to come. And that new family knew of others. This was part of a vast movement. Following the Vietnam War, many Laotians left their country. A large number crossed the Mekong River into Thailand, and were situated in the Nong Khai Refugee Camp. Many of these people were educated and from urban settings. A good number of them had been United States government employees. Of course, all were hoping for a permanent home and a good life elsewhere.

From the late 1970s through the 1990s, more than 180,000 Lao were settled worldwide.[6] Probably about 100,000 of these came to the United States and, among them, several dozen came to the Kansas City area. Many of these were sponsored by Prairie Baptist Church and the Laotian families that were there ahead of them.

The late 1980s and early 1990s were a busy time for that church and those first families who came! When there was news of the anticipated arrival of another family, Lao persons and other church people would work together to find housing, basic furniture, cookware, bedding, and employment opportunities. Others would help children enroll in school, and still others would help with addressing the needs related to getting established in a new land with a new language. In our busiest years, families that included more than twenty-five persons arrived!

None of these new residents were Christians when they came here. However, they were grateful to the church that sponsored and cared about them, and they were open to learning more. To help that happen, a church member offered a Sunday morning Bible study class that was translated for all interested persons. In time, morning worship was translated into hearing devices so the new families could participate. Shortly, Alice Shae, a missionary who was living in the area because her husband taught in the seminary, was contracted to serve as minister of Asian outreach. The discipling and worshipping continued to grow. Over time, a number of persons expressed their faith in Jesus Christ and were baptized into the membership of the church.

When Alice and her husband returned to overseas service, we sought New Church Start funding and called Ruth and Terry Rosell as ministers to work with this growing component of our church. In time, they became a separate congregation in a different building, nurturing their own life and leaders. (Their adequate little building was provided from a failed suburban church-start.)

There continued to be frequent cooperation, between the two congregations (daily Vacation Bible School for example), including meals, worship, and lifelong friendships. Many of us recall that experience in those years as a wonderful time in the life of our church, even as we also tried to heal from some bruising church conflicts that had happened shortly before all this began.

Years later (by then, I was simply a member, not the pastor), this church's hospitality took a different form. When a number of Syrian families were being settled in our area, Sherry, one of our mission committee members, went to a meeting to see how we could help. The agency leader responded, "Invite one of these families to dinner. Get acquainted. You'll discover what else you might want to do."

Our representative did one better; she recruited our church to invite several families to an American Thanksgiving dinner (not on actual Thanksgiving Day, but on a date close to it). A number of guest families and host families gathered. We were instructed to sit with each other and figure out how to get acquainted across language differences. Very soon, people were getting out their phones and showing each other family pictures. Games were planned; Uno cards were placed on every table. The man of the family where I sat had said, "No English," but we had a good time playing an improvised game with those cards. A Cub Scout had collected children's books and had arranged them by age and subject. He invited the children of our guest families to come and help themselves to these books.

A few months later, we again gathered these Syrian friends for a meal. This time our guests wanted to bring some food, and we enjoyed discovering each other's culinary creations. The mother in the young family with whom I sat wanted to be sure I tasted everything, especially the dessert she brought!

We also learned about an information clearing person connected with the refugee agency. If folks needed something or had something to give, we could let that person know. In this way, we learned of a family that needed beds, and as we moved out to another city, we made our extra beds and mattresses available. We learned that in a family of five, the three young adult sons had been sleeping on the floor. This group of arrivals from another land will likely not become members of that congregation where I belonged. More probably they will continue in their Muslim faith. Still, this welcome, hospitality, and care was noticed and appreciated. "The people at that church are good people," one of them told Sherry, our liaison person.

Perspectives from Michele

The various churches I mentioned responded to the crises and opportunities of their times, understanding that it was simply their calling to address needs related to migrations and new arrivals. I also visited with the Rev. Michele Turek, National Coordinator for Asian Ministries for American Baptist Home Mission Societies. Michele resources one of the fastest growing parts of her and my denomination's life. She supports many refugee and immigrant communities and their succeeding generations. This is a varied population, she notes, that speaks more than twenty-eight different languages. As she works with historic churches and newer ones, she sees some strategies recurring and others developing.

She provided this example: "In my home church, a local pastor's wife saw a need: a growing number of Chinese immigrants. She started a Bible study that, in time, became a church. This was 1884."

Another example illustrated a different approach: "The Japanese Baptist Church was founded by First Baptist Church, Seattle, many years ago. When people of Japanese descent were rounded up and sent to internment camps during World War II, the pastor at the time, the Rev. Emery Andrews, was commissioned by the then National Ministries to care for the Japanese and Japanese American community in the Minidoka Camp in Idaho, with the church sheltering their belongings while they were confined there. Over generations, Japanese Baptist Church was very proud of their history of being Japanese American and had a loyalty to the community that helped them so much in a desperate time. There was hospitality there that wasn't present in other places."

"But change came to their neighborhood. How does a Japanese Baptist church stay alive in a community that isn't Japanese? They reached out to people who were not Japanese and sensed that God was opening a new door. This has been a long journey for them to discern next steps for their church community. This is especially needed since the Japanese are not immigrating to the United States nearly as much anymore. Japanese Baptist Church has been turning their attention to the neighbors God has brought them, which are more multicultural. It has been difficult, at times, when the church community had long been the safe space for them as Japanese Americans."

Rev. Turek also helps immigrant communities with their succeeding generations and guides churches to be sensitive to this change and need. As children and youth grow, another culture gap occurs. Immigrant elders and children-adolescents acclimate to language and culture at different speeds and ways. She notes, "Parents may try to prevent some changes from happening, but other influences such as peers, school, and social media can't really be stopped."

Another distinction that is important to understand, she reminds us, is the distinction between immigrants and refugees: "The refugee experience is different from that of an immigrant. Refugees don't choose to leave their homeland, while immigrants might come for economic reasons, a job opportunity, social mobility, or education. Of course, the refugee experiences the loss of culture and family. Refugees, having been ripped from their homeland without much choice, may be experiencing a much more painful process."

With these new arrivals, there are many doorways into a closer relationship. Perhaps individuals or families have a need for a place to worship or a need related to some service the church can provide. Growing out of her experience, Rev. Turek offers some examples, "A host church can do many things to build relationships with migrant communities. This could be through church members themselves. Maybe a church member is a social worker who knows possible helpful agencies or resources, or an accountant who can help with navigating tax forms, or a conversation partner or tutor in English as a second language. It could be a family with similarly-aged children who can play together or build friendships or offer guidance that can ease the jarring changes of settling in a new community and country. In all this, there needs to be mutual respect and interest in each other's story. On the host person's part, this includes awareness of the context of their migration and appropriate curiosity of the individual and their family's experiences."

A Global Model for Multi-lingual and Multi-cultural Faith Communities

In 2017, the Rev. Dr. Chakravarthy Zadda came to First Baptist Church of Waukesha, Wisconsin, with the mutual agreement that he would bring his model for an intercultural faith community to life in this local church. This congregation was a small, shrinking, mostly Anglo 178-year-old church. They had been making space available for groups of various ethnicities to nest, meet, and worship in their facility.

Dr. Zadda, originally from India, is a missiologist who has received his Ph.D. from Lutheran School of Theology and had been teaching at Northern Seminary. He felt called to try this model in a church. A century and a half before, American Baptists sent missionaries to India. Now, a missionary from India was offering leadership for the church in America!

He joined First Baptist Church to provide pastoral leadership and vision. Upon arriving, he initiated the Multi-Cultural Multi-Ethnic Envision Committee (MMEC), a conversation among these varied small congregations—a Hispanic one, a Karen (a language-tribal group from Burma/Myanmar) one, the Anglo congregation, and a Telugu-speaking Indian church he founded. He explained the strategy this way: "The goal was we would meet once a month on a third Saturday, at 10 a.m., to hear the stories of each congregation representative along with a brief devotion to begin with. Then we would have fellowship over lunch together. From these four congregations there were three delegates each. For the next two years, MMEC took time to get to know the congregants from our fellow ethnic churches. Everyone was worshipping in their own spaces and with their own little group during this time. As we did so, we grew to know and trust each other. We were seeking a way to be together with none of us overtaking the others. Perhaps, we thought, we could prepare a document of how we would work with each other as one church."

Then the pandemic happened. They had to close in-person worship services for a time, while staying in touch with each other via online Zoom services.

"After Covid, we decided that we should reopen our church for in-person worship as a new congregation. We invited all these congregations to worship. Each and all had a consensus to worship together as First Baptist Multi-lingua and Multi-ethnic Family on Sunday mornings at 9:30. This is one congregation that embraces a multi-cultural worship service. When we reopened, we didn't have a document from our group, but we had shared experiences and relationships."

"This service is mostly in English with scriptures and prayers in all three languages—Karen, Spanish, and Telugu. A bi-lingual worship bulletin is published each Sunday which is both in Karen and English. That's how we strengthen our bonds—with each other and with God.

"We celebrate each other's festivals and important cultural/traditional events throughout the year. And we enjoy food from each of those cultures. Since 2018, our multicultural faith community is consistently growing and changing. We have a young family of four from the Anglo community who have joined the church celebrating multi-culturalism. A person from Taiwan has joined us, feeling at home in the multi-ethnic nature of the church. Now, Sunday worship includes reading the scripture in Mandarin. Recently, three African American families have also joined our church to enhance our diversity as the First Baptist Church family."

"There are persons from each of these communities on each of our church boards. Now everyone shares the responsibility of providing leadership as to how we carry on the life and witness of our Lord Jesus Christ through coming together as one church. First Baptist Church is celebrating our 185th anniversary this year. Unlike the traditional churches' communities, we don't have a language, culture, or history in common. We are one because we all believe in Jesus Christ as our Lord and Savior. This is the only factor that unites us."

When I asked Dr. Zadda to tell me more how he goes about this ministry, he told me, "From a missiological standpoint, Jesus both called people and related to them. This is how I based my mission from a biblical standpoint—one on one. When I started, nobody knew anybody. Jesus wanted people to know him personally. He allowed them space to eat, drink, live, and work with him. We need to see that our mission is around here, how we encounter each other, how we embrace."

I asked what the most difficult part was of living this model. "Unlearning, to learn," he responded. "The learning can go fairly fast. The unlearning, not so much."

I also asked, "What are the rewards and blessings from being part of a multi-cultural faith community?" Dr. Zadda responded, "The hope for the future. This church is learning to relate to each other and to the culture in which they presently live. This will prepare children and young people how to be a faithful part of the church and society in the American culture in which they are living and going to school." This church has started a new youth group to draw young people together on a journey discovering how to be committed to one another and remain faithful in the society in which they will live in brotherly and sisterly love.

I asked Dr. Zadda if he knew of others attempting a similar mission or using his model. He responded by telling me of Pastor Mark Hearn and First Baptist Church of Duluth (suburban Atlanta), Georgia. "Though we have learned from First Baptist Church of Duluth," he said, "we are quite unique. Our different circumstance needed a different strategy."

In brief, this is the story of that Georgia church: shortly after arriving to serve this traditional, largely Euro-American church, Dr. Hearn went to hear the mayor's "state of the city" address. In that speech, he heard a mind-altering statistic—that there were fifty-seven languages spoken in Duluth High School! Mark responded to this by committing to lead his church to "learn to cross language and cultural barriers to share the life-changing message of Jesus Christ."

He began by initiating "Project 57" (witness to all fifty-seven language groups) and continuing to offer friendship, develop outreach activities, and lead the church to embrace this vision. He based this on biblical strategies that he discerned from his participation in his denomination's (Southern Baptist Convention) worldwide mission outreach. He was bringing that mission method to bear on one Atlanta suburb! A group of church leaders met over time to articulate a new mission statement. They eventually wrote: "To be a united community of faith that loves, reaches, and disciples all people for Jesus Christ."

Some of the ways they did this included:

- Transitioning friend to family with a "Cross Class," a cross-cultural, cross-generational gathering around the cross of Christ. Mark led the first eight-week class of twelve families from six different countries. At the conclusion of this group study, he encouraged the participants to work with another family and lead the class anew with yet other families.

- Surrounding the sanctuary with the flags of the nations where someone had worshipped, participated, or joined the church.

- Creating the "One Voice Interpretation Center" that includes English as a Second Language classes in at least three different languages (with Mark learning enough Spanish to, at least one time, try preaching in it!).

- Church events that note some of the national and cultural holiday celebrations of the various national groups in the church.

- An "International Grounds Café" built in their entry lobby—international teas and coffees served in a place to meet and form friendships as they enter the church facilities.

These are just a few examples of the much effort and growing effectiveness of this growing pastor and church. Any who would like to know more should consult Hearn's two books: *Technicolor: Inspiring Your Church to Embrace Multicultural Ministry*[7] and *Hearing in Technicolor: Mindset Shifts Within a Multicultural Congregation*.[8]

FINANCIAL JUSTICE

Does financial justice need to be part of the new racial shalom that beckons us? From time to time, this discussion surfaces. At least a few of the persons and churches I interviewed or read about are investigating and acting on this issue. Here is some food for thought based on what I heard.

Ben Norquist reflects on standing on a cul-de-sac in Glen Ellyn, Illinois, in front of the small house he purchased in 2015. He decided to investigate the story of that land, from the present, going backward. He traced this land and the land surrounding it nearly a century and a half back to 1845, when Thomas Patchell had travelled from the east to purchase some cheap land to farm. In 1845, Patchell "received a patent from the General Land Office that legally transferred this parcel of land to him. With that patent, signed on September 1, 1845, by a bureaucrat in Washington, this land was claimed as private property for the first time in its history…every subsequent event depends on this moment, this piece of paper."[9] Further, the earlier Prairie du Chien Treaty of 1829 is part of the precondition for his cul-de-sac and the removal of Potawatomi villages nearby.

He reflects, "I am a child of this settler society…this shallow world of the present that buries the moral detriments of the past. When I look at my yard and street each day, I want the past to be brought to mind. I want to remember the Native communities that are a part of the history of this land…to honor them. They are still here, their ongoing stories linked to mine in ways that have yet to be revealed."[10]

In his reflection, while Norquist speaks of many implications of this history, he does not develop one of them—the economic aspect. What is the economic responsibility of those who benefitted from such histories to those who suffered from it?

As I pondered this, I came across an account of one interesting response.

In a recent article, I read this: "Every month, Terry Kelly sends a 'rent' check to the Duwamish tribe on behalf of Quest Church in Seattle, where Kelly serves as senior director of finance. The church owns the property where it holds services. But the congregation's monthly payment acknowledges and honors the Duwamish people and other original inhabitants of the land the church occupies and people who have never been justly compensated for their 'land, resources, and livelihood,' as the Duwamish 'real rent' program puts it."[11]

These two vignettes raise questions related to financial justice and how we should address the issues of inter-ethnic injustice. These, in turn, raise the topic of reparations. Who owes reparations to whom, and how should such responses be made? These are huge questions with equally large implications. No church can fully solve these issues, but there can be—there needs to be—at least conversation, investigation, and perhaps symbolic but significant responses.

Of course, this conversation also concerns the population captured, deprived of freedom, and brought where they did not want to go to work hard for no pay—endlessly for generation after generation. Where does this conversation even start? Out of his reflections and experiments, Travis Norvell responds, "You start with those you know who are close by and listen and take notes. You repent and tenderize your heart." Does a small response even matter? "Regardless of size, it would be more than you ever did before."[12]

The counsel he received from local Black leaders urged a slow, contemplative approach, with an emphasis on "reparation"—seeking to repair relationships. As he pursued this question further, he heard of one such initiative. Members of Crescent Hill Baptist Church in Louisville, Kentucky, compiled "Stokely's List," a directory of black-owned businesses. Before this, neither the church nor individual members knew where to go if they wanted to support and engage black-owned business services. Now, they have started to do so.[13]

The most thoroughgoing church reparation process I learned of was undertaken by two Evanston, Illinois, churches led by Michael Woolf, pastor of Lake Street Church, and Michael Nabors, pastor of Second Baptist Church. When I visited with Amber, she told me of this journey where she has served as a staff member. Over a period of time, these pastors and their congregations got to know each other, became friends, and learned about their joint and separate history.

Sometime after Amber and I visited, Pastor Woolf told of this process in more detail, in an article he titled, "Repairing the Redlined Body of Christ."[14] He began by noting the valuable archives of both the city of Evanston and of the church he serves. Both provide evidence of racism and discrimination in the city and in the church. Indeed, in those church archives he notes, "You will find the record of a congregation that has a wound at its center: in 1882, the Black members of First Baptist Church in Evanston, Illinois [the previous name of Lake Street Church], left to form Second Baptist Church. There they found safe harbor from the White supremacy that had relegated them to my church's balcony and asked them to contribute to the construction of buildings that were built by them but never for them. You will also find a history of a congregation alternately avoiding that wound and seeking redemption."[15]

He further notes that, while the Black members left because of racism and White supremacy at First Baptist, "they also sought to form independent Black institutions. In the late nineteenth century, the Black population of Evanston was growing by leaps and bounds, and there was need for new institutions to meet their needs—something First Baptist was ill-equipped for and uninterested in doing."[16]

Over the years, the two churches have been fairly friendly, with their ups and downs. However, in 2018, the churches became sister churches. They were committed to "eradicating racism in Evanston." This was undergirded by the understanding that these churches' story was a microcosm of their city. Further, they believed that through Christ reconciliation was possible. A key part of this was the question of property justice. As Woolf notes, his church "is not a wealthy congregation, but we do have a beautiful property in a prime location that is worth a considerable sum."

Their congregations have now acknowledged together that Second Baptist is a full and rightful partner in the ownership of the Lake Street property. Second Baptist is now on the title for the Lake Street building. They use the building for their larger events. This was not accomplished without controversy. There were a number of angry conversations. Pastor Woolf is happy to report that some who earlier opposed the plan are now ardent supporters. One told him that his view changed when he realized that we were not "giving away our church so much as we are sharing its future."[17]

Amber told me, "We are still working out what all of this means. We plan to do our own worship but also attend each other's worship and events. Each church has its own culture, style, and preferences that we care deeply about. Further, each church has its distinctive missions—Second Baptist does much work in encouraging Black seminarians, and they also have a voice in the inner-city movement. Lake Street shares a building with a homeless shelter. A lot of our ministries help support that: making meals, collecting winter clothing, volunteering, and more."

As an American Baptist press release summarizes, "Discernment continues about how that partnership will be lived out, but the work of reparation by these two faithful congregations, inspired by their prophetic leaders, is underway."

Amber and I had earlier visited about nones and her identity with them. As a postscript to describing this process, she reflected, "Doing this work and talking about this work—young people would be more likely to participate. This is the sort of thing they want to be doing. But they don't often see churches doing that."

INTERIOR WORK

A number of pastors spoke of another journey that their congregations—and they themselves—needed to take. That is an inward journey, to recognize one's own history, biases, prejudices, and growth steps that are needed.

I will quote one pastor with whom I visited, and I choose to do so anonymously: "We are overwhelmingly a white congregation, not only in racial makeup, but also in attitude. This is true whether people are aware of it or not. On the face of it—we unanimously voted a racial justice statement. However, there are things done or said that represent our bias. For example, we recently interviewed a candidate to be our minister of music. This person had a heavy accent based on her national origin. As we evaluated, concern was expressed—would people understand her? What does it mean that we ask that after we conversed just fine in an extended interview? We have a lot of internal work to do. We need to take a look at our attitudes that we may not be aware of. We will help people identify those attitudes. Many don't realize we are coming from a racial or ethnic bias. But these conversations need to happen for us to grow and move forward."

FURTHERMORE

I began this chapter with statistics and stated concerns from Bob Smietana of Religious News Service. In the book I was citing, he also offered a number of examples of pastors and churches taking constructive steps, some of them different from what my conversation partners and I experienced.

Here are two of those stories:

Interbay Covenant Church was an older congregation, and it seemed that its best days were behind it. It was founded in the mid-1950s by Swedish immigrants. In a new century, though relatively healthy, the church was aging and shrinking. In the early 2000s, the church had started renting a warehouse they owned across their parking lot to a young, multiethnic start up called Quest Church.

Over the years, two things had happened. One was that Interbay's well-loved and trusted pastor, Ray Bartel, stimulated reflection about the church and its future possibilities. With no axe to grind, he set forth possible scenarios: they could add a younger pastor and try to regrow; they could move to a new location and build a new building; or they could merge with Quest and give them their building. Whatever course they chose, he reminded them, the future would bring change.

The other thing that happened was that Pastor Bartel and Quest's pastor, a much younger Eugene Cho, often visited, drank coffee together, grew to trust each other, and became friends. Out of this long and careful process, the Interbay Covenant congregation voted to "sacrificially give themselves to Quest."

Smietana reports, "In June, 2007, the two churches merged—creating a vibrant, multigenerational, multicultural congregation that kept the Quest name. Bartel became an associate pastor, serving under the much younger Cho. Interbay Covenant had to die for its ministry to live on—a process Bartel compared to a saying of Jesus: 'Truly, truly I say to you, unless a grain of what falls into the earth and dies, it remains alone; but if it dies, it bears much fruit'(John 12:24, Revised Standard Version)."[18]

That's one way for a church to live its racial shalom—a difficult, costly, risky way to be sure—dying to birth an even greater ministry.

Another very different but fascinating story Smietana told was that of All Saints Church (Episcopal) in Smyrna, Tennessee. The church had been planted some years earlier, but after a promising start, the priest withdrew and took most of the congregation with him because of his perception of their denomination's liberal drift. The remaining twenty members were left with a near-empty church building and a mortgage they could not afford. A new priest with a business background, Michael Spurlock, was sent with the task of shutting down the church and selling the property.

However, about a year after the split, a group of about seventy refugees from Myanmar showed up and asked if they could attend the church's worship services. They were members of the Karen ethnic group and had been at odds with Myanmar's repressive government. As a result, they had been on the move in various refugee camps before coming to the United States. Ye Win, their informal leader, told Spurlock they had all been Anglicans in their home country. Their faith had carried them through all their sufferings. Ye Win told Spurlock, "Even if we are lost…away from home…isolated, we are still close to God. God never left our people."

Spurlock was skeptical. He was afraid of disappointing them if the church closed soon after they joined in. Nevertheless, he took a risk and told them they were welcome. It was hard going at first. These new refugees had many logistical needs—finding jobs, cars, furniture, and other necessities. The church's finances were already dire.

However, things began to change when Ye Win and other Karen members came to Spurlock with an idea. All Saints sits on two dozen acres, half of which is bottomland, perfect for farming. The members wondered if they might be able to plant crops at the church for food for themselves and a little income. This was an adventure itself as these refugees had to learn new ways of farming that fit the climate and the soil. After many struggles, the farming succeeded, producing thousands of pounds of radishes, squash, cucumbers, green beans, and other vegetables. Eventually the church was designated as a mission, opening up new funds. As a result, the church was saved.

As one church member put it, "We could not find God, but God found us…in the form of seventy people who came from Myanmar."

Smietana returned a decade later for another visit and follow-up story. The story of All Saints would be told in a faith-based film by Sony Pictures.[19] He recalls that "…the modest brick building…was filled with the noise of children and families settling in for Sunday services. In the pews, hymnals with lyrics in Karen sat side by side with English hymnals while copies of the Book of Common Prayer had Karen translations written in the margins."[20]

So here is another door into racial shalom: welcome those who come your way. Risk for each other, learn from each other, grow together—and the people you are rescuing just might be used of God to rescue you!

FOR REFLECTION AND CONVERSATION

1. How would you describe your church's situation regarding various racial and ethnic groups and immigrants or refugees in your area?

2. What do you see as your next steps in this regard?

3. What justice issues and what needs are being faced by people in the various ethnic groups in your community?

4. Which of the ways to greater friendships and involvement mentioned in this chapter seem most possible to you? Where would you start?

NOTES

[1] Bob Smietana, *Reorganized Religion: The Reshaping of the American Church and Why It Matters* (New York: Worthy Publications, 2022), 13-14. He is citing Census publications.

[2] Ibid., 20.

[3] Ibid., 20.

[4] Studies cited in Smietana, 197.

[5] Mindi Welton-Mitchell, email, 18 December 2023.

[6] "Indochina Refugee Crisis," https://en.wikipedia.org/wiki/Indochina_refugee_crisis accessed 9 August 2023.

[7] Mark Hearn, *Technicolor: Inspiring Your Church to Embrace Multicultural Ministry* (Nashville: B&H Publishing Group, 2017).

[8] Mark Hearn, *Hearing in Technicolor: Mindset Shifts Within a Multicultural Congregation* (Nashville: B&H Publishing Group, 2021).

[9] Ben Norquist, "My Land Acknowledgement," *The Christian Century*, November 2023, Vol.140, No.11, 44.

[10] Ibid., 45.

[11] Jose Humphreys III, "God's Economy of Generosity: How the Church Can Help Reimagine the Story of Money," *Sojourners*, November, 2023, Vol 52, No. 9, 22.

[12] G. Travis Norvell, *Church on the Move: A Practical Guide for Ministry in the Community* (Valley Forge: Judson Press, 2022), 53.

[13] Ibid., 54-55.

[14] Michael Woolf, "Repairing the Redlined Body of Christ," *The Christian Century*, March 2024, Vol. 141, No.3, 44-48.

[15] Ibid., 44.

[16] Ibid., 46.

[17] Ibid., 48

[18] Smietana, 162-164.

[19] *All Saints*. DVD, Sony, Affirm Films, 51314LIT, 2017.

[20] Smietana, 206-210.

CHAPTER 9

Mother God Comes Close

I commend to you our sister Phoebe, a deacon of the church at Cenchreae,
so that you may welcome her in the Lord, as is fitting for the saints,
and help her in whatever she may require from you,
for she has been a benefactor of many and of myself as well.

Romans 16:1-2

A great tragedy in my life became the doorway to wonderful growth and discovery. I wrote a bit about this in the first chapter. When I was almost ten years old (the year was 1944), my father died. He had been an American Baptist (then Northern Baptist) Home Missionary and the pastor of a little two-church parish in remotely settled northwestern South Dakota. His church, his family, and I loved him deeply and missed him terribly.

About a year later, the Home Mission Society sent someone else to serve our little church and parish. They sent a woman! Not only that, but they sent an eastern woman who had grown up in Cambridge, Massachusetts, and had been serving churches in Vermont. She came with a large foster family, mostly orphaned children of former parishioners. Her name was Jeanie K. Sherman.

Our town of about five hundred souls was in the middle of ranching country, in between two nearby Native American reservations. It was a rough, rustic village, with few sidewalks and no paved streets. The area had been opened for settlement a scant thirty-five years before.

Local residents were skeptical when they heard about our new pastor: "A woman? An eastern woman? She won't last two weeks." Such was the common sentiment on Main Street. However, when she arrived, she placed her foster children in the local school and went to work. People were surprised that she wore a robe and conducted worship rather formally for our part of the country. As she led worship and preached, occasionally someone would titter out loud at her New England accent that omitted some "Rs" and inserted other inflections in unexpected places. It was a strange new experience for both pastor and congregation.

But she persisted, learning about farming and ranching and taking an interest in the children and young people. The Sunday School and youth group slowly grew. She joined the library board and helped the county get a better library and, eventually, a bookmobile. Nobody knew how many miles she travelled to be at a distant hospital bedside nor how many troubled confessions and anguished conversations she heard. It was known that she was with many families when death came. She offered compassionate and reverent services in their loved one's memory. She also broke through the custom of many people being married in front of an often-drunk justice of the peace. Instead, she helped couples create beautiful church wedding celebrations and simple, lovely receptions in the church basement.

Of course, even with all this, occasionally someone would tell her, "A woman shouldn't be a minister." She would reply with good humor, "Well, you'll have to talk to the Lord about that because he called me to do this." She was the only woman among twenty-five or thirty ministers of our denomination in the state.

In an area with much prejudice, she unapologetically offered hospitality and friendship to American Indian people. She also formed a friendship with the rector of the Episcopal Indian Mission some distance away. Eventually out of this friendship, care, and witness, we had both European-Americans and Native Americans in the same congregation. This was one of the few churches in the state, maybe the only one, where this was true.

I sensed my call to ministry in this congregation. My pastor encouraged me and welcomed the use of my unpolished gifts in the church. She also counseled me about college and seminary. I chose to go to the seminary she had attended, so I could take Clinical Pastoral Education as she had done. I hoped to be as good a pastoral caregiver and counselor as she was.

She was my mentor whom I often consulted in my early days of ministry. I remember making a frantic phone call—I needed her guidance. As a very young pastor (serving a summer parish before going to seminary), I was asked to conduct a graveside service for a stillborn infant, and I had no idea what to do! I called her, listened carefully to what she told me and, at that service, probably repeated word for word what she had said.

Those skeptics on Main Street were right about one thing—she didn't last two weeks. Instead, she lasted thirty plus years! Later, she was buried in the little cemetery on the edge of that town to which she had given her best years of ministry. I met her when I was eleven and preached at her funeral when I was sixty-two. When she died, I called my best friend, Ron, to tell him. I have always treasured his response for its truth and insight: "Dick, she left a lot of gifts, and you are one of them." He was right; in many ways, I am an extension of her ministry.

All of this answered one question early for me: What about women in ministry? I didn't even have to wonder! Beyond settling that basic question, however, there was a further call for me. I knew that I was called to be friend, advocate, colleague, support—and recipient of leadership—with the multitudes of women who would join in ministry over the next decades.

RECENT HISTORY OF WOMEN IN MINISTRY

Indeed, what has happened over those decades is quite striking. In a comprehensive overview study of women in ministry, Eileen R. Campbell-Reed chronicles some recent changes:

- In 1960, women were 2.3 percent of United States clergy. In 2016, women were 20.7 percent of United States clergy.

- In the Unitarian Universalist and United Church of Christ denominations, clergywomen have numerical equity with clergymen.

- In most mainline denominations, the percentage of clergywomen has doubled or tripled since the 1990s.

- Since 2015, Roman Catholic lay ministers outnumber priests, and eighty percent of them are women.

- However, in 2017, women made up less than twenty-five percent of seminary faculty and deans and only eleven percent of seminary presidents.[1]

The Evangelical Lutheran Church of America, with about four million members in the United States, began ordaining women in 1970. The denomination now reports that women comprise forty percent of the denomination's pastors, forty-six percent of all bishop positions, fifty-four percent of associate or assistant pastors, and twenty-two percent of senior pastor positions.[2]

CONTINUED STUDY, CLARIFICATION, AND ADVOCACY OF WOMEN'S MINISTRIES

There is wide diversity of opinion on this topic across Christian denominations. In some denominations, ordination is denied to women. In others, women are accepted and embraced in leadership roles. The contrast is striking! Even churches in similar denominations disagree. For example, consider two Baptist denominations and their opposing views.

In one of these Baptist denominations, by far the smaller of the two, there was the pioneering ordination of women nearly one hundred and fifty years ago. May C. Jones was ordained, "licensed to preach" the record said, by First Baptist Church of Seattle in April 1882. This was the first, or one of the first, ordinations of women among American (then Northern) Baptists. To be sure, the circumstances were unusual. When the church's minister was travelling on denominational business, a group of church members convened an ordination council to ordain this May C. Jones. This was a lively and controversial gathering. An account of that event notes that "the larger portion of the ministers present were of the opinion that it was an unscriptural proceeding…their protest was rendered entirely unavailing by a failure to vote against the proceeding at the proper time, and the ordination was consummated." May C. Jones would serve as pastor to six churches in Washington from 1883 to 1891.[3] Whether the ordination was irregular or not, it was the beginning of the growth of women providing leadership in home missions as they had in overseas missions for quite some time.

Indeed, my pastor, Jeanie Sherman, ordained in the 1930s, didn't see herself as a pioneer. There were at least two generations of women ministers before her that she met in summer Christian youth camps, women who inspired and mentored her.

At the recent annual meeting of the other Baptist denomination, however, thousands of "messengers" voted overwhelmingly to uphold the expulsion of two churches that had ordained women to ministry. They also voted to add an amendment to their constitution (which would require a second vote at their next gathering) that a church in good fellowship in their denomination "affirms, appoints, or employs only men as any kind of pastor or elder."[4] Those who hold this position say that this is a matter of "biblical authority" and that "scripturally, only men are qualified to be ministers." This debate reminds us once again that there is a need for serious and thoughtful discussion about faithfulness to our source scripture and ways to interpret and apply scripture.

Clearly, there are differences of interpretation of the various New Testament passages on the subject. One perspective finds absolute and final authority in such verses as 1 Corinthians 14:34, "Women should be silent in the churches. For they are not permitted to speak but should be subordinate, as the law also says." Or 1 Timothy 2:11-12, "Let a woman learn in silence with full submission. I do not permit a woman to teach or to have authority over men; she is to keep silent."

Other groups understand such passages within the context of other passages describing the leadership and gifts of women in the church, often counterculturally in New Testament times. For example, among the twenty-eight people Paul greeted in Romans 16, ten were women. The chapter begins. "I commend to you our sister Phoebe, a deacon of the church at Cenchreae, so that you may welcome her in the Lord as is fitting for the saints and help her in whatever she may require from you, for she has been a benefactor of many and of myself as well." This tantalizing verse, the only place Phoebe is mentioned, has led Bible scholar Susan E. Hylen to look at Phoebe and other women in the New Testament world.[5] In her review of Hylen's book, Sally Dyck noted, "I was surprised to learn that women's agency and empowerment in the Gospels and Epistles are much greater than I'd previously considered, especially for women who had no father or husband at their side."[6]

In Romans 16, Paul goes on to mention Prisca "who risked [her] neck for my life," Mary "who has worked very hard among you," Junia who is "prominent among the apostles," the mother of Rufus who was "mother to me also," and other women.

Though Paul does not mention women prophets at this point, he does so in I Corinthians 11:5. Further, in Acts 21:9, Phillip's four unmarried daughters are described as having "the gift of prophecy." Further still, in Colossians 4:15 there is mention of Nympha of Laodicea and the "church in her house." In the opinion of many (including myself), women's gifts to and leadership in the New Testament church are clearly implied for any with eyes to see. In addition, the gospels reveal that Jesus was ministered to by women in many ways. For example, see Luke 8:1-3; 10:38-42; 7:36-50; 23:55–24:11.

There is also archeological evidence of women leaders in the early post New Testament centuries of the church. Professor Dorothy Irvin of the

College of St. Catherine points to Roman inscriptions which refer to women as *archisynagogos* (rulers of a synagogue) and *presbytera* (elders). Further, she takes note of a fresco from the Roman catacombs in which seven first-century women are celebrating the Eucharist. There is also a fourth-century fresco of a woman receiving ordination from a bishop. She also mentions a tombstone inscription for a "honorabilia femina episcopa"—"honorable woman bishop."[7]

BEING A PLACE FOR ALL TO DISCERN AND EXPLORE GOD'S CALL

In the light of all of this, it is important to make clear that all followers of Jesus are invited to ponder their calling. Doors to ministry should be open to all who discern a calling to ministry that is confirmed by their faith community.

This openness can take many forms. Early on, children or youths can be involved in ministry activities—perhaps within the church programs or on a mission outreach. As they serve and use their gifts, young people need to see both women and men serving in ministry and know that the doors of opportunity are open to both. I still meet women who never heard a female preacher until their young adult years. When they finally heard a woman preach, revelations, calls, and discoveries often happened!

Persons sensing a possible call to ministry may need guidance about what steps they may need to take educationally and within their denomination. Often, the awareness of a call comes to light when a minister or other church leader identifies gifts in another person. The church leader might mention that observation and invite the gifted person to think about and explore ways to use those gifts in ministry.

It is important to note that there are many years of silence to reverse. A friend of mine, several years my younger, expressed interest and aptitude in ministry as a child and youth. However, she was told, "No, honey, you will be a minister's wife." As she later told me, "I was both liberated and duped by the same faith community."

Advocacy, invitation, and support need to continue. I have seen outstanding women seminary students wait and wait for an employment opportunity after graduation, much longer than some less talented male classmates and colleagues. Encouraging, nominating, advocating, and adjusting the placement practices of one's denomination are necessary and needed.

COOPERATING WITH WOMEN THRIVING IN MINISTRY

At the celebration of the fortieth anniversary of the founding of the "Baptist Women in Ministry" organization, their director, the Rev. Dr. Meredith Stone, spoke and raised a number of questions, including these two: "If we imagine a world where women in ministry thrive, what would that world look like? And how would it be different than the world right now?"

Eileen R. Campbell-Reed has devoted a major portion of her career to these very questions, having personally dealt with many barriers and inequities in the past. She offers her response to these questions, speaking as Dr. Stone suggested, in future stories. As Campbell-Reed does this, she recognizes that her journey as a white married cisgender female does not include all the experiences and issues of others in this search for flourishing and thriving. She distills her response to five future statements:

1. Women thrive because churches pay equitably.

Women in ministry should receive equal compensation to their male counterparts. This should include the benefits supplementary to salary: medical, dental, vision, parental leave, continuing education, counseling, spiritual direction, retreats, conferences, and denominational events. Adequate pay and benefits will contribute to less fatigue and more energy and creativity for the tasks, needs, crises, and opportunities where they serve.

2. Women thrive because leadership is collaborative.

Any work goes better when it is upheld by supportive colleague groups, collaborators, partners, mentors, supporters, and sponsors. Ministry can be a lonely journey—how much better it is with fellow travelers down the hall or a phone call away!

3. Women thrive because we are not so angry all the time.

Anger at the limited opportunities to serve will be lessened when there is increased openness, justice, and collegial support. It will also happen when both men and women appreciate the historic role of women in changing both church and ministry.

4. Women thrive because child well-being is normative, expected, and funded.

Campbell-Reed further explains this insight: "It's one thing to *give* or *teach* pastoral care all day. To also come home to tasks like calming everyone else's anxiety, organizing the family calendar, listening to each person's troubles, and refereeing family disagreements can feel like a never-ending pile of needs that clergywomen face. It gives way to emotional and spiritual exhaustion."[8]

5. Women thrive because men focus on care for themselves and all people.

An important step for women to flourish is for men to do a better job of caring for themselves and others.

In her work of advocacy, Campbell-Reed also urges the welcome, ordination, and placement for queer pastors as well as women in ministry.

RECEIVING AND RESPONDING TO THE PROPHETIC WITNESS OF WOMEN

The welcome of women in ministry in ethnic groups may carry surprises, and some of these surprises may be upsetting. Different perspectives about this issue in different groups may surface previously ignored issues and call for needed changes. They may challenge the church to examine its calling and identity.

For example, Alexis Abernethy, Chief Academic Officer at Fuller Theological Seminary, notes the urgent prophetic voice of women in ministry. As she explains it, "Women—and men—in the church have seen abuse and suffering. They've seen the role of patriarchy in the church. They want to address constructively some of these challenges that have been facing both the church and our society. They're saying, 'Enough of this. We need to be different.' So I think a lot of these women are marshaling energy in that direction."

Abernethy notes the gifts these women bring: "Folks who've been marginalized or oppressed have a clearer radar regarding things like power and when it's abusive, or when people are being excluded. At their best, they would then not set up systems that perpetuate that exclusion—although that requires courage and energy, and people need to be attentive to that fact."

This may be a messy journey! As Emily Badgett, fellow at Candler School of Theology at Emory University, reflects on her Episcopal heritage: "The church is not perfect…It is a human institution trying to do the will of God and that means we're going to fail…The church is not always going to get things right. The whole point is people are redeemable. And the church is a redeemable place."[9]

REVISITING OUR IMAGERY AND LANGUAGE ABOUT GOD

The use of language is another important matter. How do we speak of God? Is there a way to talk about people that includes rather than excludes? Does this inclusive language also apply to how we speak of God? Do we use only male pronouns for God? Is that appropriate? In our conversing, studying, discussing, worshiping, singing, and living, how do we visualize, imagine, and name God?

Theologian Sallie McFague suggests that "God is she, he, and neither." Some try to avoid controversy by not using pronouns at all and speak only of "God." However, as McFague also points out, androgynous terms only "conceal androcentric and male assumptions behind the abstraction."[10]

Beyond pronouns, it is helpful to explore biblical metaphors and images for God. Since the biblical world was typically patriarchal and because Bible translation was most often done by males, male language may dominate our metaphors and images for God. In contrast, there are biblical images for God that have often been missed or obscured. The images that the Bible provides create a common spiritual language for us and help our souls understand. Further, we need a collage of images to stretch our imagination, our devotion, and our worship. As others have noted, focusing on only one image can be idolatrous. Instead, Bible writers offer a vast variety of metaphors for God—neuter, masculine, and feminine.

Neuter images for God are many and varied. Among many others, God is like a wall, a shield, a fortress, a rock, a sword, a word, glory, morning dew, and a light.

Masculine images for God are also many and varied. Among many others, God is like a mighty king, a warrior, a deliverer, a father, and a brother. (To be sure, the images of warrior and deliverer are not necessarily exclusively masculine.)

Because they have been neglected more often, feminine images for God require careful attention. First, let's consider a speculative image—and then we will look at some more certain ones. Sue Monk Kidd was intrigued by the phrase *El Shaddai* in scripture. The phrase is used forty-eight times in the Bible. Traditionally translated as "the almighty," or "God of the mountain," *shad* is also a Hebrew word for breast. The ending *ai* is a feminine ending. So, according to Kidd, *El Shaddai* might mean "God, the breasted one."[11] Further, the Hebrew word for womb or uterus is *rehem*. The plural is *rehemim*, which usually means not "wombs" but "compassion"—in other words, womb-love or divine motherly compassion (Jeremiah 31:20).

There are also many references to God as mother. We see this in Hosea 11:1-3 or in Isaiah 66:13a: "As a mother comforts her child, so I will comfort you..." As mother, God provides food for the children of Israel in the wilderness (Exodus 16) as well as clothing (Genesis 3:21). God is also portrayed as midwife and nursemaid. (Isaiah 46:3-4). Another biblical image is of God as a mother bird, caring for her young. Jesus used this image for himself—a mother hen who longed to gather her chicks (Matthew 23:37).

There are also two key Bible terms for God that are feminine nouns. One is *ruah*—spirit, the life of God, the divine essence, God's immanent presence. (It occurs in the Bible 378 times.) The other word is *hokmah*, Wisdom, which is often spoken of in Godlike ways. This term is both a female term and a term that is often personified as a woman. Sue Monk Kidd notes: "She [*hokmah*] is said to order all things as well as to permeate or inspirit all things. She is referred to as a teacher, a lover, at one with trees and plants. She is the one who mediates God's love...Theologian Elisabeth Schussler Fiorenza had suggested that Wisdom is the God of Israel expressed in language and imagery of the Goddess."[12]

In the Book of Proverbs, Wisdom (*hokmah*) speaks: "The LORD created me at the beginning...when there were no depths...no springs...before the hills...when he had not yet made earth and fields...and I was daily his delight, playing before him always, playing in his inhabited world, and delighting in the human race. And now my children, listen to me." (Proverbs 8:22-32)

All of this is important because, as Elizabeth A. Johnson puts it, "The symbol of God functions." That is to say, as Sue Monk Kidd notes, "These symbols or images shape our worldview, our ethical system, and our social practice, how we live and relate to one another."[13]

It may be that the growing number of women in ministry will be able to engage us more deeply in this soul-stretching exercise.

REPORTED EXPERIENCES OF CURRENT WOMEN IN MINISTRY

In addition to what I have learned from my own journey and the insights of respected women scholars, I also learned much from the Gen X and Millennial pastors that I interviewed. Of the approximately thirty pastors I interviewed, a dozen were women. While my questionnaire had inquiries about women in ministry and inclusive language, some responded to those questions and others did not. In the interviews, I allowed the respondents to pursue the issues that were most pressing to their interests and experience.

Just two of the women I interviewed were the first women pastors in their setting, although the transitional pastor before Meredith arrived was also a woman. As she recalls, the biggest issue the congregation had was not her gender but the shift from a full-time pastor to a part-time one. This shift resulted in a significant financial impact for both the church and the new minister. Meredith worked as a receptionist in a chiropractic office to supplement the salary she was receiving.

Jessica reflected on her experience: "I serve a little church in upstate New York. Our Area Minister gave them my information. They said, 'We are not sure we want a woman pastor,' but I have been here, at Community Baptist, for three years. They like it, find it refreshing. I haven't had a bad experience as a woman in ministry. I did have to find another job to supplement my income. I also teach refugees English. I feel like I am part of their community. I feel very loved."

In some cases, I learned about churches who do not ordain or welcome women ministry leaders. For example, Joanna, who serves a Mennonite church in a university community, recalled, "I met a woman whose church would not allow her to preach. So I asked her to come preach." There was no flack or second-guessing Joanna on this in her faith community. She continued: "My congregation could not comprehend why a church would do this (exclude a woman minister from preaching). It was hard for them to get their heads around it. We have a long history of women congregation leaders. Ordination is something they just assume."

I also asked about support for family responsibilities. Edris serves a small church part time and is also a "stay-at-home mom." Her experience of family support within the capabilities of this little community is mostly good, but somewhat mixed. She tells me, "I was the first female pregnant pastor in the whole association."

She recalls, "When pregnant, I was treated very well. I was provided maternity leave. It was something like up to twelve weeks over the course of a year with full pay. They were open to me bringing the baby to meetings and church events. They threw me a surprise baby shower. That was pretty amazing! But then, there were comments when I chose to breast feed (I always covered up), but people were not too happy about it." On the whole, she feels accepted and supported in her dual roles of parent/homemaker and pastor.

I also asked about the language used in worship and about the images used to describe and address God. Several pastors—both women and men—reported discomfort and resistance, at least by some, when introducing or engaging inclusive language and varied metaphors as mentioned earlier in this chapter. For example, Joanna has addressed these topics a few times in worship, but mostly it's just an expectation that they use gender-neutral terms for God. Jessica speaks of "God as Creator" but doesn't go beyond that. Kathy experiences resistance and criticism by some people when she uses inclusive images.

Michael preached a sermon speaking of the Holy Spirit as "she." As he builds a relationship with a congregation, he communicates that they are free to disagree and to think for themselves, and they respond to him with curiosity and openness. Tim responded to my query this way: "In terms of language, I am the biggest pusher of using inclusive language for God. I try to quote women. We have used the Women's Lectionary for the Whole Church by Dr. Wil Gafney. She was my Hebrew Bible professor." It seems there is much learning and exploring needed for this theological and spiritual growth to take deeper root.

Earlier, I mentioned Eileen Campbell-Reed's paired advocacy for the inclusion of women and of queer pastors in ministry. With some religious groups, this is a denomination-wide decision. In others, decisions about who can be ordained and serve is decided by smaller entities, perhaps the individual congregation or a judicatory. While I did not have a specific question on this question in my interviews, the issue came up often. Amber stated it well: "In the continual struggle for gender equity and gender justice, it is too bad we don't include binary and gay women in ministry. I think we can be bigger than that. More than that, we need to include trans and nonbinary people."

That comment illustrates the thoughtful searching, innovation, and openness that I heard often in my interviews.

A DIFFERENT EXPERIENCE AND PERSPECTIVE

Before concluding this chapter, I want to report and reflect on one more experience. For the last year, as I have been completing and revising this manuscript, I have also taken part in a monthly online group convened by my friend and former colleague, Eileen Campbell-Reed. I have quoted her often in this chapter. She gathered our conversation group in the context of a new book she was writing about women in ministry; the working title was *Baptized and Ordained*.

Each month, we conversed about our experiences and responded to a portion of a chapter of the book Eileen was writing. My impression is that there were as many as twenty of us who participated at least some months. We were from at least three countries—the United States, Canada, and Great Britian. As far as I could tell, I was the only male. While there was much good conversation, my main takeaway was that many women's experiences of entering or practicing ministry were quite troubled. These women contended with more pitfalls than my Gen X and Millennial women pastor respondents had mentioned to me!

Both in Eileen's chapter excerpts and in women's shared experiences in the group, I heard of some having difficulty being nominated for seminary education or being licensed or ordained. Others mentioned "mini-aggressions"—failure to honor their ministry in any number of ways. Still others spoke of being assigned a difficult first placement out of seminary and, perhaps, a long delayed or non-existent second placement. Many struggled with acceptance of inclusive language for God, or they simply chose not to address that battle. It was a harsher picture of the experience of women in ministry than I had discerned from the people I interviewed.

Both on behalf of the women discerning a call to ministry and the ministries they will enrich, a caring and encouraging attitude is important! There is much change that is still needed.

FOR REFLECTION AND CONVERSATION

1. I began by sharing my memory of the first woman in ministry I knew. What are your memories in this regard? What influence do those memories have on you?

2. Where are you, and where are those in your circle—family, church, friends—regarding your feelings and attitudes about women in ministry?

3. What Bible teachings on this subject do you find most compelling?

4. In your setting, what is done to help men in ministry thrive? What is done to help women in ministry thrive?

5. In your opinion, where is the prophetic vision of women in ministry most needed?

6. What metaphors and images for God are most enriching and meaningful in your spiritual and theological life? How are you experiencing inclusive language for God? How is this integrated into your worship and spiritual leadership?

7. What did I fail to notice in this regard? What needs to be discussed more to understand the circumstances of women in ministry?

NOTES

[1] Eileen R. Campbell-Reed, *State of Clergywomen in the U.S.: A Statistical Update*, 2018. https://cdn.eileencampbellreed.org/wp-content/uploads/Downloads/State-of-Clergywomen-US-2018-web.pdf.

[2] A.J. Willingham, "More Women Are Aiming to Become Church Leaders. Together, They Could Change American Christianity." https://www.cnn.com/2023/07/30/us/women-church-leadership-united-states-cec/index.html.

[3] Thanks to Anita Peebles for providing this information in correspondence on 22 February 2024. The information about this ordination is on pages 19-20 of *Welcome Home: A 150-Year History of Seattle First Baptist Church*, 1869-2019, copyright 2020 by Seattle First Baptist Church, ISBN: 978-0-578-73170-4.

[4] Southern Baptist leaders voted to further restrict the role of women in ministry : NPR, accessed 7 January 2025.

[5] Susan E. Hylen, *Finding Phoebe: What New Testament Women Were Really Like* (Grand Rapids: Eerdmans, 2023).

[6] Sally Dyck, "We Still Need Books about Biblical Women's Liberation," *The Christian Century*, August 2023, Vol 140, No.8, 83.

[7] "Forgotten Women: Female Priests of the Early Church," in *Feminism and the Church Today Fact Sheet* published by National Ministries, American Baptist Churches, U.S.A., vol 5, no. 1 (March; 1981), 13.

⁸ Eileen R. Campbell-Reed, "How Do Women Flourish in Ministry?" https://eileencampbellreed.org/2023/07/03/3mmm-episode-204-how-women-thrive-in-ministry/ https://eileencampbellreed.org/2023/07/10/3mmm-episode-205-how-women-thrive-in-ministry-part-2/

⁹ Willingham, "More Women Are Aiming to Become Church Leaders. Together, They Could Change American Christianity." The quotes from Abernethy and Badgett are taken from this essay.

¹⁰ As quoted in Sue Monk Kidd, *The Dance of the Dissident Daughter* (New York: HarperOne, 1992, 1995), 136, 140.

¹¹ Ibid., 146.

¹² Ibid., 148.

¹³ Ibid., 152-53. Kidd is quoting and reflecting on Elizabeth A. Johnson, *She Who Is: The Mystery of God in Feminist Theological Discourse* (New York: Crossroad, 1993), 4.

CHAPTER 10

A Visible Church for an Invisible People

*"Neither this man nor his parents sinned;
he was born blind so that
God's works might be revealed in him."*

John 9:3

When I moved to a new city a few years ago, I went to a worship service the following Sunday with the nearest faith community. While the content of the worship—scripture, hymns, and all—felt familiar, there was much that was new to me. The usher who greeted me had a walker close at hand. She handed me a several-page stapled worship folder printed in a large font. Along with the order of worship, this folder also told me that there was telecoil available to amplify sound into my hearing aids. In the worship space, the rows of moveable chairs were quite far apart.

As the community gathered, I saw why the seating arrangement was arranged that way. Several people entered with walkers or in wheelchairs, either pushed by someone or self-propelled, and there was room for them. Near the front of the chapel, several people in wheelchairs—a few nearly reclining—were brought in by assistants. Some of these helpers sat close by to be available for any need.

During the worship time, persons reading the scripture were able to use walkers and come up gentle inclines to the lectern. As the worship service continued, worshippers were never asked to stand, kneel, or move about. At the offertory time, the ushers with their walkers moved up and down each row with the offering plates.

When it was time for the Lord's Supper, the minister came to each individual to distribute a wafer to dip into the chalice of wine and/or put it in their mouth. When he had served nearly everyone, he came around a second time with a different chalice, this time with grape juice for those who needed or had requested this accommodation.

When worship concluded, staff and other helpers brought those needing assistance back to their accommodations. Others visited with friends for a few minutes before going their various ways. No one had to climb a step to come to worship or return to their residence—there were ramps and elevators from each residence hall.

Where was I? You have probably surmised. I was at the worship service in a retirement community with its several levels of care—independent living, assisted living, memory care. This is where I now reside.

It might seem strange in this book on present and future ministry to begin a chapter with a story from a retirement community. However, I (as an older adult) am your future, and you are my past. To ignore the elderly may make a more difficult world for your future self! Not only that, but the American—and world—demographic is already leaning toward more older people and fewer children and youth. Obviously, ministry today must include elders as well.

The topic of this chapter, however, is not merely the elderly who are a subset of a larger population. This chapter's focus is on the special opportunities of ministry with a population that is often ignored—people with various disabilities. While our ministries may experience declining numbers and less response among populations we once served, there are other people who need our care and compassion and who might respond to loving care and sensitive witness.

Consider these realities in today's world:

- A recent survey reported that nineteen percent of the current American population (nearly 1 in 5 people) has a disability. Half of these people have a disability that can be described as severe.

- On a world scale, over a billion people, fifteen percent of the world's population, have some form of disability. According to the World Health Organization, this is "the world's largest minority."

- It is estimated that only five to ten percent of the world's disabled are effectively reached with loving gospel witness. This means that this is one of the largest unreached, underreached, and hidden people groups in the world.[1] As one example of this, two different studies of deaf and hard of hearing people conclude that from ninety-five to ninety-nine percent of deaf people are unchurched.

- According to one survey, over ninety percent of parents with special needs children said the most helpful support was "a welcoming attitude toward people with disabilities," but eighty percent said that attitude was not present in their church.[2]

As striking as these statistics are, as we shall see, they *understate* the reality.

RESPONSES FROM THE PASTORS I INTERVIEWED

When I asked present-day pastors about this, I heard about their awareness and efforts to make a place for everyone who came their way, including persons with disabilities. Several spoke of making their facilities more accommodating. If they had built or remodeled within recent decades, safer access and more accessible facilities were built into the design. Congregations in older buildings may have added a ramp or two. Michael's congregation installed a chair lift, for example, and has taken other steps to make their space accessible and welcoming for those with mobility or cognitive challenges.

A number spoke of efforts to make a place for a person with a specific issue.

- On two occasions, a person was elected deacon in the community where James served. One new deacon was blind and the other had cerebral palsy. They were willing to serve, but they did not feel able to participate in the distribution of the communion elements. James covered that part of their responsibility. Not being able to serve the community elements did not prevent them from offering their gifts to the spiritual care of people in their community.

- In their sanctuary, Joanna's small congregation has a table with materials and activities for families with children with special needs so that all have ways to be involved.

- In this same vein, Peter had served as children's minister in a larger church that had welcomed children and youth with various cognitive needs. He recalled, "These autistic children are going to come into youth groups. I had one mom ask me about our church. Another mother said that three churches in a row had told her not to bring her kids back. We were attentive to policies and how we relate to each young person so that all will feel safe."

- Molly's congregation was in the beginning stages of attempting to be more welcoming and inclusive. They were providing travel assistance so a family with blind members could be present and participate. Recently, a family with a deaf person had become members. The congregation was exploring having a sign language interpreter at least the first Sunday of the month to serve this family and reach out to others.

- Jessica's congregation includes a couple of older members who may be on the autism spectrum. As she offers personalized care to her members, she has learned both how to be responsive to these persons and their interests and how to balance this with other needs in congregational life.

- Jeremy teaches in a college and serves a congregation part time. He has learned much from the college's policies and practices. He notes, "Students with learning disabilities are provided accommodations. They may take their tests in an isolated room or have extra time for their testing. Or they may have assistance with note taking. They are still responsible for mastering the content, but there is help in leveling the playing field." He also participated in a community group that helped with a Make a Wish Group for older people. One elder wanted to learn to sew, another wanted to visit family in California they had not seen in years, and another wanted to take a balloon flight. He concludes, "That has given me extra awareness of some of the things going on in access and made me aware how much the church is or is not accessible to persons."

- Jonathan attended a disability conference and has increased his intentionality in leading his congregation to be more inclusive. However, this congregation encountered an unexpected and difficult issue. One person has had psychotic episodes to which he attached religious significance. These episodes have felt dangerous enough that a restraining order has been placed on him. Jonathan reflects, "This experience rang false for several church members. We are supposed to be welcoming and affirming, but we are excluding this person. Perhaps there is a hard lesson to be learned here. We can vastly expand our vision and inclusiveness, but perhaps we cannot do all."

What might be involved in a journey of expanding these churches' ministries in reaching out to persons with disabilities? I will paint this picture with a broad brush and then suggest some resources for further discovery.

BEGIN WITH A REDEMPTIVE THEOLOGY OF DISABILITY

Four persons who are active in this area of life offer important theological perspectives on disability.

Nancy Eisland

The late Nancy Eisland, writing as a person of faith and a theologian, also contended with disability. She challenged the "Disabling Theology" of disability found in some scripture that connects sin and disability and excludes the person with disability. Rather, she explored a "liberatory theology of disability" that includes both political action and reconception of symbols. This liberatory theology includes both how we think, believe, and worship and also how we work politically to influence the treatment of disabled and other embattled individuals.[3]

Empowering symbols from within one's faith heritage are vital for marginalized people. These must not only "change the way that people with disabilities conceive of our experiences and, in particular, our relationships to God" but also must "alter the regular practices, ideas, and images of the able bodied."[4] To this end, Eisland offered a "contextualized Christology" of "Jesus Christ as disabled God." As people who struggle with their own pain and limitations try to live out their faith and calling, they look to Jesus, "the disabled God who embodied both impaired hands and feet and pierced side and the Imago Dei."[5]

She pointed to the Eucharist as a worship expression of this truth: "Do this in remembrance of me." Whom do we remember? We remember "the disabled God who is present at the Eucharist table—the God who was physically tortured, arose from the dead, and is present in heaven and on earth disabled and whole." But to faithfully express this, persons with disabilities must be able to participate fully, not isolated from the rest of the "body."[6]

Thomas Reynolds

Another person who has thought deeply in this vein is the theologian Thomas Reynolds. Reflecting on his life as he has cared for and advocated for his son, Chris, Reynolds has come to a clear understanding of how universal our needs and problems are. According to Reynolds, those with no disability needing immediate attention are really only temporarily and partially able! Indeed, much of our society is blissfully unaware and lives in what he has termed "the Cult of Normalcy."[7] As Reynolds notes in his theology of disability, "All humans are only partially and temporarily able-bodied. We are subject to limitations, suffering, and finally death…"[8]

Reynolds contends that our wholeness is not the product of our independence and self-sufficiency. Rather, it comes from "the genuinely inclusive communion that results from sharing our humanity with one another in the light of the grace of God." This includes the recognition that all of us are "finite…contingent, and vulnerable."[9] Therefore, he proposes turning our viewpoint upside down "by privileging disability." In his view, "the so-called deformed and dysfunctional become the normative fulcrum for understanding the human…Not ability but disability is basic." All too often we respond to people based on appearance and achievement. In reality, we all share something much more basic: "vulnerable personhood."[10] Out of this understanding, wherever we are in this picture, all of us have gifts and all of us have needs. Each of us needs welcome and hospitality, and each has welcome and hospitality to offer.

If I hear these two theologians accurately, they reveal an alternative view and the important reminder that we need to welcome and relate to each other because of what the identifiably disabled have to teach and offer us!

Lamar Hardwick

The Rev. Lamar Hardwick has recently claimed these same truths. He writes, "I do not believe that the fact that I am autistic is an offense to God. I do not believe I should seek to be anything other than human. This is who I am and how God created me."[11] He applies a viewpoint that is foundational for many persons with disabilities and those who love them, including their church families.

Such an understanding is a hard-fought conclusion for him. He had experienced both inner pain and outer difficulty in being a minister until he was diagnosed with autism at the age of thirty-six. He would preach powerfully, but then he would stumble and miss social cues with those who spoke with him after the sermon. He recalled, "People said I looked angry or mean, that I am standoffish. I would hear people say things like, 'He walked past me, and he didn't speak,' all the things that I knew I would never intentionally do." Though he had heard all this before, now he felt a new urgency. He sought out a diagnosis. In 2014, a clinical psychologist confirmed he was on the autism spectrum.[12]

Based on his experience, Hardwick says that what the disability community most needs from the church is a group of people "that intentionally includes them as being image bearers of God."[13] That is his starting place for a theology of disability, a fresh discovery and experience, very much like the viewpoints of Eisland and Reynolds. Since then, Hardwick has written and spoken widely, equipping the church in this new direction. His latest book is *How Ableism Fuels Racism: Dismantling the Hierarchy of Bodies in the Church*.[14]

Amy Kenny

Amy Kenny, author of *My Body Is Not a Prayer Request: Disability Justice in the Church*, carries this conversation forward. She warns about "theological ableism." Kenny describes it this way: "When we limit our understanding of faithfulness or of holiness to nondisabled people, it limits our understanding of God, and it allows for us to be fooled into thinking that independence is a virtue, and non-disability is somehow holy, or good.[15] When well-meaning people tried to pray her disability away (she uses a wheelchair), it made her feel diminished and defective.

Rather, Kenny suggests that her disability can be a way to reveal God to others. She mentioned Moses, Elijah, Timothy, Zacchaeus, Paul and even (agreeing with Eisland) Jesus as persons in the Bible who dealt with disabilities and were used of God.[16]

Indeed, she writes, "Maybe what needs healing isn't my body, but society. Maybe people will come to appreciate that disability is not a sad form but a cultural identity with its own wealth of lessons just like my nephew and nieces do." (She earlier commented that these young relatives think her scooter makes her "cool." They think it is exciting to see her zip around.) She concludes: "Maybe what will be healed is ableism."[17]

CONTINUE WITH THE BASICS OF WELCOME, RESPECT, AND HOSPITALITY

As we aspire to be a welcoming community, a foundational question is this: Who is making decisions about the life and witness of a church, including ministry with people with disabilities? It is essential that persons with disabilities and/or their family members are on that leadership/decision making board. This is necessary for mutually respectful decision-making and strategy. Without shared leadership, these ministries may easily lapse into paternalism.

Building on that foundation, one place to begin may be clear communication that starts as one approaches and enters a church facility. Large signs that guide people to worship, study areas, offices, elevators, accessible pathways, dining room, and restrooms are an important step. Even more, hospitable people are needed. These are people who are cordial, welcoming, and able to respond to a query by accompanying a person to the place, activity, or individual they are seeking.

When worship or some other activity is underway, it is wise to be attentive to how the experience will be available to all who are present. Perhaps closed captioning, sign language interpreters, audio recordings, or large-print texts will be needed for some participants.[18] In that regard, the worship I described at the beginning of this chapter responded to some, but not all, of those possible needs.

Physical accessibility needs to be examined and changed when possible. Can persons safely reach worship, education, social, and dining spaces? Is it easy to access restrooms? Is it possible to provide access to places where worship leadership will happen? It may be difficult to adapt older buildings; still, creativity and effort are needed. I recall a church where each week a child would have the honor to enter the sanctuary, go up three steps, and light the candles on the communion table. This beautiful ritual signaled the beginning of worship. One Sunday, the communion table was moved down to the main floor—and a child in a wheelchair, her eyes shining, lit those candles!

Perhaps there are people who need a room where remote worship is still available. Some are uncomfortable with involuntary touch, including handshakes and hugs. Other parts of worship might also make some uncomfortable, so a separate room where the worship service is broadcast or displayed may be needed. These rooms might be similar to rooms some churches provide for parents with infants and small children.

Further, we need to be sensitive to our language and attitudes. It is not appropriate to pray for a person with disability and ask for their healing without their request and permission. It is never right to suggest that blindness, deafness, epilepsy, mental illness, or any other condition is the result of sin. It is important that we live and speak the theology that we suggested as our foundation—that all are created in the image of God, that all are loved by God, that all have dignity, and that all have gifts to offer.

We also need to create an atmosphere that encourages learning about various disabilities. We can provide room for discovery and growth. Areas to consider might include: issues and hardships these folks experience, successes and accomplishments they might celebrate, and what they might need from a faith community and caring friends. Even though these might be sensitive areas, silence and ignoring these subjects serves no one! Perhaps persons with a disability or a family member can be assisted in learning how to share this information with others to the benefit of all of us.

Finally, we need to commit to the long haul. At best, we will only partially succeed in being as inclusive as we hope we are. Likely, we will often fail. But we are called to persist. There may be healing experiences of caring, friendship, and community—even when we make mistakes. Our ultimate hope is that people will be touched with gospel love.

Cindy brought her combined perspectives as a pastor and occupational therapist to building a caring community when she was called to be a servant leader for a church that was at a low point. Part of the growth the church experienced was among people with varying disabilities.

When I asked her about method or strategy, this is how she responded:

> I do not have any specific printed out strategy. The methods we use are to foster a sense of welcome and acceptance for each individual that enters the door. We have various ways we adapt our service, such as not requiring people to read a lot. We do not go around the room in Sunday School class and ask that each person read a paragraph of the lesson. We have the tablets that transcribe speech to the written word for persons with hearing impairments. The words of the music are both printed on a page in the bulletin and on the screen. I enlarge the print on paper for people who need it.

We also spend time playing together, talking around the fire pit, and working together in our community garden, trying to find a task that each can do and that builds relationships, drawing each person into the church family. We also welcome discussions and recognize that people are coming from many different life experiences."[19]

Clearly, people are responding to a caring invitation and welcome!

LOOK FOR AND INITIATE THE STRATEGIES THAT FIT YOUR MISSION

In this process of hospitality, welcoming, and listening, doors of opportunity may open. Consider these possibilities:

Respond to One Family's Need

A church might begin by asking one family or individual what would be most helpful and welcoming. This might be a family with a child who needs extra attention and care. There seems to be an increase of children with hyperactivity or attention deficit disorder. It may be very difficult to worship as a family or to place that child in Christian education where the child is welcomed. Special concern and response may be needed.

Support an Existing Agency or Group

A church's mission might be to reach out to an agency or organization serving a given population and offering whatever support or help might be needed. Perhaps the organization needs a place to meet or hold an activity. Maybe the need is help with a fund-raising project or refreshments for a gathering. An agency might need volunteers, such as a driver for Meals on Wheels. There might be a need to offer one-on-one support to a participant.

Provide a Respite Time

A church might offer a regularly scheduled respite time. One church offered just such a service. They publicly announced that on the same Friday each month from 6:00 to 9:00 p.m. they would provide an evening with one-on-one care and group activities for persons with disability to give parents or other family members time to use as needed. For that evening, they served a meal, offered art activities and games, and provided the care and attention that each person needed. This ministry was welcomed and well-received![20]

Create and Offer a Needed Support Group

A church might provide a support group to respond to a need not being met elsewhere. Christ the King Lutheran Church in South Bend, Indiana, did this. They sent teams into their surrounding neighborhood to listen and ask where the church could help. They heard about loneliness and isolation—and especially about the loneliness related to mental illness. To respond to these needs, they secured funding and then initiated a group called "Fresh Hope." The group meets every Wednesday. In offering this support, the church has connected with the Fresh Hope for Mental Health organization founded by the Rev. Brad Hoefs[21] that provides guidance, consultation, and resources to churches aspiring to such ministries.

Hillary Doerries, one of the leaders at Christ the King, reflects: "Groups like this deal with really, how are we going to be human and how are we going to do it together? It's starting new conversations in the church with people who haven't known how to talk about it before."

A closely related second group, "GriefShare," was started at about the same time. It was founded by a woman whose husband died in a car accident. Out of her struggle and experience, she saw this group as a way for people to gather and speak about other hard things they face in life. The two groups work hand in hand to respond to hurts and loneliness that might have otherwise been missed. These groups have been supported by worship experiences in the church that highlight these issues and provide related spiritual and religious perspectives.[22]

Support or Establish a Church for a Special Population

To take this a step further, perhaps the need is for a faith community that focuses specifically on a population of people with specific needs. Founding or supporting a church for otherwise untouched persons might be a strategy to address this need. For example, there is a community called "Beloved Everybody" whose website announces, "Creating spaces in L.A. where people with and without intellectual disabilities can be celebrated and form mutual, authentic friendships." This community was founded by the Rev. Dr. Bethany McKinney.

"Beloved Community" describes its mission this way: "We believe communities miss out unless they make space where everyone is able to fully participate and belong, and to lead and share their gifts. And not only to share gifts they have, but to share the gift that they are, through their presence." This gathered group offers faith community, social events, and opportunities for creative expression, both in person and remotely. This work is a new worshipping community of the Presbyterian Church (U.S.A.).[23]

Debbie Buckholz has focused on ministry with the deaf and hard of hearing in three different settings. First, she took part in a deaf ministry within a church. Second, there was an experiment of serving as a co-pastor with a minister in a hearing church. These two experiences had both joys and real difficulties. Finally, in 2010, Buckholz and the people in the ministry founded the Deaf International Community Church (DICC).

She describes their method:

> This stand-alone Deaf church has been the most successful out of the three types. The service is done entirely in American Sign Language (ASL) and Deaf culture, while at the same time doing the best we can to meet the needs of those who attend. Currently, DICC provides a Deaf/Blind ministry, Zoom ministry, and transportation ministry. The transportation ministry picks up local Deaf people as well as the Deaf refugees who mostly live forty minutes away. At DICC, people in the Deaf world will find deep access of various ways to be included through language, culture, and visuals that cannot be found in a hearing church.[24]

As important and helpful as this is, there are struggles. One struggle is financial sustainability. Another struggle is finding the best way to relate to CODAs—an acronym for Child of Deaf Adults. Buckholz notes that only ten percent of deafness is hereditary. That means that about ninety percent of the children of deaf adults are hearing. Similarly, ninety percent of the parents of deaf children are hearing. So there is this double need. There is first a need for deaf people to experience worship and spiritual life in their language and culture. Then there is also a need for other family members to experience worship, life, and ministry in a hearing environment. Ultimately, Buckholz visualizes a new and different model:

Therefore, I believe the best possible design for a successful and thriving church for the Deaf community to attend is a church built for and around the Deaf world and the hearing world, all within the same building; a church where no one is minoritized and left in the margins; a church where true equity is found and the vision of an equity plan is fully shared between the Deaf pastor and the hearing pastor; a church where healthy choices for learning, spiritual growth, worship, fellowship, and community building are accessible for both the Deaf and hearing participants.[25]

This beautiful vision will require a special group of people willing to enter into full partnership and begin to build a new and different kind of organization. Perhaps this will happen in some post-pandemic congregation looking for a new mission!

EXPECT WONDER, EXPERIENCE LOVE

Wonderful gentle things can happen when people enter this realm of ministry with love and openness. As this chapter draws to a close, I will tell two stories. One story is told from the perspective of a person with a disability. The other story is about a family that includes a person with a disability. (I read the first story while studying and co-leading a course on this topic at a seminary. I am not able to relocate the source.)

There was a Roman Catholic family with a teenage son who had Down Syndrome. Every weekend they went to a mass where he eagerly served on the hospitality and ushering committee. He would stand by a door welcoming people with a big warm smile and then help with receiving the offering. When the mass was over, he would help clean up the sanctuary, picking up loose papers. After that, he would rush over to join his family as they went somewhere to eat.

One Sunday, however, he did not rejoin his family shortly after mass. They waited for him for quite a while. Worried, they went to look for him. They found him seated with an elderly couple, and they were earnestly talking with him. This couple had just learned that their infant grandson has Down Syndrome, and they had come to mass heartsick that morning. Who should welcome and greet them but this radiant young man! They came up to him when the service was over to talk with him and ask him questions. In turn, he was telling them about what he enjoyed in life and what he loved, including serving his church. If there was one person in that whole faith community this couple needed to talk with—and be guided to—it was this young man!

The second story was told to me by my friend and colleague in ministry, Jenny Hatfield-Callen. This is the story she tells:

> When my son was five or six years old, we almost stopped going to church completely. My son had been diagnosed with attention deficit hyperactivity disorder (ADHD). He would later be also diagnosed with Fetal Alcohol Spectrum Disorder (FASD). As a single mother, I had adopted my first and only child when he was four days old. I was told that the birth mother was a teenager who had minimal prenatal care.
>
> As a single mother, I was trying desperately to balance parenting, work, finances, and family and still keep my life intact; it was difficult. Weekends provided some respite, but church involvement was hard. Joseph was difficult to get to sleep and even harder to wake up in the morning. Then, once he was fully awake, he was like a streak of lightning, running from one thing to the next, not wanting to get dressed or get ready for church. If we did get to church, he was not the calmest, most cooperative child. He was busy, and unless I brought along many distractors, he would also be a bit noisy. It was always an experience to keep Joseph in church long enough for 'children's time,' after which he could go to the nursery.
>
> Often it was too much, and we just did not go. After too many absences from Sunday service and fellowship (these things are noticed in a smaller, aging congregation), I received a call from my pastor asking if everything was ok. He said that my son and I were missed in church. I explained the difficulties. While I loved going to church and Sunday school, the stress of all the preparation at home was overwhelming.
>
> Then this wonderful pastor came up with a plan for Sundays. He suggested that I get up and get myself dressed and ready for church. I asked him about my child. The pastor said to let him sleep and to pack a bag for him with his Sunday clothes, his breakfast, and anything else he might need in the morning. He said that I should wrap him in a blanket, put him in his car seat, and drive

to church. I asked if someone would watch him until the nursery opened. The pastor assured me that the church would be more than happy to pay for an extra hour of salary for the nursery attendant to have someone to watch Joseph. When Joseph did wake up, he explained, the nursery attendant would feed him the breakfast we brought and get him dressed. Then they would come and find me in adult Sunday school.

WOW! What a gift! This pastor had come up with a plan that would meet the needs of my child and, at the same time, get both of us back into church. As a parent, I would never have been so presumptuous to even think of asking for the level of help the pastor was suggesting. But he offered, and it was such a great gift. As a single parent, this provided two hours of time (Sunday School and church service) when I would have help with my child. It was time that I could be with other adults and share in study and worship, two hours of less stress and shared responsibility for Joseph.

Empowered in this way, Joseph and I became regular attenders. That was our precious church home until we moved to another state, where we found another church and again became faithful members. I will forever be grateful for this wonderful pastor who kept us in church, and I will never forget the generosity of this pastor and the congregation who gave us the gift of acceptance, welcome, and hospitality.

That is not the end of the story. Joseph grew into a fine young man. He served in the military, lived through some sorrow and pain in his life, and now manages a car repair service. Jenny pursued further education, including theological studies, and eventually devoted her career to helping families who had members with a disability find the support and care they needed. For years, she was a Certified Information and Referral Specialist for the University of Missouri Kansas City Institute of Human Development. Those who contacted her appreciated her deep empathy and practicality born of her experience as a caregiver for a person with a disability.

Jenny also persuaded her seminary to offer an occasional elective course called "Welcoming Persons with Disabilities in Faith Communities." She recruited me to collaborate with her to teach and coordinate that course. Without that caring pastor, this chapter would not exist.

FOR REFLECTION AND CONVERSATION

1. How do you personally relate to the thought that we are all only temporarily and partially able bodied? What disabilities and what unique abilities do you discern in yourself? What disabilities and unique abilities do you discern in the people you hold dear?

2. What moments of recognition did you experience in this chapter? What ministries are you already rendering with persons with disabilities and their families? How might these be expanded to those people and to the wider community?

3. What effective ministries with disabled persons and their families are you experiencing? Where are you confused or frustrated in trying to do so?

4. What invitations did you hear? What possibilities did this chapter birth?

5. What more do you need to know? Where might you go to learn more?

NOTES

[1] Lamar Hardwick, *Disability and the Church: A Vision for Diversity and Inclusion* (Downers Grove: Intervarsity Press, 2021), 102-103.

[2] "5 Statistics We Can't Ignore: Disability and the Gospel," The Banquet Network, September 4, 2018, www.thebanquetnetwork.com/blog/2018/8/28/5-statistics-we-cant-ignore?rq=statistics. As cited in Hardwick, 103.

[3] Nancy L. Eisland, *The Disabled God: Toward a Liberatory Theology of Disability* (Nashville: Abingdon Press, 1994), 90-91.

[4] Ibid., 91.

[5] Ibid., 98-99.

[6] Ibid., 107, 113-14.

[7] Thomas Reynolds, *Vulnerable Communion: A Theology of Disability and Hospitality* (Grand Rapids: Brazos Press, 2008), 46 ff.

[8] Ibid., 29.

[9] Ibid., 18.

[10] Ibid., 104-5.

[11] Hardwick, 11.

[12] https://religionnews.com/2024/02/08/meet-the-autism-pastor-lamar-hardwick-preacher-author-cancer-warrior/ accessed 19 February 2024.

[13] Hardwick, 71.

[14] Lamar Hardwick, *How Ableism Fuels Racism: Dismantling the Hierarchy of Bodies in the Church* (Brazos Press, 2024).

[15] As quoted in https://religionnews.com/2022/07/29/disability-theology-how-religious-beliefs-can-help-or-hinder-accessibility/. accessed 19 February 2024.

[16] Ibid.

[17] Amy Kenny, *My Body Is Not a Prayer Request: Disability Justice in the Church* (Grand Rapids: Brazos Press, 2022), 154.

[18] In this section I am summarizing suggestions from several sources. One of the most helpful and succinct is Kathryn Post, "Ten Ways to Make Your Worship Space Lest Ableist," from a series of articles published by the Religious News Service, https://religionnews.com/2022/07/29/10-ways-to-make-your-worship-space-less-ableist/

[19] Cindy Boyer, email correspondence, 8 June 2023.

[20] Zoom conversation with Cindy Boyer, 6 June 2023.

[21] https://freshhope.us/

[22] Brenda Martin, "A Place of Fresh Hope: Mental Health Ministry Has People Talking About Issues," *The Living Lutheran*, Volume 8, no.1, May/June 2023, 26-27.

[23] https://www.belovedeverybody.org/

[24] Debbie J. Buckholz, Redesigning a Deaf Church to Meet the Needs of the Deaf Community, A Dissertation Submitted to the Faculty in Partial Fulfillment of the Requirements for the Degree Doctor of Ministry at Central Baptist Seminary. 6 December 2021, 71-72.

[25] Buckholz, 73.

CHAPTER 11

A Humble Journey

MARRIAGE, FAMILY, GENDER, AND SEXUALITY

I praise you, for I am fearfully and wonderfully made.
Wonderful are your works; that I know very well.
Psalm 139:14

I once co-wrote a book whose title I did not understand! It happened like this: my friend Joe Leonard and I had been working on a book about all the changes we were seeing in the American family and what that meant for the church. Joe contributed from his perspective as a family life staff member, first for our denomination and then for the National Council of Churches. I wrote from my experience of being a pastor (and pastoral counselor) of a local church.

We were observing many things: the growth of the two-paycheck two-career marriages and "latchkey" children…the vast impact of no-fault divorce legislation…decisions about officiating at weddings of divorced persons and ministry with remarried families…the increasing isolation of nuclear families…changing sexual norms with new and improved contraception…non marital cohabitation…and more. Together, we wrote the book and submitted it to a publisher. Our working title was "The Church and the Changing Family."

The publisher accepted our submission. During the process of editing, designing, and naming our project, however, their entire publishing enterprise moved from one city to another. There were changes in staff and assignments and, of course, there was some confusion. Our manuscript moved toward publication without our involvement in those steps.

Finally, copies of our newly published book arrived in the mail. I was exhilarated! But then I saw the title: *Ministry with Families in Flux.*[1] I had no idea what a "flux" was. As I looked in the dictionary, I learned that "flux" could mean "the action of flowing or flowing out," or "continuous change." The book sold rather well. Whoever chose the title for the book had good instincts. We were told that the book was bought by many military chaplains, particularly chaplains of those being deployed to Iraq in the early 1990s. They understood exactly what a family in flux was!

A friendly early critic pointed out to me that, for all its helpfulness, the book had a big omission. We had said nothing about gay people or the unions and families they established. "Say whatever you believe about the subject," she said, "but say something." It was a fair and helpful criticism.

Seven years later, Joe and I wrote an update in the light of all that was continuing to happen in family life over those years. That publisher gave it the title *A New Day for Family Ministry*.[2] That time, largely because of Joe's experience of membership in a church that had for twenty-five years welcomed gay and lesbian Christians into membership and leadership (and a little from my own experience), we gave at least brief attention to this population.

All of this happened thirty or more years ago. My point is that we used that title, "ministry with families in flux," too soon. That description fits now even more than then! So, let's explore how families are changing and then consider our present ministry and ministry opportunities with them.

DECLINING AND DELAYED WEDDINGS AND MARRIAGES

Recently I heard that a young adult friend, a staff member in the community where I live, had just received an engagement ring. The next time I saw her I congratulated her. She responded, "Well, we have been together seven years. It's about time." I asked if they had wedding plans. She responded, "Oh no, we haven't even started to talk about that!"

Her response reveals a growing pattern of relationship and commitment. When Joe and I were investigating and writing on these topics about thirty years ago, these new patterns were just beginning to surface. We were reading studies about the growth of cohabitation and its impact on an enduring covenant in marriage. Preliminary studies were inconclusive.

Today, seven percent of the population is cohabiting without marriage, up from three percent in 1995. Among adults between the ages of eighteen and forty-four, fifty-nine percent have cohabited at one time.[3] This has become quite normal.

Back then, I experienced a church controversy about whether to allow an unmarried cohabiting couple to teach the senior high Sunday School class. (In this situation, the couple was eager to be married, but an angry ex-spouse kept delaying the divorce. Out of spite, this person was making it impossible for the couple to be married.) Would that couple be allowed to give leadership a Bible study class today?

A related concern was the technology of sex and the corresponding behavior changes. The first oral contraceptive pill was approved in 1960 by the Centers for Disease Control. This made possible the separation of sexual intercourse from conception. (As I write this, the Federal Food and Drug Administration has just approved an over-the-counter birth control pill, as have dozens of other countries before.) Oral contraception also led to an increase of persons having sexual intercourse, as well as persons having sexual intercourse at earlier ages. A recent study of high school seniors reported that over fifty percent have had intercourse, but many have avoided conception.[4] Other scientific advances such as in vitro fertilization separate conception from intercourse in the other direction.

Society—the media, celebrities, the general population—seems to be eager to create and engage in new patterns of sexual conduct. But what moral, ethical, and spiritual guidance is a pastor to offer these days—whether it is requested or not? And what should be the basis of that guidance? How do our historic faith, moral guidance, and contemporary science speak to these matters?

If marriage happens, both men and women are typically older at the time of marriage than in previous generations. And often marriage, when it happens, has been preceded by a time of living together. When the time for the wedding comes, what will it look like and where will it happen? What form will it take? Who will conduct the ceremony? For much of my ministry through the late twentieth century, I was one of the many "gatekeepers" to marriage. If a couple wanted me to conduct their wedding ceremony, I insisted on counseling time together before the wedding. I wanted to discuss with the couple what a wedding ceremony means, and I wanted to assist them in planning it. I especially encouraged their attention to the covenant they would be making with each other.

There was another purpose behind my desire to meet with the couple: I wanted to help them explore the meaning of marriage and help them build a strong marriage relationship together. I hoped and believed that strengthening and enriching their marriage was a compassionate faith witness on my part. And I also wanted to increase the probability that that their marriage would endure. Over time, I discovered helpful resources to shape our time together. Often, I was quite busy meeting with couples! The majority of these weddings were in a church or at a nearby outdoor setting.

Today, however, weddings do not require the participation of a pastor. Many other people can preside over a wedding and pronounce a marriage. Of course, there have always been civil ceremonies, presided over by a public official. Recently, however, online "ordinations" are readily available. With a simple application and (sometimes) a fee, a person can secure an "ordination certificate" (with absolutely no prerequisites) that allows that person to conduct weddings. Also, some wedding ceremonies today are known as "destination weddings," far removed from communities where couples live and work.

FRAGILE MARRIAGES AND FAMILIES

Increasingly, these are second—or subsequent—marriages. And often these marriages may be fragile and of uncertain duration. One report notes that forty to fifty percent of first marriages end in divorce, while sixty-seven percent of second marriages and seventy-four percent of third marriages do.[5]

Remarriages and stepfamilies are delicate and complicated entities! My friend Carole, who has lived, counseled, and written about these matters, recalls an experience. Her family had just moved to a new community. She went into a bank and said to the bank officer, "I'm Carole Della Pia-Terry, and I'd like to open a new account here." The bank officer responded to her name by saying, "That sounds more like a corporation than a family!"

Carole admitted that this bank official was more accurate than he knew. She said, "There are thirty-one people who own a piece of me. And those are just the main ones. There are many more minor characters in this family structure." She was thinking of her children, her new spouse's children, both partners' extended families, ex-spouses and in-laws, and more.[6]

One of the pastors I interviewed was experiencing this kind of marriage and family chaos on a church level. Kathy was trying to schedule a time when all the interested children and youth would be able to take part in a confirmation class. However, the complicated schedules of custody for children in remarried families, each with their own nuances and schedules, made it nearly impossible to find a time to meet! And who knows what the children in such complex family structures are experiencing?

GAY AND TRANSGENDER PEOPLE'S PASTORAL CARE AND FAMILY LIFE NEEDS

There is still more to consider in the changing marriage and family scene. In a 2022 cross-generational Gallup Poll, the question was asked "Which of the following do you consider yourself to be? You can select as many as apply." The choices provided were "Straight or Heterosexual; Lesbian; Gay; Bisexual; Transgender." Among the overall adult population, those who self-identified as other than heterosexual was 7.2 percent, a number similar to results from recent years, but double what it was when Gallup first started asking this question a decade ago.

The answers, however, varied with the generations. Researchers noted, "Adult members of Generation Z, those born between 1997 and 2004 who were aged eighteen to twenty-five in 2022, are the most likely subgroup to identify as LGBT, with 19.7% doing so. The rate is 11.2% among Millennials and 3.3% or less among older generations."[7] From generation to generation, we see changes in gender and sexuality self-perception.

I am among those on the beginning end of the learning curve on all this, but let's reflect and continue our conversation. This subject can be broken down into several sub-topics. First, there is the distinction between gender and sexual orientation. Second, there are questions about how this self-awareness is experienced in childhood and youth years as compared to the self-awareness of adults. Still another aspect of the conversation involves the political atmosphere in which all of this is happening. Finally, there are questions about the response of churches to these new realities and relationships.

How does a church discuss, decide, and grow into new responses? How do biblical and theological perspectives speak to these questions? Further, how does the church desire to be seen and experienced by people in the younger generations? In all of this, there is the need for guidance and the commitment to maintain Christian community even when Christians disagree with each other. Is it possible for us to stay together through our differences?

Gender

Based on his wide experience, social worker Irwin Krieger provides a basic perspective on gender. He notes, "*Gender identity* is a person's inner sense of being female, male, neither, or both." Sex is assigned at birth (natal gender), based on the appearance of the baby's genitals. However, for a small number of individuals, the anatomy is not entirely male or female (sometimes called sexually ambiguous). There are clear expectations about gender expression and behavior in any society. Many children and youths are *cisgender*. What that means is that their assigned sex, their gender identity, and their gender expression are all male or all female. On the other hand, *transgender* persons have a gender identity and/or gender expression that does not conform. Some identify fully with the opposite—male or female—but other trans people have *non-binary gender identities*—neither male nor female, or a blend of the two.[8]

As Robin Marantz Henig notes, it is even more complex than that. Gender, she notes, is an amalgamation of a number of elements. These include "chromosomes (those Xs and Ys), anatomy (internal sex organs and external genitals), hormones (relative levels of testosterone and estrogen), psychology (self-defined gender identity), and culture (socially defined gender behaviors). And sometimes people who are born with the chromosomes and genitals of one sex realize that they are transgender, meaning they have an internal gender identity that lines with the opposite sex—or even occasionally with neither gender or no gender at all."[9]

Indeed, there are cultures that recognize and name a third gender—in South Asia (*hira*), in Hawaii (*mahu*), in Mexico (*muxe*), and among some Native American peoples (*two-spirit*).[10] Other studies have suggested that gender is even more complex—that there may be five or even seven genders!

These self-perceptions that do not directly relate to traditional categories may arise as early as preschool. They may persist or may change over time. When any of this happens, it is an extremely uncomfortable place for a child or youth. There are concerns related to feelings about their own body and identity, how they may be treated, and whether they might be harassed or bullied by others. There may be confusion, depression, and perhaps suicidal ideation.

Two of the pastors I interviewed are parents of children who are exploring a different gender identity than the one assigned at their birth. One pastor's child is an early teen and the other is an eight-year-old who had named their gender two years earlier and maintained it consistently. One of these families lives in a state where it is safe to do this. However, the other family lived in a state where increasingly repressive legislation has been and is being passed. These parents feared that their child could be taken from them, and they have moved to a state they consider to be safer.

For the present, both sets of these parents are simply being supportive and following their pediatricians' guidance. If their children's gender self-identification and gender dysphoria persist, the future might hold counseling with a gender identity specialist. Following this, if indicated, they could choose medical interventions. One such intervention consists of puberty-blocking hormones that would "suspend the bodily changes of puberty, giving the teen more time to decide on a future course." For teens with "persistent gender dysphoria," there are cross-sex hormones that "help masculinize a female body or feminize a male body."[11] Generally, surgical interventions are not considered until adulthood.

Sexual Orientation and Gender

Then there is the distinction between gender preference and sexual orientation. As Austen Hartke notes, "*Sexual orientation* is about whom you are sexually and romantically attracted to. Being gay, lesbian, bisexual, or any other sexuality has to do with your relationship to others, while being trans has to do with your own internal gender identity and sense of self."[12]

While these are two different matters, they both deserve attention, discussion and conversation among people in Christian churches. We might wonder if it is possible to welcome all people and if it is possible to be supportive. These topics are certainly discussed in many places throughout our culture. A justice issue for LGBTQ+ people involves the right to marry with all the protections and obligations of other people's marriages. Legally, there has been progress on this in recent years.

A Wikipedia article summarizes recent developments:

> In June 2015, the Supreme Court ruled in the landmark civil rights case of *Obergefell v. Hodges* that the fundamental right of same-sex couples to marry on the same terms and conditions as opposite-sex couples, with all the accompanying rights and responsibilities, is guaranteed by both the Due Process Clause and the Equal Protection Clause of the Fourteenth Amendment to the United States Constitution. On December 13, 2022, DOMA [Defense of Marriage Act] was repealed and replaced by the Respect for Marriage Act, which

recognizes and protects same-sex and interracial marriages under federal law and in interstate relations.[13]

This legal action has occasioned vigorous—and sometimes divisive—conversation in many churches. If the law of our land allows for marriages of same-sex couples, should the church and its ministers be ready to provide this pastoral service when asked? On the other hand, if our reading of the Bible so leads us, should we refuse? Timothy Bonner and Matthew Sturtevant have both experienced and explored these conversations. They have shared their conclusions and guidance for other churches wanting or needing to have the same discussion.[14]

Divisions and Processes for Christian People

For some, there is no discussion or conversation needed. There has long been reliance on six or seven widely scattered Bible passages that speak of same sex activity. From these passages, some conclude that such activity or orientation is forbidden and that there is no room for discussion. Generally, these passages include Genesis 19:1-38; Leviticus 18:22, 20:13; Romans 1:25-27; 1 Corinthians 6:9-11; 1 Timothy 1:9-10, and Jude 6-7. Some also cite Genesis 1-2. Some people may want to be "welcoming but not affirming," calling for kindness and acceptance but wanting to help persons change their sexual orientation or at least their behavior.

Others find these scattered and diverse passages in a huge Bible less binding, particularly in the light of all that has been learned and discovered about human sexuality. There is the need for respectful conversation among Christians as they seek to be faithful and redemptive among all people.

Distinguished Christian ethicist David Gushee recently wrote about his changed and growing conviction on these topics. He talks about what he has come to believe and how he arrived at his conclusions:

> I believe the moral call of God to Christians in this *kairos* moment is to include LGBTQ+ persons on the same terms as any other person or group. I believe that this is not fundamentally about changing our Christian sexual ethic—because the heart of my sexual ethic, at least, remains unchanged and traditional—the framework is covenantal and marital and the norm is lifetime covenant fidelity.

So the issue for me is not sexual ethics *per se*, but about widening the circle of who is included in a sexual ethic that hasn't changed.

However, Gushee points out that the question is broader and even more basic: "It is the crucial question of who is fully included in Christian community and the reach of the gospel of God's love for humanity in Jesus Christ. The issue is about the nature of the gospel and the church far more than it is about sexual ethics."[15]

In a series of five essays, Gushee tells how he came to this conclusion. To retell it briefly, he came to know faithful, loving, forgiving Christians who were also LGBTQ+. He also was reminded of his core understanding of the gospel—God's love for the world and all humanity. Furthermore, he noted the growing cultural acceptance and progress for gay people as compared to widespread Christian resistance. Ultimately, he concluded that the view of culture was closer to the correct view.

This led him to reject the perception that LGBTQ+ acceptance was apostasy or cultural decline, but rather the door for more people's participation in gospel-shaped communities. Along with this, he felt convicted of complicity in his previous teaching that led to contempt for or rejection of gay people. As he continued his journey, he reexamined the Bible passages we mentioned earlier. Space does not allow detailing all he found in that part of his exploration. I will just mention that he saw the divine creation in Genesis 1-2 as open to reinterpretation in the light of what we now know about sexual and gender diversity. For example, he came to understand that Genesis 2:18, "Then the LORD God said, 'It is not good that the man should be alone...'" can speak more broadly than he previously thought.

He also concluded that Romans 1 was not so much about human sexual behavior as it was "about knocking down either Gentile or Jewish pridefulness in the divided Roman Christian communities—while also demonstrating awareness of Roman imperial debauchery." This led him to the conclusion that "the broader themes of the Christian ethical tradition, as I had interpreted it, must lead to full acceptance and inclusion of LGBTQ+ Christians. Perhaps the most familiar bit of ethical instruction in the whole Bible is this text: 'In everything, do to others as you would have them do to you.' This is Matthew 7:12, the 'Golden Rule.' It still speaks so beautifully to this and every issue."[16]

Through my years of ministry, I came to the same conclusion as Gushee. My process was not as rigorous as his. Instead, my viewpoint surfaced quite simply as I loved, cared for, and heard the stories, struggles, and pain of the people I served as pastor. It is sad to see how divisive this topic of conversation has become. There are denominations that are being torn apart over this subject. In other places, people are leaving their churches because of official positions. Some are leaving because the official positions are too open. Others are leaving because official positions are not open enough!

My hope is that this might be a gentle, loving, and respectful journey. Change is hard for any of us, particularly those of us who have believed and behaved in a certain way for many, many years. At the same time, there are people of all ages who are hurting and struggling with gender and sexuality issues. Silence needs to be broken. If an entire congregation cannot have the conversation, perhaps there can be a safe space for those who need it and for those who are willing to talk and listen.

Advocate Susan Cottrell writes, "LGBTQ+ people experience depression, self-harm, substance abuse, suicidal thoughts at alarmingly high rates—and the root cause of this is *family and faith-based rejection*." She notes that "twenty-five percent of LGBTQ+ homeless youth became homeless the very day they came out to their Christian parents. Fifty-seven percent of transgender youth without supportive parents attempt suicide. When even just one parent is supportive, that number drops to four percent. THAT is what is at stake here. That's the power a parent holds in their hands."[17] She is speaking about family acceptance. I am writing to encourage pastors and churches to create places that can provide parents and families with refuge.

RESPONSES AND INVOLVEMENT I HEARD

Christian churches have many responsibilities here. For some, it is to have earnest conversations among themselves. For others, it is to make known where those conversations have led them. A number of the pastors I interviewed expressed resistance in doing this. Several spoke of "don't ask, don't tell" atmospheres. Some mentioned that older adults might be interested and concerned for their grandchildren's situation, wanting to be kind and understanding, but not wanting to give voice to that in a systematic way.

At least two of these pastors told about church decisions that were discussed, decided, and publicized. Jason C serves in a denomination where local congregations decide on such issues. He had led his congregation in an earlier series of study sessions and conversations. He recalls, "When we began speaking about whether I could officiate at weddings of gay people, I asked if the congregation wanted to do a study on the issue. Members declined, feeling that they had had enough study on the issue. Instead, the Session publicized and held a listening session where people could share their perspectives. This helped people feel like they were heard. In that setting, they were able to hear that there was a variety of perspectives within the body. At the end of the day, the Session voted to leave it up to the pastor's discretion whether a couple could be married in the church. The Session knew about my inclination. It was only later, after a year or two, that we explicitly adopted the statement of being fully affirming and welcoming of all."

Evan came to a church that had gone through a slow process of study, discussion, and discernment during a time between pastors. This process was even slower because of Covid. The congregation reached their statement on nondiscrimination, sought a pastor who would lead in that direction, and then called that pastor—Evan. After his arrival, they publicized their statement.

When I asked how that position had been received, Evan answered: "It's been a year that we have had this statement in place. Folks have come and found us because of our statement. We have some LGBTQ people in leadership in our music team. We have invited folks. We will continue have more LGBTQ folks coming and leading in all facets." Evan so admires the way this church went through this process before calling him. "There was this real spirit that we will make this decision together, and even if we don't agree, we will stay in fellowship with each other."

PASTORAL OPPORTUNITIES

What are the implications of all of this for ministry? What caring and serving opportunities can we find here?

Wedding Availability

Many of the pastors I spoke with had not conducted any weddings; others had conducted a few. The delay of marriages, destination weddings, and the plethora of wedding planners and officiants all seem to be making a pastor-led, church-hosted wedding more and more rare. As Rob observed, "The wedding industry has become such there is no need for church anymore. It has taken the conversation for marriage away from the church which comes off as being completely irrelevant on this topic."

While reflecting on this, I happened on an interesting article about the "minimony."[18] The article described a growing movement among couples to avoid the lavish, wildly expensive wedding in favor of a small gathering with friends. This trend was called the "minimony." The article pointed out various businesses that were providing these events "for less than the cost of an iPhone."

The article concentrated on the opportunity provided by a couple, Tess Sweet and Dan Gambelin, who bought an old chapel, redecorated it, and called it "The Old Brown House." There, they offered to provide amenities for simple weddings. This included a collection of used veils and wedding dresses for the bride. Both business partners had obtained Universal Church ordinations and had also created a simple "madlibs" way for couples to create their own wedding vows. The article cited a sociological study claiming that lesser cost weddings had been sociologically demonstrated to result in a slightly larger chance for longevity for the marriage. In the same way, honeymoons were also associated with increased chance of longevity for the marriage.[19]

This essay described the "minimony," using madlibs-aided vows, of one couple: "My dearest Jen," the groom said, "together with you, my life is amazing, fun, and damn near perfect." "My dearest Will," she said to him, "Together with you, my life is full of music and joy and love."

The article explained that Sweet and Gambelin are still nailing down specifics on pricing, but that they plan to offer weddings for around $600. This is, indeed, less than the price of a new iPhone and less than a third of the average rent for a studio apartment in Los Angeles. The couple added that they intend to never turn someone away because of cost, describing their special place as a "nontraditional, nonconformist, sliding-scale wedding chapel."[20]

Apparently, business is booming! In a secular world, they are compassionately meeting a real need. But they are not providing anything that a pastor and a church with warmth and Christian hospitality could not provide as well. In addition, we can offer a spiritual perspective and supportive community as well. It seems simple enough to make oneself and one's church available for this type of ministry, and then to publicize it.

The guidance and ceremony may be an opportunity for outreach ministry and may be a way to be a caring force in the world.

Relationship Support

When the opportunity to be the pastor for a wedding comes, it is wise to ask if the couple is open to conversations about marriage and relationship. It might be helpful to share with the couple what Forbes Advisor researchers learned when they asked one thousand people experiencing divorce what might have preserved their marriages. Here were the top five answers:

1. A better understanding of the commitment of marriage prior to marrying

2. A better understanding of the values and morals of their partner prior to marrying

3. Waiting longer to start a family

4. Seeking professional help from a therapist or couples' counselor

5. Waiting longer to get married.[21]

If the couple is open to conversation, you have an opportunity. It will be good to be equipped with a means for doing that yourself or to be able to refer them to someone who can provide that kind of help. For the last dozen years or so of my pastoral and teaching ministry, my go-to resource was *Prepare/Enrich*.[22] This resource provides inventories and methods for guiding fruitful couple's conversation. This resource offers training as well as a list of nearby professionals who have already been trained. I have used both of these options to good effect. This is a widely available, researched, and trusted method. And, of course, there are many others.

There may be other occasions where another kind of conversation group will meet a need and be an important ministry. An example of this would be a grief support group. There might also be helpful group possibilities for persons who have experienced a divorce. And remarried families might benefit from learning and sharing with others who are part of a similar experience.

Moral Guidance, Witness, and Teaching

Years ago, I sensed that there was a lack of discussion about how to make moral decisions about sexual and relationship behavior in our changing age. At that point, I was grateful to discover Marie Fortune's *Love Does No Harm: Sexual Ethics for the Rest of Us*.[23] In the book, she offered (and then developed) five helpful guidelines:

> 1. Is my choice of intimate partner a peer, that is, someone whose power is relatively equal to mine?
>
> 2. Are both my partner and I authentically consenting to our sexual interaction?
>
> 3. Do I take responsibility for protecting myself and my partner against sexually transmitted diseases and to insure reproductive choice?
>
> 4. Am I committed to sharing sexual pleasure and intimacy in my relationship?
>
> 5. Am I faithful to my promises and commitments?[24]

Using available resources, a pastor can initiate and sustain important conversations that will lead to rich and enduring experiences and relationships.

Celebrations

One family life practice that pastors described to me was their participation in various family life celebrations—anniversaries especially, but also births, graduations, and home dedications. One pastor told me that a church family so repeatedly and insistently invited her to a big anniversary party that she decided that she had been adopted into the family! Only good things can come from that kind of continued pastoral relationship.

Advocacy

Jennifer, a pastor who is the parent of a transgender child reflected, "Other pastors ask if they can just be quietly supportive. But our state legislature is considering and passing one repressive measure after another. There is a group of us clergy who go and give testimony at legislative hearings on those measures. It is mostly rabbis and me. We need stronger backing and support from those who care about us and support us in our right to care for our child without outside interference."

Commitment to Support Parents' Decisions About Family Size

There is another reality in family life that we have not mentioned yet. In June, 2022, the United States Supreme Court overturned the fifty-year-old ruling on Roe v. Wade to the effect that the federal constitutional right to abortion no longer exists. This ruling leaves it to each state to regulate the matter, meaning that nearly half the states now prohibit or restrict abortion in a number of ways. Increasingly, decisions about having children—when and how many—have become important and difficult family discussions. Personal decisions about the ability to care for a child have led, in some cases, to decisions to have fewer children, to have children later in life, or not to have children at all. Pregnancy can surface both financial and health questions for both mothers and children.

Pastors need to know where they stand on this issue. In my view, these decisions need to be entrusted to a woman, her family, her support community, and her medical care professionals.

Personal Support, Family Support, and Advocacy of Transgender and Gay Persons

It is the responsibility of pastors and church to offer healing from the hurt, isolation, and even despair of life that sometimes comes as persons deal with their own identity and that of others. Molly notes, "More than half of what new members appreciate is my sign that says: 'I am called to be pastor to all people.' Families are looking for churches that are open to people struggling with their gender and sexual identity. I support families as they work on this with their physicians."

Jonathan reflects, "I find people respond positively to a welcome for who they are, not for a mask they have to put on. Knowing the danger of suicidality is enough for me to care about trans people. God does not want more dead suicidal teens. Being a place of welcome is one of the best ministries we can do."

Not all will agree with the conclusions that those pastors have expressed—and the conclusions that I have reached. Hopefully, all concur that an atmosphere of caring, respect, and compassion for those struggling with any of these topics is a value we all share.

I was touched when I read the story of Asher O'Callaghan who grew up in the Church of Christ. For much of his early life, he struggled with his dual identity of being gay and being a Christian. He tried to leave his sexual identity behind, including working with a counselor who used conversion therapy techniques unsuccessfully. After college, he enrolled in graduate school, seeking a Ph.D. in religion, hoping to look at his life issues from a safer distance. However, fellow students invited him to their church, and he went with them. It was a Welcoming and Affirming Lutheran church.

He recalls,

> It was the first time I'd ever experienced liturgy, and it was weird and wonderful. What really got me was the communion table. They said, "Everyone without exception is welcome to the table." And I went, not thinking much of it, but then, every single week I found myself thinking, "I need to go back." Not because I felt a sense of duty or obligation but because I felt it sustaining me…I felt it was holding my life together.[25]

Church and family are two entities that can harm—or two entities that can heal and sustain. May we choose to be part of a healing story!

FOR REFLECTION AND CONVERSATION

1. What are the best things you are doing to sustain and support families in your ministry setting?

2. What suggestions, ideas, or opportunities did this chapter suggest to you? What invitations did you hear?

3. Where did you disagree? Where did you agree—but wonder if your congregation would agree? What will be your ministry strategy?

4. Where are you and your church community on the topics of gender? Sexual orientation? Family planning, including abortion? What conversations are needed?

5. What did I miss?

NOTES

[1] Joe Leonard and Richard Olson, *Ministry with Families in Flux* (Louisville: Westminster John Knox Press, 1990).

[2] Joe Leonard and Richard Olson, *A New Day for Family Ministry* (Bethesda: The Alban Institute, 1996).

[3] Julianna Menasee Horowitz, Nikki Graf, and Gretchen Livingston, "The Landscape of Marriage and Cohabitation in the U.S.," Pew Research Center, 6 November 2019.

[4] Over Half of U.S. Teens Have Had Sexual Intercourse by Age 18, New Report Shows, CDC Report.

[5] The High Failure Rate of Second and Third Marriages | Psychology Today, accessed 7 January 2025.

[6] Richard P. Olson and Carole Della Pia-Terry, *Help for Remarried Couples and Families* (Valley Forge: Judson Press, 1984), 70-73.

[7] "US LGBT Identification Steady at 7.2%" https://news.gallup.com/poll/470708/lgbt-identification-steady.aspx, accessed 17 June 2023.

[8] Irwin Krieger, *Helping Your Transgender Teen: A Guide for Parents*, 2nd ed. (Philadelphia: Jessica Kingsley Publishers, 2011, 2018), 19-21. Italics in the quote and in the paraphrase are his.

[9] Robin Marantz Henig, "Rethinking Gender," *National Geographic*, January, 2017, Vol. 231, No.1, 56.

[10] Krieger, 73.

[11] Marantz Henig, 69.

[12] Austen Hartke, *Transforming: The Bible & the Lives of Transgender Christians* (Louisville: Westminster John Knox Press, 2018), 23. Italics his.

[13] "Same-sex marriage in the United States," https://en.wikipedia.org/wiki/Same-sex_marriage_in_the_United_States. Accessed 17 June 2023.

[14] Timothy J. Bonner and Matthew B. Sturtevant, *From Distrust to Trust: Controversies and Conversations in Faith Communities* (Valley Forge: Judson Press, 2023).

[15] David Gushee, "How Minds and Hearts Change: 10 Steps in My Journey Toward Full LGBTQ+ Inclusion—Part 1." https://goodfaithmedia.org/how-minds-and-hearts-change-10-steps-in-my-journey-toward-full-lgbtq-inclusion-part-1/, accessed 9 July 2023.

[16] Gushee listed and elaborated on these steps in a series of five articles published on Good Faith Media in mid-June of 2023, the last of which is https://goodfaithmedia.org/how-minds-and-hearts-change-10-steps-in-my-journey-toward-full-lgbtq-inclusion-part-5/.

[17] Susan Cottrell, How a Parent's Journey Can Help Us Be More Inclusive (patheos.com) https://www.patheos.com/blogs/freedhearts/2022/06/09/parentjourney/?utm_source=Newsletter&utm_medium=email&utm_campaign=Best+of+Patheos&utm_content=57&lctg=32930&rsid=&recipId=32930&siteId=7DF2956C-D2F1-40D4-A777-98E450E58360 accessed 10 June 2023. Italics and capitalization are hers. Persons might also be interested in her support organization, FreedHearts, https://www.freedhearts.org/.

[18] Marisa Gerber, "How to throw a wedding for less than the cost of an iPhone — the minimony craze" https://www.latimes.com/business/story/2023-06-21/wedding-couples-choosing-affordable-minimony-elopement.

[19] Andrew Francis-Tan and Hugo M. Mialon, "A Diamond is Forever" and Other Fairy Tales: The Relationship Between Wedding Expense and Marriage Duration," *Economic Inquiry* (ISSN 0095-2583) Vol. 53, No. 4, October 2015, 1919–1930. https://www.csus.edu/faculty/m/fred.molitor/docs/wedding%20expenses%20and%20marriage%20duration1.pdf.

[20] Gerber.

[21] Aditi Shrikant, "Poll: What do you think could have saved the marriage?" https://www.msn.com/en-us/money/personalfinance/63-of-divorcees-say-this-is-the-no-1-thing-that-would-have-saved-their-marriage-and-it-s-not-more-money/

ar-AA1fpKiG?ocid=msedgdhp&pc=U531&cvid=f1d91fa5ca724c0b936dc1dadcf85c27&ei=19 accessed 18 August 2023.

[22] https://www.prepare-enrich.com/.

[23] Marie Fortune, *Love Does No Harm: Sexual Ethics for the Rest of Us* (New York: Continuum, 1995).

[24] Fortune, 38-39.

[25] Quoted in Hartke, 133.

CHAPTER 12

Faithfulness in a Frail Creation

WHAT CAN A CONGREGATION DO?

In God's hand are the depths of the earth;
The heights of the mountains are God's also,
The sea belongs to God, for God made it,
and God's hands have formed the dry land.

Psalm 95:4-5 (An Inclusive Version)

As I was working on this chapter in the spring of 2023, the United Nations Panel on Climate Change came out with its most urgent warnings yet. They referred to our planet as a "ticking time bomb."

As Sara Kaplan in the *Washington Post* reported,

> The world is likely to pass a dangerous temperature threshold within the next ten years, pushing the planet past the point of catastrophic warming—unless nations drastically transform their economies and immediately transition away from fossil fuels, according to one of the most definitive reports ever published about climate change. The report released Monday by the U.N. Intergovernmental Panel on Climate Change (IPCC) found that the world is likely to surpass its most ambitious climate target—limiting warming to 1.5 degrees Celsius (2.7 degrees Fahrenheit) above preindustrial temperatures— by the early 2030s. Beyond that threshold, scientists have found, climate disasters will become so extreme that people will not be able to adapt. Basic components of the Earth system will be fundamentally, irrevocably altered. Heat waves, famines and infectious diseases could claim millions of additional lives by century's end.[1]

During this same time, there have been waves of tornadoes destroying whole communities and taking lives across wide swaths of the American continent. Recently, Wisconsin, where I live, experienced devastating tornadoes in February for the first time in history. In other parts of the country, there have been long-term droughts. At the same time, in other places there has been grave concern about the impact of hurricanes and rising oceans on coastal cities. This is occasioned both by huge deluges of rain and long-term trends of glacial melting.

THE "ATMOSPHERE" OF CREATION CARE AND CLIMATE CHANGE

With such a clear global threat, we might assume that everyone will want to do everything possible to avoid this catastrophe. But our assumption would be wrong. There is widespread disagreement about climate change and global warming. The range and extent of this disagreement has been documented by the Yale Program on Climate Change Communication. This group has conducted nationwide surveys twice a year on American attitudes on the climate for more than a decade. They have discerned six Americas as far as attitudes about climate change. They are:

- The Alarmed
- The Concerned
- The Cautious
- The Disengaged
- The Doubtful
- The Dismissive[2]

How are Americans distributed among these various viewpoints? These trends have changed somewhat over the last ten to fifteen years. The Alarmed group has nearly doubled in that time. The Concerned, Disengaged, Doubtful, and Dismissive groups have remained approximately the same.[3] At the time of this writing, over half of the population is in the Alarmed or Concerned categories, and less than half are spread out among the other four categories. Millennials and Gen Z are about seven percent higher in the Alarmed and Concerned categories than older adults. Hispanic-Latinx and Black respondents are twelve to fifteen percent more Alarmed and Concerned than white persons. Women of Color register as the most Concerned.

Another division exists over opinions about the cause of climate change—whether it is from natural causes, or whether it has been caused or exacerbated by humans. Although ninety-seven percent of published environmental scientists believe climate change is caused by human activity, popular opinion does not seem to follow this. The percentage of those in public surveys who say climate change is mostly or entirely the result of human activities has been declining in recent years, falling from sixty percent affirmation of this view in 2018 to forty-nine percent in 2023. Now, nearly four in ten adults believe that climate change is caused equally by humans and natural changes (up five percentage points from 2021), while fourteen percent say it is mostly or entirely the result of natural changes.[4]

Sometimes these differences of opinion are even more pronounced within churches. Those in the mainstream and progressive parts of Christianity are more likely to acknowledge the reality of climate change and believe that there is a human cause than those in the more conservative or evangelical parts of Christianity. This is true despite the fact that there are concerned and creative leaders—and excellent resources—that address climate concerns from all across the theological spectrum. Here are some examples:

- Evangelical Environmental Network: https://creationcare.org/

- Young Evangelicals for Climate Action: https://yecaction.org/

- Interfaith Power and Light: https://interfaithpowerandlight.org/ and

- Climate Caretakers, Climate Stewards USA: https://climatestewardsusa.org/climate-caretakers/

Christians take seriously a Bible that tells us that we live in a world and a universe created by God. Christians also know that God entrusted humans with the privilege and opportunity of stewardship. Yet, this is a world that, according to many respected leaders, is under threat.

There are probably at least two reasons that explain why Christians are not more unified in their response. The first reason may be the fear that any involvement may be seen closely tied to big government and governmental involvement in our lives. A second reason may be a person's fear that climate activism will be necessarily linked to other social issues with which one does not agree.

BEGINNING RESPONSES

What can we do about this issue and the impasses around it? Climate scientist (and self-described evangelical) Katherine Hayhoe responds, "The number one thing we can do is talk about climate change."[5] When Yale investigators asked the people they surveyed how often they heard someone talk about climate change, the most frequent answer was once or twice a year! This topic needs discussion. We need to conquer our fear of talking about it. Worship, sermons, discussion groups, forums, Sunday School classes, and informal conversations around the coffee pot can open up exploration.

We should give one another permission to disagree on this subject. Indeed, some people may be reluctant to engage the issue, while others might be moved to activism. A caring community can give permission for some to engage in actions while others hold back. Christians need to grow in the ability to discuss differences among themselves (on many topics!) without shaming those who hold other opinions. We also need to avoid shaming those whose work, employment, or business may be among those seen as contributing to global warming.

For example, Kate Forer, pastor of a Saratoga Springs, New York, congregation deeply involved in environmental sustainability, speaks of a dairy farmer in her church. He struggles with the way some facets of his farm work intersect with climate challenges. "I don't think he feels like he's ever treated 'less than' in our congregation," she says. "The thing is, we recognize and name that the climate crisis is so big that none of us can do everything, and all of us have to stretch ourselves more than we think we can. So, we have to work together and be kind to each other while challenging and calling our community forward in the work."[6]

There are a wide variety of ways that churches can participate in constructive activities that address climate change. Many of these activities are simply good practices, commendable in themselves, and do not require direct reference to climate change out of respect for those who disagree.[7] The following list of possibilities may feel overwhelming! It might be helpful to break this list into these categories: (a) what we are already doing; (b) what seems immediately doable; (c) what doesn't apply to our setting; (d) what we should think about, discuss, and explore; and (e) what we would never consider.

Materials and Supplies

Possibilities for change include rechargeable batteries for microphones and hearing aids and energy efficient light bulbs and lighting (both inside and outside), perhaps with timers or motion sensors. Beeswax candles are a possibility as are environmentally friendly cleaning supplies and ice melt. We might eliminate the use of some materials, such as Styrofoam, plastic water bottles, and plastic tableware. It might be possible to prepare coffee more efficiently and some might consider a return to dishwashing (by hand) together.

While she hopes for more, this is where Molly sees her congregation's engaging. She comments, "They have done the low hanging fruit. We have mostly efficient lighting all over the church and we are getting rid of Styrofoam. Nobody is opposed to it, but nobody seems to want to do more."

Paper

How can a church use less paper? We install electric hand dryers in bathrooms. If a church has worship bulletins, it might consider exchanging larger bulletins for small, inserted pages for the variations and recent news. If a church has the capability for projected images, perhaps paper bulletins are not necessary at all. Further, a church can offer the option of electronic rather than paper copies of many items in a church's life: directories, minutes, agendas, newsletters, and annual or quarterly reports. Several of the pastors mentioned moving to paperless worship with all relevant items available on screens or on participants' phones. Some simply urge people to use both sides of a piece of paper, and then to recycle it.

Building Audits and Building Use

There are at least three audits, maybe four, that a congregation may want to make of its building to help it not only manage energy more efficiently but also to point the way forward for possible expanded ministries.

First is an energy audit. Sometimes, a local electric company will provide this or refer to other agencies that provide this service. This can include assessment of the building's insulation and air sealing, the efficiency and cleanliness of the heating systems, and information about more efficient heating or cooling methods. Anita mentioned that this was one of the places her church was engaging this topic—evaluating their gas-fired boiler and the heating efficiency in their building. Energy conservation may also mean wise and maximal use of the church building, rather than being mostly empty except for a few hours a week. The church building can become an expression of how a church relates to and serves the community.

G. Travis Norvell suggests a second kind of audit. He advises inviting someone who is not a part of your faith community, perhaps not a part of any faith community, to see your building with new eyes. What does your building offer that may meet community needs? Some possibilities might include high ceilings…an acoustical environment suitable for recitals, chamber orchestras, choirs, or other music groups…open space…a library of books probably not available elsewhere…a kitchen, perhaps even an industrial grade kitchen with large utensils…various size rooms…office space…roofs that soak up the sun rays…perhaps a playground…perhaps open spaces for parking, activities, or greenspace.[8]

The church that Norvell serves, Judson Memorial Baptist Church, in Minneapolis, Minnesota, participated in that kind of audit with the goal of increasing their building use as much as possible. Within the last year, several different music groups have used their space for practice or performance. The church has hosted the Martin Luther King, Jr., Community breakfast and community conversations. They also house a pre-school, Meals on Wheels, four licensed counselors, offices for a philharmonic orchestra, two Girl Scout troops, a watercolor painting group, and a women's strength training group. Clearly, many in their community are served by their building. And they look for even more possibilities.[9] They have also actively investigated how the exterior of their building can communicate more clearly who they are and what they stand for.

A third audit involves investigating the local watershed and the church's impact on the water in its community. This audit might lead, for example, to a decision to install rainwater collection tanks for gardens. Or the church may consider other ways to preserve water and protect the environment.

While doing these three surveys, it might be good to consider a fourth. In chapter 9, we explored the possibility of reaching out for more effective ministry to persons with disabilities. If a congregation becomes committed to and involved in this ministry, there may be building considerations related to access and lighting. Surveys that anticipate as many futures as possible will be more effective in guiding to the future.

Transportation and Access

Churches can be creative in energy use by exploring transportation options for people attending worship services and other activities at their church building. Bike racks and ready access to storage space for parents coming with strollers can encourage those who can ride or walk to church. Public transportation (with possible lobbying for more Sunday morning options) or church vans and buses might be good choices. Or a church could plan worship at times that are served by public transportation. Perhaps a group of churches could combine by sharing vans and routes to offer people ways to be present with their own church communities. Those who drive their own cars can be encouraged to offer rides to others or carpool. Creativity addressing transportation issues may mean that elderly persons, those with various disabilities, those too young to drive, and those who cannot afford a car might be able to take part in church activities.

Grounds and Parking

A church should also consider its parking facilities and church grounds. Norvell invites reflection on what a parking lot is and what it can be. He notes that a parking lot "is a flat, impervious surface with a single purpose: the temporary storage of automobiles."[10] Each parking spot is ten by twenty feet. However, with imagination, a parking lot—and other grounds—can be so much more, and this in turn can enhance both the church's effectiveness and outreach and its climate care. Norvell muses, "What if a church parking lot functioned more like a bridge than a wall? What if it functioned like a plaza where the faith community re-neighbors itself to its once familiar home?"

Here are a few possibilities he noted and imagined:

- A parklet with a few chairs and tables for neighbors to congregate and have coffee.

- A straw bale garden. Straw bales can simply be laid on the asphalt or other surface, and with the proper method and care become a fruitful vegetable garden.[11]

- Community garden plots—raised or in ground—can be made available to interested individuals to grow food for themselves and to share with others.

- A parking lot can be made available to be a site for a Saturday morning farmers' market.

- A church might paint a labyrinth on its parking lot and, from time to time, offer opportunities for prayerful, contemplative walking with spiritual presence and counsel available.

- In the San Francisco Bay area, churches have invited people who live in their cars to park in their parking lots for the night. This might be a safer place for them, and the church might also offer kitchen, bathroom, and laundry access. In the process, this kind of service might build a sense of community.

- Parking lots and other grounds can be playgrounds, basketball or pickle ball courts, and other recreation and play sites.

- There are churches and individuals who have transformed their lawns into vegetable and fruit gardens.

- In the Minneapolis area where George Floyd was killed, Calvary Lutheran Church "transformed its parking lot into a community center offering food, clothing, medical supplies, and water. [And later it] hosted voter registration drives and functioned as a staging area for protesters and marches."[12]

Investment Strategies

If churches or individuals are fortunate to have investments, there are two possible strategies that can have a positive impact on the environment. One idea is to take steps to move investments away from fossil fuel industries or any other activities that are harmful to the climate. The other possible strategy is "shareholder activism." Shareholders have the right to vote at annual meetings, raise questions, and advocate for environmentally friendly strategies. Christopher James, who is an executive with an investment firm, chose this course. His organization used their votes and were able to place three board members on the ExxonMobil board. These board members had experience in transitioning away from fossil fuels and had a part in modifying and reducing the corporation's goals for oil production. He points out that large and small investors have a voice at a company's annual meetings and should "sharpen their elbows and raise their voices."[13]

Recycling and Composting

Collectively and individually, we can recycle materials using community recycling programs. In addition, we can compost food scraps, other wasted food, and coffee grounds that would otherwise go to overcrowded landfills. (The community where I live offers a composting collection and processing service for a modest fee.) But our planet needs more. In the March 2020 *National Geographic*, Robert Kunzig and others wrote of "The End of Trash." The subtitle of that article asks, "Can we save the planet by reusing all the stuff we make?" The article describes a "circular economy" which "aims to end trash by not producing it at all."[14]

He goes on to describe actual experiments in Europe to recycle, refurbish, reuse, and repair. These efforts focus on metals, machines, energy, clothes, and food. However, even its most enthusiastic proponents admit that this effort is moving too slowly in a world dominated by consumerism. It may take generations to turn this around.

Kunzig reflects, "Building a circular economy will require an enormous cultural shift on the scale of the industrial revolution." He further ruminates, "A world without waste sounds impossible. But the vision of a circular economy—where we use resources sparingly and recycle materials endlessly—is inspiring businesses and environmentalists alike. Can we make it happen? Can we afford not to?"

In the meantime, he offers a "What You Can Do" List:

- *Restrain yourself.* Fly and drive less. Eat all the food you buy. Wear the clothes you already have. Avoid single-use plastics.

- *Repair and reuse.* Buy fewer higher quality products and repair them when they break. Donate the clothes you don't wear.

- *Recycle everything.* Compost food waste (or feed it to your pig). Recycle everything you can—and lobby for more recycling.[15]

- As an aside, Kunzig notes, "All the trash we make is not a sign that we're evil. It's a sign that we're a little dumb."[16] Perhaps we can be a little less dumb with a few projects, such as:

- An annual clothing swap.

- A food table where any who grow food and have excess can leave it for others to take.

- A tool and implement collection where people can make available tools and equipment they have and borrow and use what others have provided.

Solar Panels

A church building may have large expanses of roof with the appropriate angles and exposures for installing solar panels and generating electricity. While churches are nonprofit organizations and therefore do not receive the tax benefits for doing so, there is still benefit in produced electricity and planet care. There are churches who have more roof space than they will use in their own solar installation and make available a "community garden" type of experience where others can install solar panels there.

Initiatives, Guidance, and Assistance with Members

The energy audits we mentioned earlier for the church building have usefulness for the homes of every member of a church's parish. A group of volunteers from a church could offer such assessments and help with weatherproofing and other energy saving activities, particularly for elderly or persons with disability, or for any who may need help moving in a more planet friendly direction.

Activities with/for Children and Youths

A well-known saying tells us, "We do not inherit our planet from our ancestors. We borrow it from our grandchildren [or children]." This may be a place where some people enter this conversation. People who are not already recycling may decide to do it for their children or grandchildren. And activities that allow children or grandchildren to enjoy creation and outdoor activities, to clean up trash, or to plant gardens or trees might lead to other further involvement.

BACK TO WHERE WE STARTED: EDUCATION, CONVERSATION, AND WORSHIP

Many media resources may be helpful for our conversation, discussion groups, and Sunday School classes. For example, the NPR series "Global Weirding with Katharine Hayhoe"[17] is a series of brief ten-minute illustrated presentations by this evangelical climate scientist addressing important questions: "How do we know climate change is real? What do all of these crazy hurricanes have to do with global warming? What does the Bible say about climate change? Won't plants and animals adapt? Aren't you climate scientists just in this for the money?" Such a series might have many uses in carrying on the needed conversations.

A group might find it interesting to go to the website for Project Drawdown.[18] People might explore and discuss what scientists have studied and calculated about the changes that would have the biggest impact on planet change. There may be local community leaders, other churches, or individuals who can help personalize and localize climate response where you live as well as offer doorways into involvement.

Others might be drawn to a discussion of a good book on the subject. We have already mentioned climate scientist and evangelical Katharine Hayhoe. Her book, *Saving Us, A Climate Scientist's Case for Hope and Healing in a Divided World*[19] offers much food for discussion and thought. Also worthwhile is Pastor Ken Whitt's *God Is Just Love: Building Spiritual Resilience and Sustainable Communities for the Sake of Our Children and Creation*.[20] Anita's church offered a study group on *Active Hope: How to Face the Mess We're in with Unexpected Resilience and Creative Power*.[21] There are, of course, many other excellent book resources; these are just a starting place.

RESPONSES BY MY INTERVIEWEES

Several pastors and churches with whom I visited were involved in climate care in several ways.

Joanna notes, "Care for creation is one of five pieces of our church's mission statement. We tried to pay attention to climate concerns when we did our building expansion. Dr. Ruth Rosell (a pastoral theology professor and climate activist) is coming to preach on climate justice, a week from Sunday. We don't have a large involvement, but we are a part of mission care involvement. The group we are part of is Mennonite Creation Care Network."

Amber spoke of engaging climate concerns in her regional staff leadership: "One of the places I am is helping the church recognize that we are a justice-oriented region. Any justice work we do is and needs to be ecojustice. If we are working on racial justice, climate change is affecting your community. If we are addressing gender justice, we know that vulnerable people will be most affected by climate. Climate concern needs to be central in our justice ministry."

Tim reported, "A group of members in our church started a Green Team. This is a group of people who are concerned about climate change, creation care, climate care, and are passionate about these things politically. They are trying to connect these concerns to faith perspectives and a theology of climate change."

Anita shares a variety of involvements that engage her congregation: "We are always keeping on our toes—are we doing sustainable practices in our kitchen? Twice a year we have a worship focus, one is a service of grief and mourning for the challenges of climate change, and one is a celebration of the world."

"We also actively participate in Interfaith Climate Action which sponsors educational events, supports climate-friendly legislation and policy, and opposes actions that would increase global warming. This coalition has also recreated 'Green Buildings Now' to aid the transition from fossil fuel to nonpolluting heating systems and the establishment of a safe haven at a nearby United Church of Christ campus. This will be available for residents in case of climate emergencies such as heat or cold or wildfire smoke."

Her interfaith coalition has also:

- Lobbied legislators and participated in a youth led climate march
- Planted trees to celebrate Tu Bishvat, the Jewish New Year of the Trees
- Participated in "Taming Bigfoot," a friendly competition to reduce our personal carbon footprint
- Cosponsored prayer vigils with Faith Action Climate Team members
- Hosted book study groups."[22]

WORSHIP, PLAY, AND SERVE OUTDOORS

There are movements and opportunities where individuals or a church can bond with and join with others in their relating to and caring for the natural world. These may include outdoor worship of our God of all creation as well as other activities. Two of these are the Wild Church Network,[23] and Holy Hikes, another eco-ministry network.[24] Outdoor activities including worship, nature retreats, and service projects may be an important doorway to further conversation and action as well as being enriching in themselves. The involvement of children and youth in these activities will be important for their own growth and for the growth of our church communities.

AND SO

If the United Nations Panel quoted at the beginning of this chapter is right (and I believe it is), we all have a most important task. Our task is to do what we can to save our planet from becoming inhospitable to humans and other life. This task is urgent; radical change is needed now.

May our churches be part of the healing and not the destruction! May our churches be part of the solution and not the problem!

FOR CONVERSATION AND REFLECTION

1. Where are you in your thoughts and activities as regards environmental stewardship? Where is your church?

2. Has your faith community experienced disagreements about global warming? Uncomfortable silences? What have you done to engage this conversation? What more, do you believe, needs to be done?

3. What outside worship, picnics, retreats, and camps are part of your church life? What other activities feel interesting and possible? How do these contribute to your plant awareness and advocacy?

4. Which of the activities mentioned above has your church engaged? What others might be possible and helpful?

NOTES

[1] Sara Kaplan, "World is on brink of catastrophic warming, U.N. climate report says," https://www.washingtonpost.com/climate-environment/2023/03/20/climate-change-ipcc-report-15/.

[2] https://climatecommunication.yale.edu/about/projects/global-warmings-six-americas/ accessed 6 April 2023.

[3] https://climatecommunication.yale.edu/about/projects/global-warmings-six-americas/.

[4] Zack Dawes, Jr., "Fewer in U.S. Say Climate Change is Driven Primarily by Human Causation." https://goodfaithmedia.org/fewer-in-u-s-say-climate-change-is-driven-primarily-by-human-causation/ 23 April 2023. He was summarizing an EPIC report from the University of Chicago, https://apnorc.org/wp-content/uploads/2023/04/EPIC-factsheets.pdf.

[5] https://www.christiancentury.org/article/interview/climate-scientist-talks-respectfully-climate-change-skeptics, accessed 15 April 2023.

[6] As reported and quoted in Anna Woofenden, "Thinking big (and small); What Does It Mean to Be a Green Church?" *The Christian Century,* August 10, 2022, Vol 139, No.16, 23.

[7] In addition to previous reading, the following list is derived primarily from three sources: Woofenden's just-mentioned essay in which she and friends propose forty possibilities; G. Travis

Norvell, "Reimagining the Church Parking Lot," *The Christian Century*, March 23, 2022; and G. Travis Norvell, *Church on the Move: A Practical Guide for Ministry in the Community* (Valley Forge: Judson Press, 2022).

[8] Norvell, *Church on the Move*, 47.

[9] Ibid., 50.

[10] Norvell, "Reimagining the Church Parking Lot," 23.

[11] Norvell, *Church on the Move*, 22, tells of the experience of Joel Karsten of Roseville, MN.

[12] Ibid., 24.

[13] Christopher James, "Every Investor Must Vote," *Time*, 17-24 January 2022, 20.

[14] Robert Kunzig, "The End of Trash," *National Geographic*, (March 2020), 42-71. I have also summarized this information in my book *The Grandparent Vocation: Wisdom, Legacies, and Spiritual Growth* (Lanham: Rowman & Littlefield, 2023), 113-114.

[15] Ibid.

[16] Ibid., 71.

[17] https://www.npr.org/podcasts/961315153/global-weirding-with-katharine-hayhoe.

[18] https://www.drawdown.org/.

[19] Katharine Hayhoe, *Saving Us, A Climate Scientist's Case for Hope and Healing in a Divided World* (New York: Atria/One Signal Publishing, 2021).

[20] Ken Whitt, *God Is Just Love: Building Spiritual Resilience and Sustainable Communities for the Sake of Our Children and Creation* (Canton, MI: Read the Spirit Books, 2021).

[21] Chris Johnstone and Joanna Macy, *Active Hope: How to Face the Mess We're in with Unexpected Resilience and Creative Power* (Novato, CA: New World Library, 2022).

[22] https://www.seattlefirstbaptist.org/climate-action/ accessed 2 October 2023.

[23] https://www.wildchurchnetwork.com/page-18079.

[24] https://holyhikes.org/

CHAPTER 13

Figure Skating on Thin Ice: Navigating the Political Divide

He has told you, O mortal, what is good,
and what does the Lord require of you
but to do justice and to love kindness
and to walk humbly with your God?
Micah 6:8

Throughout this book we have looked at many opportunities, tasks, and issues present in the church. Many of these involve caring for those within the church community or in the neighboring environs. But the church also has the responsibility to respond to larger crises and issues—crises and issues that affect whole regions or even a nation. Sometimes, church people work well together even when there are theological or denominational differences. At other times, church people can be deeply divided. Let's look at both of those situations and consider some possible responses.

INFRASTRUCTURE COOPERATION

Often, various religious bodies, denominations, individual churches, and religious agencies unselfishly offer their gifts to provide infrastructure support to communities where the larger governmental programs may be insufficient. For example, a recent study showed that about half of congregations have food pantries or other food distribution programs. According to Feeding America, about two-thirds of that organization's sixty thousand partner food pantries or meal programs are faith based.[1]

During the pandemic, many churches responded to the crisis with new community support services. For example, churches provided transportation to medical appointments, calls to check on isolated persons, and elder care assistance. In addition, churches and religious groups often tutor children, resettle refugees, offer clinics, run shelters for battered women, host Thanksgiving dinners, and more—all in informal cooperation and mutual support of each other.

This level of community involvement leads Bob Smietana to conclude, "In some ways, the infrastructure of religion matters more than the spiritual part."[2] This is both evidence of the good that religious folks can offer and a cause for concern because the number of those involved in "organized religion" is drastically decreasing.

Ryan Burge, pastor and sociologist. has noted, "The average American doesn't realize all the things that churches do to make society less awful. It's one of those things you don't know what you had till it is gone."[3] The societal contribution of churches can best be seen in two specific areas: caring for communities after a major disaster response and shoring up community infrastructure by providing care services not otherwise available.

Again, Bob Smietana notes, "At a disaster site, it's common to see people who are usually at odds—say atheists and evangelicals, Muslims and Jews, liberal Christians and their more conservative relatives—all working side by side."[4] There may be times of conversation and witness, but only after the splintered trees are felled, the damaged homes secured, and the victims and workers fed. These massive responses are anticipated and prepared for by approximately forty faith-based groups who together comprise the National Voluntary Organizations Active in Disaster. These are the leaders who devote the planning, forethought, and preparation needed to bring care and response to where it is most needed.

For these multi-faith organizations, there is grave concern about the aging and shrinking of their core of dedicated volunteers. What will happen when disaster strikes if there are not enough volunteers to comfort, support, and make things a little less awful? New creativity is needed to recruit, guide, and train cadres of volunteers (willing, but possibly untrained) who will show up to help. Earlier we mentioned that one of the ways of attracting young spiritual but not religious people was to offer a chance to participate in activities of care and healing. Perhaps this appeal can help to fill the gap of aging volunteers in preparing for and responding to disaster times.

POLITICAL DIALOGUE AND DEBATE

This brings us to a part of discourse and response to human need where our nation is severely divided: politics. The Rev. Father Richard Rohr has said, "There is no such thing as non-political Christianity."[5] Whether one agrees or disagrees probably depends on the understanding of "politics." The root of the word "politics" is the Greek word *polis*, which means community or citizens. The *Merriam Webster Dictionary* offers three definitions of politics:

> a: the art or science of government
>
> b: the art or science concerned with guiding or influencing governmental policy
>
> c: the art or science concerned with winning and holding control over a government.[6]

If by "politics" we mean definition a. or b. (understanding what government is, how it works, and attempting to influence it for the greater good), then I agree with Father Rohr. When we get to definition c., then we are clearly dealing with partisan politics. It is all too easy to move on from that definition to strong opinions about who is fit to govern and who is not.

Homiletics professor Leah D. Schade has suggested that, for the sake of preaching and addressing these topics in church communities, there might be better words to use than "politics." She suggests that perhaps one of these terms or some combination of these terms may be better: "Issues of public concern, community matters, the common good, civic concerns, communal issues, societal matters, discerning public issues, how we live together in community."[7]

Whatever way we put it, there are harsh divisions in America and in Christian churches over these topics. A recent survey showed that at least half of the people questioned said that they preferred to go to church with people who share their (partisan?) politics. Even more than that, it has been observed that when people leave their former religion behind, politics can become their religion. Some politically convinced people do not want their children to date or marry someone in a different political party. Cooperation or compromise even on lesser polarized issues may be seen as betrayal.

If a church must pass a political litmus test, invitations to church and recruitment of members become even more complicated! Sadly, when we fall into this divisiveness, we may contribute to the increasing polarization of our county. That's why I gave this chapter the title I did. For a minister to address major political concerns these days is, indeed, like trying to skate difficult patterns, hoping not to fall through very thin ice!

Lilliana Mason, political scientist at Johns Hopkins University, speaks of "mega-identities" where one's "political, cultural, regional, and religious beliefs are all combined." Various "mega-identities" compete with each other and are suspicious of each other. People who hold different views may not be welcome. Mason is concerned that we are falling more and more into this pattern and thus losing what she calls "cross-cutting identities." This is where a person's political, social, and religious patterns may have variations and don't fall into predictable patterns.

Many of us can recall a past when this was true. There were folks in our church, job, community organization, or bowling league who thought differently and belonged to a different political party than we did. Still, they were "basically well-intentioned human beings," and we could all live with various positions and decisions. Currently, Mason notes, our polarization is a "bumpy part of the road" as we transition from America's past to its future. She is hopeful that we as a nation can probably get to a smoother road, "if the wheels stay on the car" until we get there.[8]

GEN X AND MILLENNIAL PASTORS' INVOLVEMENT

I asked the pastors with whom I visited how their leadership in this political climate was going. Did pastors experience freedom to speak on prophetic issues they believed they should address as Christian leaders? Were there people of both major political parties in their congregations? If so, could those members talk with each other? Did they respect each other? Clearly, respectful conversation across our deep divides is needed in these troubled times. Is it happening in our churches?

The answers I heard were diverse, both regarding the pastor's involvement and the ways these issues play out in church life. There are some pastors who do not address possibly controversial topics from the pulpit but will respond to direct questions. For example, Jessica has responded to one-on-one questions, such as "What about gun control?" or "What about unborn children?" Others discover they can have church-wide discussions on local issues more easily than on national issues. Some of these discussions can be quite heated. Topics such as policing, abolishment of prisons, mental health concerns, climate issues, school topics, and affordable housing have been addressed by the pastors I spoke with.

Some pastors have addressed broad perspectives from which politically sensitive topics should be considered. Cody reflects, "On July 4, I preach that we are called to be Christian Americans, not American Christians, and we need to recognize the difference. In our church life, there are two things that happen pretty regularly: explanation and conversation. Such as presenting an opportunity to understand more about separation of church and state and making sure we are God followers."

James attempts to build a community of free and open communication. He reflects, "If our churches are homogenous in any way, they are not reflecting our community. If our churches cannot say everyone is welcome here regardless of political stripes, we fall short. When I speak on social justice issues, this means I will have to field uncomfortable phone calls. I also must be willing to explain myself and be wholly respectful of other people. I don't preach in such a way that I have cornered the market on truth. I want people to be free to disagree with me. I am not willing to let our church become an exclusive political organization."

Michael responded in a slightly different way to my question about engaging political issues: "There are two pieces of me that come into play on this question. In general, there is not anything more politically explosive than quoting Jesus. The other part of it: I don't beat around the bush. I have not been the least bit shy to talk about issues that are important faith issues. I have spoken privately and publicly about the health care system, Christian nationalism, and racial violence. One of the things I learned in observing people during the pandemic was that when I tried to be nuanced, people would not connect the dots. Being subtle was the equivalent to being misunderstood. I don't have the energy to beat around the bush anymore."

Jonathan recalls an experience related to the risk of prophetic preaching: "In my former church, I did a sermon for our remote worship site after the murder of George Floyd. It was fiery, but I let it ride. The recording of that sermon was retained on that church's web site. When I was in consideration for my present position, this video was viewed by members of the search committee. Some saw it as a reason I should not be considered—I was too political. My response—if the church refuses to speak to the world around it, people don't see the church as speaking to them either. Further, I gave that sermon to a church I had served for four years. I believed I was giving a sermon to the congregation where we were. Eventually, this church called me in spite of those misgivings."

Of all the pastors I interviewed, a group in the church served by Jason C. appears to have the most open way of carrying on these conversations:

"This is a men's breakfast. We read about ten verses of scripture at each meeting. After discussing those verses, we may have vigorous conversations, including conversations about politics and government. These conversations are friendly, not toxic. There are no personal confrontations or attacking. We hold each other accountable for that. Again, for the times, these discussions are very respectful."

Others find such conversations hard to get underway. Molly, who has come to her present position recently, hears hesitancy in addressing issues with political implications. She told me, "The last election, our church did experience some conflict in how they disagreed. There was a real fear that this would spill over into church-wide conflict, and they don't want to hurt the fragile peace. I have had some conversations about this. There are some who say that I should stay away from this. Others want me to help them learn how to talk about issues and discuss them. This is an interesting conversation to have before the next election." I have not visited with her more recently to hear whether or not they attempted these conversations.

Joanna wryly observes this about her congregation: "If we are diverse, the diverse are not saying much."

These are difficult conversations indeed, and they are so important! Significant issues deserve reflection, discussion, and involvement of citizens. And our nation needs our divided citizenry to start talking with each other rather than isolating and demonizing the other!

A POSSIBLE STRATEGY TO BRIDGE THE GAP

Homiletics professor Leah D. Schade has developed a method to carry on this prophetic conversation in politically divided churches and regions. She has experimented with this method, improved on it, and taught it to her students as well as to parish pastors. She titles it: "Preaching in the Purple Zone," with a subtitle, "Ministry in the Red-Blue Divide."

Schade readily admits that she has made missteps while engaging this process in her ministry. She also acknowledges that this process has hazards. However, she has also witnessed gratifying growth in the ability of congregations to explore important but controversial topics and move toward constructive citizen engagement, both as individuals and as a congregation.

I will first give a brief overview of this method and then discuss some aspects of it in more detail. In a word, she slows down the process of what we might think of as prophetic preaching. Indeed, she slows it down considerably with steps, conversations, and community reflections.

Step 1: Explain the Reason for These Conversations

The preacher begins with a sermon and possibly other teaching strategies. In this first step, a sermon (or perhaps, a more detailed class) lays the foundation for addressing important societal issues. For example, this might include biblical stories of people of faith who engaged topics of public concern. The sermon or discussion group might also retell the church's story of engaging controversial issues, perhaps in other times and places. The purpose of this sermon and/or study session is to prepare the congregation for a process of prophetic dialogue.

Step 2: Choose the Topic or Issue That Will Be Discussed First

Next, the minister selects the topic or issue that will be addressed over the coming weeks. In doing so, the minister will decide between a "cool" (less controversial), "warm," or "hot" (riskier, with potential of offending) topic. Many considerations will go into this choice. These will include such matters as the length of the pastor's service with the congregation, the comfort and security of the pastor's relationship with the congregation, the nature and health of the congregation (how adverse it is to conflict, for example), and the congregation's history in dealing with various issues in the past.[9]

It may be wise to seek wisdom from others in making this selection—perhaps close friends, advisors, or a church committee can offer assistance. Some of the topics selected in her examples and case studies included immigration, health care, end of life decisions, climate change, health care accessibility, hunger, mental illness, and gun violence.

Step 2a: Examine, Discuss, and Develop a Personal and Congregational Theology of Conflict

Simply raising such topics will open the door for some degree of conflict. Schade encourages pastors to explore their own and the congregation's "theology of conflict." In its most basic form, she says a theology of conflict "is what we believe about the relationship between God and human conflict." She provides a series of questions to assist in exploring this important topic that may well be part of this journey: "What does God think about human conflict? What does the Bible reveal about God and human conflict? What is God's role in human conflict? How does God regard *power differentials* when it comes to conflict? If all parties are on a level playing field, how does God interact with us when it comes to conflict? Is it possible to be in conflict and yet remain connected to the Body of Christ? What is the role of the Holy Spirit in the midst of our conflict?"[10]

Step 3: Engage the Topic and Each Other

Then the minister will lead the church in a process that includes a series of events. These events include: (a) a sermon on the topic selected; (b) a forum on the topic; and (c) a second sermon. This second sermon includes some reporting and reflection on the forum but goes beyond that.

Step 3a: The Sermon

The minister has introduced the need to theologically address public issues, has developed and articulated a theology of conflict for both the pastor and the faith community, and has selected and announced the subject to be explored. The next step in this process will be for the pastor to preach the first sermon, a "prophetic invitation to dialogue."

Schade provides this counsel about the first sermon:

> ...*the preacher does not take a stand on the issue.* Instead, (the preacher) acknowledges the complexity of the topic, considers many voices and perspectives, and frames it within a scriptural and theological context. In addition, the preacher specifically invites listeners to participate in a deliberative dialogue about the topic and explains how the Holy Spirit is part of this process of discernment within the Body of Christ.[11]

Step 3b: The "Deliberative Dialogue"

National Issues Forums

Sometime in the next week or so after the first sermon, a "Deliberative Dialogue" (forum) is conducted. For this step, Schade has chosen to work with the Kettering Foundation, and the National Issues Forums Institute (NIFI) that they created. According to Schade, this "nonprofit, nonpartisan research foundation trades insights from its research with a broad network of institutions, organizations, and individuals from over eighty countries...

striving to understand how citizens and political systems can work together." Their primary research question is: "What does it take to make democracy work as it should?"[12] While it is a secular organization, it collaborates with forum facilitators, including clergy and lay religious leaders. They have prepared resource and process guides on several dozen topics, including each of those that I have mentioned.

The Makeup of the "Deliberative Dialogue"
Sometime after the first sermon, a diverse group of persons of varying ages and viewpoints are invited to this "deliberative dialogue" that will be enriched by the NIFI resource guide. Schade points out this is not a debate and not a panel presentation. It is a carefully structured forum that will meet for at least ninety minutes. If more than ten people are taking part, she recommends breaking parts of the discussion down into smaller groups of three to six people so that all can participate and be heard. It is important for this forum to include the variety of viewpoints in the congregation. It is also important that there is room for all to share and for no one to dominate the conversation. It may be important and necessary to actively recruit people who may have different points of view so that an authentic conversation on the topic can occur.

The "Deliberative Dialogue" process
In the dialogue itself, participants will:

- identify where the issue personally touches each person present;
- analyze the issue;
- consider options;
- reflect on recurring themes, shared values that were discovered in the process, and common ground among the participants; and
- consider next steps.[13]

This conversation could have many benefits and could surface some basic civic needs. For example, this may be an opportunity to rekindle ordinary citizens' interest in civic engagement. Ultimately, this could help to revitalize civic life in our nation. Schade hopes, furthermore, that barriers can be removed—barriers that inhibit citizens from discussing and acting on pressing issues in our society. She hopes further that this may be a means for Christian people to be the "yeast in the bread" as they work for a more just and equitable society.[14]

Step 3c: The Second Sermon

The process is completed with a second sermon which Schade describes both as a "Communal Prophetic Proclamation" and "collaborative preaching." Part of this sermon will report about and reflect on the Deliberative Dialogue. Important questions to consider include: How did this topic affect people personally? Did the group have times of tension and/or points of contention? What common themes and shared values did the group identify? Were there any "aha" moments? Were further steps suggested? What were some of the personal responses to the experience?[15]

While there needs to be adequate and fair reporting, this is also intended to be a sermon based on some fitting biblical text. Schade points out that a fitting text can relate to themes and images connected to the topic. Or the text could be a prophetic passage on a related subject. Or one might choose a dialogical text—a passage that includes a conversation.[16]

This thoughtful and carefully designed process can lead to multifaceted growth:

- personal growth,
- growth in a community's ability to converse on difficult topics and address difficult topics, and
- growth in citizen involvement.[17]

For some, this process might lead to wider conversations and perhaps a replication of this process that might include a group of churches or other community groups. Of course, there is also the possibility that the process may lead to disagreement, frustration, and alienation. Schade anticipates this possibility and provides some suggestions about handling negative reactions to the sermon—or negative reactions to any part of this process.

First, she suggests "breathing and pausing," and then saying "thank you" to the person expressing discomfort. Then she suggests meeting with that person. In that meeting, it is important to ask and listen carefully, and to avoid debating content. The use of reflective listening will be helpful. If possible, it will be good to identify common biblical and Christian ground with the antagonist. And, of course, it will be essential to express appreciation for their sharing and affirm your care for them. A good follow-up question might open additional doors for communication: "Would you like to know why I decided to preach about this (or guide the congregation to explore this)?" If needed, an apology for any unintentional offense may be appropriate. A conclusion to the conversation should focus on a possible way forward.[18]

As she does the things described above in these sections, Schade is practicing the theology of conflict that she has earlier described. In doing so, she often refers to Dr. Dale P. Andrews' concept of "prophetic care." This is an understanding of prophetic preaching that is not distinct from pastoral care but, rather, an expression of pastoral care.

Schade summarizes Andrews' contribution:

> When pastors care for their people, they call out sin (including systemic sin) for the way it harms individuals, families, communities, the nation, and the planet. And when they are prophetic, it stems from their deep and empathic—even suffering—love for God's people. All of this is done, he explained, in the spirit of *bridge building*—seeking ways to span the seemingly uncrossable polarizations between people of different political orientations, religions, races, ages, genders, physical/mental abilities, and socioeconomic strata.[19]

I found Schade's concepts and process to be tremendously important, hopeful, and helpful. This carefully conceived and skillfully developed process holds promise for constructive and healing witness and dialogical conversation for prophetic pastoral leaders. I commend her book for your thoughtful consideration, application, and practice. It just might hold the wisdom we need for being faithful ministers in one of the most difficult arenas of being a Christian and a pastor these days.

FOR REFLECTION AND CONVERSATION

1. In what ways do you, your church, and your ministry involve yourselves in the infrastructure needs of your community? Are these efforts by you and your church alone, or do you partner with others? If so, who are your partners? What other needs and possible responses and partnerships do you discern?

2. Have you ever been involved in disaster relief efforts? Were there other groups also involved in this effort? If so, who were they? What was the range of religious groups who were participating?

3. How do you respond to Father Rohr's contention that "there is no such thing as non-political Christianity"? How do your respond to the Rev. Dr. Schade's suggestion that there may be better words than "political"?

4. As best as you can tell, what is the political spectrum of the people in your congregation?

5. How do you see your congregation's—and your—ability to have constructive conversations about political concerns where there might be a difference of opinion?

6. What is your response to the process described in *Preaching in the Purple Zone*? What might be your first step to investigate it?

7. If you and your faith community could have a positive impact on some issue in your community, state, or nation, what would that issue be? What might you and your faith community do to make a start? What allies might participate with you?

NOTES

[1] Bob Smietana, *Reorganized Religion: The Reshaping of the American Church and Why It Matters* (New York: Worthy Publishing, 2022), 45.

[2] Ibid., 46.

[3] Quoted in Smietana, 48.

[4] Smietana, 50.

[5] Quoted in Chuck Poole, "Concerning Religion and Politics," https://goodfaithmedia.org/concerning-politics-and-the-gospel/ 4 August 2023

[6] "Politic, Definition and Meaning," *Merriam Webster Dictionary*, https://www.merriam-webster.com/dictionary/politics. accessed August 10, 2023.

[7] Leah D. Schade, *Preaching in the Purple Zone: Ministry in the Red-Blue Divide* (Lanham: Rowman &Littlefield, 2019), 38.

[8] Lilliana Mason, in an NPR interview by Danielle Kurtzleben, "What If We Don't Need to 'Fix' Polarization?" https://www.npr.org/2021/03/19/979369761/is-todays-bitter-partisanship-a-step-toward-a-more-equal-democracy as summarized by Smietana, 126-127.

[9] Schade, 78-79.

[10] Ibid., 79-81. Italics hers.

[13] Ibid., 85. Italics hers.

[14] Ibid., 99.

[15] Ibid., 102-112.

[16] Ibid., 98-99.

[17] Ibid., 122-129.

[18] Ibid., 187-189.

[19] Ibid., 182. Italics hers

Finally, Sisters and Brothers...

Finally, brothers and sisters, whatever is true...honorable...just...
pure...pleasing...commendable,
if there is any excellence and if there is anything worthy of praise,
think about these things.
As for the things that you have learned and received and heard and noticed in me,
do them and the God of peace will be with you.

Philippians 4:8-9

We now approach the end of our journey through the past, present, and possible future of the Christian church and its ministry. Our journey has been informed by personal stories, the wisdom of scholars, and the insights of younger pastors serving today. Our journey has highlighted experiences, emotions, losses, hopes, opportunities, and issues. Hopefully, there has also been discovery and insight in our conversation.

In the opening pages, I confessed my disappointment about the shrinkage and reverses that have happened over the course of my—and many others'—parish ministries. That shrinkage has continued. In my title, however, I promised you "hopeful conversations." I stand behind that promise, and in these concluding paragraphs I will name some of what I have discovered that gives me hope.

I am hopeful to see such spiritual vitality and compassion in the pastors with whom I visited. They are learning how to how to lead and experience authentic worship that balances traditional and contemporary spirituality with various types of music. The variety includes worship combined with table fellowship, a symphony of various languages, or worship outdoors that praises and honors the God of all creation and peoples. Through the deep study of scripture or through respectful and gentle conversations with seekers, these young pastors are fulfilling their calling.

I am hopeful to see so many churches adapting to our nation's changing ethnic makeup and learning to expand their community wider and wider. Cooperative enterprises and conversations, the building of faith communities, and openness to reparations suggest that our growth will continue to be ethnically and racially diverse.

I am hopeful when I see the ways churches are responding to the pressing and growing problem of widespread loneliness and isolation. Care, counseling, and support for those wrestling with the pains of addiction and incarceration address a vital need. Worship and gatherings that incorporate warm community building, frequent meals and potlucks, varieties of support groups, and a spirit of welcome and invitation all touch and fill an urgent emptiness. Of course, there is need for even more reaching out with listening and care.

I am hopeful at church efforts to join in activities and projects that provide care and healing for our frail planet. For example, churches helping to make buildings and homes become more energy efficient. They are creating community gardens, reducing waste, repurposing otherwise unused space in church buildings or parking lots, and engaging in outdoor worship and community repair. All of this and more is an important start to healing our world.

I am hopeful that, more and more, creative church leaders are finding the way to communicate who we are and what we stand for in a world populated by the spiritual but not religious and those who are feeling nudges that they are not quite done with faith and God. Worship, Bible studies, spiritual counsel, and community groups open doors to encounters with God in Christ and these continue to touch people at a place of deep need.

I am so grateful for the many who, when a disaster occurs, are there with portable kitchens, tools and equipment, and muscle grease to give practical assistance and help people recover.

I am overjoyed to see church leaders welcome, affirm the gifts, and call on the leadership of people with disabilities. People testify about the richness and rightness of this. While they hoped to be helpful to others, they were even more enriched themselves by this broadening vision and experience.

I welcome the church leaders who are making at least beginning efforts to respond to those individuals and families who are living with gender and sexual identity questions. This is slow, hard work for us who may need to rethink what we believed and how we have read certain scripture passages for a long time. But it is important and healing work for many people, some in despair of life itself. Also, I welcome greater sensitivity and support for single persons as well as divorced and remarried families—and other helpful family ministries.

I am particularly hopeful as I think of the more than thirty Gen X and Millennial pastors whom I got to know as we visited about their work and as they answered my questions for this project. They are more at home in this world of the spiritual but not religious, of the "nones" and "dones" than I will ever be. They nimbly offer their leadership and gifts with churches diminished in numbers and resources. Further, they engage the problems, questions, and disbelief of their era of ministry, and they do it with grace and joy.

I especially appreciate the perspectives of the women who shared their stories of ministry with me. They are part of a movement, more widespread, confident, and more at ease in their role than might have been true earlier. Still, they come with an awareness of resistance and discrimination—sensitivities that can awaken and inform the rest of us.

In chapter thirteen, I described the contribution of seminary professor Leah Schade and her book, *Preaching in the Purple Zone*. I am hoping that this scholar, the model she developed, the resources she accessed, and the case studies she described will be helpful. It will be good if this example will start some conversations that in turn can help us to talk with each other across our political divides. May it be that this exploration might yield a measure of discovery and insight. In turn, may these conversations point the way to good though difficult conversations, respect, reduced polarization, and community.

I have spoken of hope inspired by ministers' and churches' creativity. It is also enhanced by their witness, including their worthy projects. Furthermore, I experience hope from faithful people living out their commitments in difficult times.

It is true that we are diminished in size and likely to remain a small movement. But as Margaret Mead noted, decades ago, "Never doubt that a small group of thoughtful, committed citizens can change the world; indeed, it's the only thing that ever has."[1] At the beginning of our Christian story, Jesus told his early band of followers—and us—that we are to be just such an influence, small communities enhancing the larger whole. Jesus said that we are to be salt, light, and yeast. This book has been a description of my conversation partners' and their efforts to be just that: salt, light, and yeast.

But there is more. We have hope because of the promises and faithful care of our loving God. The present circumstance of the church is, in many ways, not dissimilar to the church in the first century. Like those early followers of Jesus, we are quite tiny, powerless, with meager resources, in a sometimes hostile and sometimes indifferent world. Our prospects are uncertain. It was a fragile situation in the first century. But that fragile story didn't come to an end. In fact, that story continued—and it continues even today. And, surely, there is more to come!

Today, the media frequently tells the story of the church's decline and the dilemmas that we face. We have mentioned their projections of the future based on current trends. There are also many personal accounts from people who have left the church. Social scientists, historians, and religious scholars have weighed in on various reasons people trust traditional religious teachings and practices less. All of this is probably true, and yet it is not the whole story. I have been telling the other side.

Years ago, I saw a pin that had a list of letters on it: "pbpginfwmy." When I asked what it meant, the wearer answered, "Please be patient. God is not finished with me yet." And God is not yet finished with us!

In a recent *Christian Century* article, Debie Thomas spoke beautifully to this situation. She said that when she enrolled in seminary last year, friends were concerned about her naivety. They offered this counsel: "You understand the church is dying, don't you?"

She reflects that there is a church that needs to die—the church that is "aligned with Christendom and wedded to Whiteness, colonialism, patriarchy, wealth, entitlement, and prestige." However, she continues, there is also still hunger for "coherence, for awe, for connection, for meaning, for wonder." In other words, we still need what Jesus' life, death, and resurrection offers us. Furthermore, the church has been most Christlike when it ministers from the margins. To be sure, there will be painful deaths of churches, shrinking budgets, part-time minister positions, vocational uncertainties, and much more.

Still, she asserts,

> I am convinced that in all of these holy things, God will still be with us. The church, which is God's and not ours, will still be with us. And the Spirit who reigns over the church in all of its deaths and resurrections will do what she has always done: blow where she

wills, full of mischief and mystery. She will show us the way forward when we least expect to find our footing one more time. She will teach us once again how to laugh. And she will make all things new.[2]

Trusting in that prophetic vision, these words from the Apostle Paul's offer encouraging exhortation: "let us not grow weary in well-doing. For in due season we shall reap, if we do not lose heart." (Galatians 6:9, RSV).

Grace and peace! Shalom and farewell!

NOTES

[1] https://www.brainyquote.com/quotes/margaret_mead_100502.

[2] Debie Thomas, "Which church is dying?" *The Christian Century*, Vol. 141. No.9 (September 2024): 32-33.

Appendix

This is the questionnaire I sent to the Gen X and Millennial pastors who agreed to talk with me. I would ask them to tell me a little about their ministry. Then I would ask their response to question 1. After that, I would ask them to respond to any of the other questions that are related to their ministry. We would talk for an hour to an hour and a half. I would take notes as we spoke. The authors quoted in this book have confirmed the accuracy of their comments, and they have given me permission to share their stories.

Thank you for talking with me!

I am working on a project—with the working title *Rowing Together Through the Rapids*—in which I seek wisdom about church and ministry today.

I attempt to do this through the bifocals of my experience as a pastor and pastoral theologian and your—and your colleagues'—experience of church and ministry today.

And so, I will ask a series of questions. I ask you to select a few—some of these of greatest interest-involvement to you—and talk with me about them.

1. How has the growth of "nones-dones" affected your ministry? What about the pandemic?

2. What is your best experience in addressing the spiritual hungers of both those alienated from church-historic faith and those in your congregation?

3. What are the most frequent loneliness-hunger for community-pastoral counseling-pastoral care issues you experience and respond to?

4. What worship experiences, innovations, experiments have been enriching in your ministry?

5. Are you experiencing biblical illiteracy among the people you encounter? What strategies are you using to engage it?

6. Is your congregation interracial or interethnic? Is your congregation addressing issues of justice and healing around racial issues? What are you experiencing as regards race and ethnicity?

7. Where are you and your congregation as regards the ordination of women, the leadership of women, inclusive language about God and humanity, the feminization and womanist-ization of theology?

8. How is your congregation doing as regards to relating-including people with other- or dis-ability? Do you have specific ministries for given populations of people in the disability community? If so, how is it going?

9. Have you considered resigning and finding a new career? If so, how often, how urgently, and how recently? How are you and your congregation doing on rest and renewal practices for minister and congregation?

10. What is your pastoral experience in dealing with the changed marriage, family, sexuality and gender spectrum in society today?

11. What is your and your church's stance and involvement as regards climate care and global warming?

12. What is the makeup of your congregation politically? All or most of one party or a variety? What is your experience of discussion of issues of national or local importance where people of different political parties might disagree?

13. What did I fail to ask you that is important to know to understand your ministry experience today?

Bibliography

"Affordable housing rises where a church building once stood" https://faithandleadership.com/affordable-housing-rises-where-church-building-once-stood, accessed 7 September 2024.

All Saints. DVD, Sony, Affirm Films, 51314LIT, 2017.

Ahlberg, David. "Loneliness on the rise as public health threat," *Wisconsin State Journal*, 16 July 2023, A1.

Anderson, Bernhard W. *Understanding the Old Testament*, 4th ed. Englewood Cliffs: Prentice-Hall, 1986.

Austin, Thad S. and Katie R. Comeau. *Caring for Clergy: Understanding a Disconnected Network of Providers*. Eugene, OR: Cascade Books, 2022.

Bass, Diana Butler. *Christianity after Religion: The End of Church and the Birth of a New Spiritual Awakening*. New York: HarperOne, 2012.

Bass, Diana Butler. *Christianity for the Rest of Us*. New York: Harper Collins, 2006.

Bass, Diana Butler. *The Practicing Congregation: Imagining a New Old Church*. Herndon: Alban Institute, 2004.

Bass, Dorothy C. ed. *Practicing Our Faith*, 2nd ed. San Francisco: Jossey-Bass, 1977.

Berglund, Brad. *Reinventing Sunday: Breakthrough Ideas for Transforming Worship*. Valley Forge: Judson Press, 2001.

Bloom, Matt. *Flourishing in Ministry: How to Cultivate Clergy Wellbeing*. Lanham: Rowman & Littlefield, An Alban Book, 2019.

Bolsinger, Tod. *Canoeing the Mountains: Christian Leadership in Uncharted Territory*. Downers Grove: IVP Books, 2015.

Bonner, Timothy J. and Matthew B. Sturtevant. *From Distrust to Trust: Controversies and Conversations in Faith Communities*. Valley Forge: Judson Press, 2023.

Bonczar, Thomas P. and Allen J. Beck. "Lifetime Likelihood of Going to State or Federal Prison," Bureau of Justice Statistics, March 1997.

Brown, Claire and Anita Peebles. *New Directions for Holy Questions: Progressive Christian Theology for Families*. New York: Morehouse Publishing Company, 2022.

Buckholz, Debbie J. *Redesigning a Deaf Church to Meet the Needs of the Deaf Community*, A Dissertation Submitted to the Faculty in Partial Fulfillment of the Requirements for the Degree Doctor of Ministry at Central Baptist Seminary. 6 December 2021.

Burge, Ryan P. *The Nones: Where They Came From, Who They Are, and Where They Are Going*. Minneapolis: Fortress Press, 2021.

Cafferata, Gail. *The Last Pastor: Faithfully Steering a Closing Church*. Louisville: Westminster John Knox, 2020.

Campbell-Reed, Eileen R. "How Do Women Flourish in Ministry?" https://eileencampbellreed.org/2023/07/03/3mmm-episode-204-how-women-thrive-in-ministry/ https://eileencampbellreed.org/2023/07/10/3mmm-episode-205-how-women-thrive-in-ministry-part-2/

Campbell-Reed, Eileen R. *Pastoral Imagination: Bringing the Practice of Ministry to Life*. Minneapolis: Fortress Press, 2021.

Campbell-Reed, Eileen R. "No Joke! Resisting the 'Culture of Disbelief' That Keeps Clergy Women Pushing Uphill." *CrossCurrents*, July 14, 2019. https://cdn.eileencampbellreed.org/wp-content/uploads/No_Joke_Campbell-Reed_Rev_4-25-2018_Submitted_Version.pdf

Campbell-Reed, Eileen. "Pandemic Pastoring: What It Was Like; How it Changed Us; Where We Go from Here." https://cdn.eileencampbellreed.org/wp-content/uploads/PandemicPastoring-Report-FULL-9-1-2022.pdf. Accessed 19 August 2023.

Campbell-Reed, Eileen R. *State of Clergywomen in the U.S.: A Statistical Update*, 2018. https://cdn.eileencampbellreed.org/wp-content/uploads/Downloads/State-of-Clergywomen-US-2018-web.pdf.

Campbell-Reed, Eileen R. *Baptized and Ordained*. Forthcoming.

Cottrell, Susan. "How a Parent's Journey Can Help Us Be More Inclusive." https://www.patheos.com/blogs/freedhearts/2022/06/09/parentjourney/?utm_source=Newsletter&utm_medium=email&utm_campaign=Best+of+Patheos&utm_content=57&lctg=32930&rsid=&recipId=32930&siteId=7DF2956C-D2F1-40D4-A777-98E450E58360. accessed 10 June 2023.

Cox, Harvey. *Fire From Heaven: The Rise of Pentecostal Spirituality and the Reshaping of Religion in the Twenty-first Century*. Reading: Addison-Wesley, 1995.

Cox, Harvey. *The Future of Faith*. New York: HarperOne, 2009.

Dawes, Zack Jr., "Fewer in U.S. Say Climate Change is Driven Primarily by Human Causation." https://goodfaithmedia.org/fewer-in-u-s-say-climate-change-is-driven-primarily-by-human-causation/ 23 April 2023.

Doucleff, Michaeleen. *Hunt, Gather, Parent: What Ancient Cultures Can Teach Us about the Lost Art of Raising Happy, Helpful Little Humans*. New York: Avid Reader Press/Simon & Schuster, 2021.

Dyck, Sally. "We still need books about biblical women's liberation," *The Christian Century*, August 2023, Vol 140, No.8, 83.

Eisland, Nancy L. *The Disabled God: Toward a Liberatory Theology of Disability*. Nashville: Abington Press, 1994.

Elsdon, Mark, ed. *Gone for Good? Negotiating the Coming Wave of Church Property Transition*. Grand Rapids: William B. Eerdmans Publishing Company, 2024.

Enns, Peter. *The Bible Tells Me So: Why Defending Scripture Has Made Us Unable to Read It*. New York: HarperCollins, 2014.

Enns, Peter. *How the Bible Actually Works*. San Francisco: HarperOne, 2019.

Erlacher, Jolene Cassellius. *Millennials in Ministry*. Valley Forge: Judson Press, 2014.

Evans, Rachel Held. *Searching for Sunday: Loving, Leaving, and Finding the Church*. New York: Nelson Books, 2015.

"5 Statistics We Can't Ignore: Disability and the Gospel," The Banquet Network, Sept. 4, 2018, www.thebanquetnetwork.com/blog/2018/8/28/5-statistics-we-cant-ignore?rq=statistics.

"Forgotten Women: Female Priests of the Early Church," in *Feminism and the Church Today Fact Sheet* published by National Ministries, American Baptist Churches, U.S.A., vol 5, no. 1 March 1981.

Fortune, Marie. *Love Does No Harm: Sexual Ethics for the Rest of Us*. New York: Continuum, 1995.

Foster, Richard. *Celebration of Discipline*. New York: HarperCollins, 1978.

Fowler, Gene. *Church Abuse of Clergy: A Radical New Understanding*. Eugene: Cascade, 2020.

Francis-Tan, Andrew and Hugo M. Mialon. "'A Diamond is Forever' and Other Fairy Tales: The Relationship Between Wedding Expense and Marriage Duration." *Economic Inquiry* (ISSN 0095-2583) Vol. 53, No. 4, October 2015, 1919–1930.

Frykhom, Amy (interviews Katharine Hayoe). "Climate Scientist Talks Respectfully to Climate Change Skeptics." https://www.christiancentury.org/article/interview/climate-scientist-talks-respectfully-climate-change-skeptics, accessed 15 April 2023.

Gallagher, Nora. *The Sacred Meal*. Nashville: Thomas Nelson, 2009.

Gerber, Marisa. "How to throw a wedding for less than the cost of an iPhone—the minimony craze." https://www.latimes.com/business/story/2023-06-21/wedding-couples-choosing-affordable-minimony-elopement.

Gushee, David. "How Minds and Hearts Change: 10 Steps in My Journey Toward Full LGBTQ+ Inclusion—Part 1."

https://goodfaithmedia.org/how-minds-and-hearts-change-10-steps-in-my-journey-toward-full-lgbtq-inclusion-part-1/, accessed 9 July 2023.

Harader, Joanna. *Expecting Emmanuel: Eight Women Who Prepared the Way*. Harrisonburg, VA: Herald Press, 2022.

Hardwick, Lamar. *Disability and the Church: A Vision for Diversity and Inclusion*. Downers Grove: Intervarsity Press, 2021.

Hartke, Austen. *Transforming: The Bible & the Lives of Transgender Christians*. Louisville: Westminster John Knox, 2014.

Hayhoe, Katharine. "Global Weirding with Katharine Hayhoe." https://www.youtube.com/channel/UCi6RkdaEqgRVKi3AzidF4ow. Accessed 12 March 2024.

Hayhoe, Katharine. *Saving Us, A Climate Scientist's Case for Hope and Healing in a Divided World*. New York: Atria/One Signal Publishing, 2021.

Haythorn, Trace. "Plenary Address," Spiritual Caregivers Conference, sponsored by the American Baptist Home Mission Society, Kansas City, Missouri, 19 September 2022.

Hearn, Mark. *Technicolor: Inspiring Your Church to Embrace Multicultural Ministry*. Nashville: B & H Publishing Group, 2017.

Hearn, Mark with Darcy Wiley. *Hearing in Technicolor: Mindset Shifts Within a Multicultural Ministry*. Nashville: B & H Publishing Group, 2021.

Holy Hikes, https://holyhikes.org/.

Horowitz, Julianna Menasee, Nikki Graf, and Gretchen Livingston. "The Landscape of Marriage and Cohabitation in the U.S.," Pew Research Center, 6 November 2019.

Hugenot, Jerrod H. *How to Call Part Time Pastors in ABCNYS Churches* (And guidance for churches considering the emerging opportunities to share a pastor with another church) https://www.abc-nys.org/uploads/1/1/8/7/118772542/parttimeandsharingpastorsguide__.docx

Humphreys, Jose III. "God's Economy of Generosity: How the Church Can Help Reimagine the Story of Money." *Sojourners*, November 2023, Vol 52, No. 9, 22.

Hylen, Susan E. *Finding Phoebe: What New Testament Women Were Really Like*. Grand Rapids: Eerdmans, 2023.

"Indochina Refugee Crisis," https://en.wikipedia.org/wiki/Indochina_refugee_crisis accessed 9 August 2023

James, Christopher. "Every Investor Must Vote," *Time*, 17-24 January 2022.

James, William. *The Varieties of Religious Experience*. New York: Penguin Books, 1902, 1982.

Jesudason, Peniel, Rufus Rajkumr, Joseph Prabhaker Dayann, eds. *Many Yet One? Multiple Religious Belonging*. Geneva, Switzerland: WCC Publications, 2016.

Johnson, Elizabeth A. *She Who Is: The Mystery of God in Feminist Theological Discourse*. New York: Crossroad, 1993.

Jones, Robert P. *The End of White Christian America*. New York: Simon & Schuster, Reprint Edition, 2017.

Kaplan, Sara. "World is on brink of catastrophic warming, U.N. climate report says," https://www.washingtonpost.com/climate-environment/2023/03/20/climate-change-ipcc-report-15/ .

Kataria, Madan. TED Talk accessed October 26, 2017, https://www.youtube.com/watch?v=5hf2umYCKr8.

Keen, Sam. *Fire in the Belly: On Being a Man*. New York: Bantam Books, 1991.

Kenny, Amy. *My Body Is Not a Prayer Request: Disability Justice in the Church*. Grand Rapids: Brazos Press, 2022.

Kerygma Bible Study Resources for Groups—The Kerygma Program. https://kerygma.com/.

Kidd, Sue Monk. *The Dance of the Dissident Daughter: A Woman's Journey from Christian Tradition to the Sacred Feminine*. New York: HarperOne, 1992, 1995.

Kinnaman, David and Gabe Lyons. *Unchristian: What a New Generation Really Thinks About Christianity and Why It Matters*. Grand Rapids: Baker Books, 2007.

Krieger, Irwin. *Helping Your Transgender Teen: A Guide for Parents, Second Edition*. Philadelphia: Jessica Kingsley Publishers, 2011, 2018.

Kunzig, Robert. "The End of Trash." *National Geographic* March 2020, 42-71.

Kurtzleben, Danielle. "What If We Don't Need to 'Fix' Polarization?" https://www.npr.org/2021/03/19/979369761/is-todays-bitter-partisanship-a-step-toward-a-more-equal-democracy.

MacDonald, G. Jeffrey. *Part-Time Is Plenty: Thriving without Full-Time Clergy*. Louisville: Westminster John Knox, 2020.

MacLaren, Brian D. *Do I Stay Christian? A Guide for the Doubters, the Disappointed, and the Disillusioned*. New York: St. Martin's Essentials, 2022.

Macy, Joanna and Chris Johnstone. *Active Hope: How to Face the Mess We're in with Unexpected Resilience and Creative Power*. Novato, CA: New World Library, 2022.

Malina, Bruce. *The New Testament World: Insights from Cultural Anthropology*, 3rd revised edition. Louisville: Westminster John Knox, 2001.

Marantz Henig, Robin. "Rethinking Gender," *The National Geographic* (January 2017); 48-72.

Martin, Brenda. "A Place of Fresh Hope: Mental Health Ministry Has People Talking About Issues." *The Living Lutheran* Volume 8, no.1, May/June 2023, 26-27.

McLoughlin, William G. *Revivals, Awakenings, and Reform*. Chicago: University of Chicago Press, 1978.

Mead, Loren B. *More Than Numbers: The Way Churches Grow*. Herndon: Alban Institute, 1993.

Mead, Loren B. *The Once and Future Church Collection*. Herndon: Alban Institute, 2001.

Mead, Loren B. *The Parish Is the Issue: What I Learned and How I Learned It*. New York: Morehouse, 2015.

Mercadante, Linda A. *Belief without Borders: Inside the Minds of the Spiritual but not Religious*. Oxford: Oxford University Press, 2014.

Merritt, Jonathan. "America's Epidemic of Empty Churches," What Should America Do With Its Empty Church Buildings? - *The Atlantic*, accessed 9 September 2024.

Miles, Sara. *Take This Bread*. New York: Ballantine Books, 2008.

Mollenkott, Virginia Ramey. *Women, Men, and the Bible*. Nashville: Abingdon, 1977.

Newell, John Philip. *Sacred Earth, Sacred Soul: Celtic Wisdom for Awakening What Our Souls Know and Healing the World*. New York: HarperOne, 2021.

Norquist, Ben. "My Land Acknowledgement," *The Christian Century*, November 2023, Vol.140, No.11.

Norvell, G. Travis. "Reimagining the Church Parking Lot," *The Christian Century*, 23 March 2022.

Norvell, G. Travis. *Church on the Move: A Practical Guide for Ministry in the Community*. Valley Forge: Judson Press, 2022.

O'Donohue, John. *Anam Cara: A Book of Celtic Wisdom*. New York: Harper Perennial, 1997.

Olson, Richard P. *Celebrating the Graying Church: Mutual Ministry Today, Legacies Tomorrow*. Lanham: Rowman & Littlefield, 2020.

Olson, Richard P. *Side by Side: Being Christian in a Multifaith World*. Valley Forge: Judson Press, 2018.

Olson, Richard P. and Carole Della Pia-Terry. *Help for Remarried Couples and Families*. Valley Forge: Judson Press, 1984.

Olson, Richard P. and Joe H. Leonard, Jr. *Ministry with Families in Flux*. Louisville: Westminster John Knox, 1990.

Olson, Richard P. and Joe H. Leonard, Jr. *A New Day for Family Ministry*. Bethesda: The Alban Institute, 1996.

Olson, Richard P., Ruth Lofgren Rosell, Nathan S. Marsh, and Angela Barker Jackson. *A Guide to Ministry Self-Care: Negotiating Today's Challenges with Resilience and Grace*. Lanham: Rowman & Littlefield, an Alban Institute Book, 2018.

Palmer, Chris. "Bodies in Silence: A worship practice Zoom can't replicate," *Christian Century*, 12 January 2022, 12-13.

Pew Research Center. "Modeling the Future of Religion in America," https://www.pewresearch.org/religion/2022/09/13/modeling-the-future-of-religion-in-america/ accessed 8 December 2022.

Pierce, Yolanda. *In My Grandmother's House: Black Women, Faith, and the Stories We Inherit*. Minneapolis: Broadleaf Press, 2021.

Pilch, John. *The Cultural Dictionary of the Bible*. Collegeville, MN: Liturgical Press, 1999.

"Poems of Grace." https://www.poemsofgrace.com/ accessed 4 January 2024.

"Politic, Definition and Meaning," *Merriam-Webster Dictionary*, https://www.merriam-webster.com/dictionary/politics. accessed 10 August 2023.

Poole, Chuck. "Concerning Religion and Politics." https://goodfaithmedia.org/concerning-politics-and-the-gospel/ 4 August 2023.

Post, Kathryn, "Ten Ways to Make Your Worship Space Lest Ableist," part of a series of articles published by the Religious News Service, https://religionnews.com/2022/07/29/10-ways-to-make-your-worship-space-less-ableist/.

Proeschold-Bell, Rae Jean and Jason Byassee. *Faithful and Fractured: Responding to the Clergy Health Crisis*. Grand Rapids: Baker Academic, 2019.

Putnam, Robert and David Campbell. *American Grace: How Religion Divides and Unites Us*. New York: Simon & Schuster, 2010.

Putnam, Robert and Shaylyn Romney Garrett, *The Upswing: How America Came Together a Century Ago and How We Can Do It Again*. New York: Simon & Schuster, 2020.

Rendle, Gil. Quietly Courageous: *Leading the Church in a Changing World*. Lanham: Rowman & Littlefield, an Alban book, 2019.

Reynolds, Thomas E. *Vulnerable Communion: A Theology of Disability and Hospitality*. Grand Rapids: Brazos Press, 2008.

Root, Andrew. *Churches and the Crisis of Decline: A Hopeful Practical Ecclesiology*. Grand Rapids: Baker Academic, 2022.

"Same-sex marriage in the United States." https://en.wikipedia.org/wiki/Same-sex_marriage_in_the_United_States. Accessed June 17 2023.

Schade, Leah D. *Preaching in the Purple Zone: Ministry in the Red-Blue Divide*. Lanham: Rowman & Littlefield, 2019.

Shrikant, Aditi. "Poll: What do you think could have saved the marriage?" https://www.msn.com/en-us/money/personalfinance/63-of-divorcees-say-this-is-the-no-1-thing-that-would-have-saved-their-marriage-and-it-s-not-more-money/ar-AA1fpKiG?ocid=msedgdhp&pc=U531&cvid=f1d91fa5ca724c0b936dc1dadcf85c27&ei=19 accessed 18 August 2023.

Skovholt Thomas M. and Michelle Trotter-Mathison. *The Resilient Practitioner: Burnout and Compassion Fatigue Prevention and Self-Care Strategies for the Helping Professional*, 3rd ed. London: Routledge, 2016.

Smietana, Bob. *Reorganized Religion: The Reshaping of the American Church and Why it Matters*. Brentwood: Worthy Books, 2022.

Sparks, Susan. *Laugh Your Way to Grace: Reclaiming the Spiritual Power of Humor*. Woodstock, VT: Skylight Paths, 2010.

Sparks, Susan. *Preaching Punchlines: The Ten Commandments of Comedy*. Macon, GA: Smyth & Helwys, 2019.

Springtide Research Institute. *The State of Religion & Young People: Navigating Uncertainty*. Springtide Research Institute, 2021.

Taylor, Barbara Brown. *Always a Guest: Speaking of Faith Far From Home*. Louisville: Westminster John Knox Press, 2020.

Temple, William. 1944 BBC Broadcast.

The Chosen," https://watch.thechosen.tv/

The Flourishing in Ministry Project, *Flourishing in Ministry: Emerging Research Insights on the Well-Being of Pastors*. Notre Dame, IN: University of Notre Dame, 2013.

Thomas, Debie. "Which Church Is Dying?" *The Christian Century*. September 2024, Vol. 141, No.9.

Thompson, Marjorie. *Soul Feast: An Invitation to the Spiritual Life*. Louisville: Westminster John Knox, 1995.

Thumma, Scott. "Exploring the Dynamics and Challenges of Congregational Size," *Theology Today* 78, no.3 (October 2021). https://journals.sagepub.com/doi/pdf/10.1177/0040576211030245.

Tickle, Phyllis. *The Great Emergence: How Christianity Is Changing and Why*. Grand Rapids: Baker Books, 2008.

"US LGBT Identification Steady at 7.2%." https://news.gallup.com/poll/470708/lgbt-identification-steady.aspx, accessed 17 June 2023.

Welton-Mitchell, Mindi. email, 18 December 2023.

White, James Emery. *The Rise of the Nones: Understanding and Reaching the Religiously Unaffiliated*. Grand Rapids: Baker Books, 2014.

Whitt, Ken. *God Is Just Love: Building Spiritual Resilience and Sustainable Communities for the Sake of Our Children and Creation*. Canton, MI: Read the Spirit Books, 2021.

Wild Church Network. https://www.wildchurchnetwork.com/page-18079.

Willingham, A.J. "More Women Are Aiming to Become Church Leaders. Together, They Could Change American Christianity." https://www.cnn.com/2023/07/30/us/women-church-leadership-united-states-cec/index.html.

Wolsey, Roger. "Sensing the Sacred—Lectio Divina—a Spiritual Experience of Scripture," https://www.bing.com/search?q=mapquest+driving+directions&cvid=f2883eb71973461fb95a0200a0599047&aqs=edge.6.69i64i45018.162315938j0j4&FORM=ANAB01&PC=HCTS accessed March 16, 2023.

Wolsey, Roger. *Discovering Fire: Spiritual Practices That Transform Lives*, Independently Published.

Woofenden, Anna. "Thinking big (and small); What Does It Mean to Be a Green Church?" *The Christian Century*, 10 August 2022, Vol 139, No.16.

Woolf, Michael. "Repairing the redlined body of Christ," *The Christian Century*, March 2024, Vol. 141, No.3, 44-48.

www.ingramcontent.com/pod-product-compliance
Lightning Source LLC
Chambersburg PA
CBHW070842160426
43192CB00012B/2270